Henry James
and Pragmatistic Thought

Henry James and Pragmatistic Thought

A Study in the Relationship

between the Philosophy

of William James

and the Literary Art of Henry James

by Richard A. Hocks

The University of North Carolina Press

Chapel Hill

The poem on pages 109-10 is from The Poetry of Robert Frost
edited by Edward Connery Lathem. Copyright 1936 by Robert
Frost. Copyright © 1964 by Lesley Frost Ballentine. Copyright © 1969 by Holt, Rinehart and Winston, Inc. Reprinted
by permission of Holt, Rinehart and Winston, Inc.

Library of Congress Cataloging in Publication Data
Hocks, Richard A   1936-
    Henry James and pragmatistic thought.

    1. James, Henry, 1843-1916—Criticism and interpre-
tation. 2. James, William, 1842-1910. I. Title.
PS2124.H57   813'.4   73-16271
ISBN 0-8078-1225-0

To my parents, Harry and Marie Hocks,
to my wife Elaine,
and to my children, Rick, Bob, Steve, and Mary

Contents

Preface

The person who makes the decision, for whatever reason, to set about writing in a substantive way of both literature and philosophy of the the first rank doubtless lays himself open to a certain degree of criticism from both sides. Attempting, therefore, to keep in my mind both the hypothetical philosopher-reader with his considerable stake in the various doctrines of William James, as well as the thoughtful Jacobite with at least an equal stake in the superb later fiction of Henry James, I have endeavored throughout this book to do the fullest justice I can for both types of person and the kinds of issues most important to them.

In this regard I should perhaps point out that in my examination of the work of the Jameses I have availed myself constantly of the copious criticism and scholarship pertaining to Henry, but have not done so—or at least to nowhere near the same extent—with respect to William. This is for two reasons: first, I consider this study, rightly or wrongly, to be essentially a work of literary scholarship and criticism, which is my field, rather than philosophical scholarship; second—and far more important—because the key which the thesis of this entire book turns on is above all else our grasping and understanding William's thought through Henry's own eyes. If such a statement already begins to sound as though I were fibbing above to my hypothetical philosopher, let me also add this: the necessity just spoken of has not precluded my assuming responsibility for evaluating Henry's grasp and understanding of William's philosophy; it is an extraordinarily good grasp (though perhaps not the usual *sort* of grasp), and one immeasurably beyond what is usually made out.

Doing justice to both sides is also what has prompted me to embark on the "ambulatory" method adopted in the middle of this book, specifically the fourth and fifth chapters utilizing the

1914 letter of Henry James to Henry Adams. The rationale for this admittedly unusual methodology is to be found in the first chapter, the definition and exposition of ambulation itself in the third chapter—both well in advance of my actual use of the method in chapters four and five. I only add this extra warning here because, as a structural method, ambulation does have its disadvantages unless the reasons for it are fully understood and appreciated: it seems repetitious, is, in fact, deliberately circular; and until—or unless—the reader is eventually "gripped" by it, he may resent so many times having to return to the point of departure. Hopefully, the reader, whether Williamite or Jacobite, will come to recognize the purpose for such a procedure as that devised in the chapters involving the letter to Henry Adams.

Finally, although the Coleridge facet of this study—and in that context Owen Barfield's elucidation of Coleridge in the first chapter—does not really come into its own, so to speak, until Part 3 and even then remains secondary to the main topic of the brothers' relationship, it can serve to remind us once again that philosophy and imaginative literature meet most closely in aesthetics. This is presumably why aesthetics is the one subject studied with equal interest and importance in both disciplines. I would like to hope that this book will have helped to do its part in continuing to bring the two disciplines just mentioned even closer together in their natural meeting-ground of aesthetics.

Acknowledgments

It is a pleasure for me to acknowledge my gratitude and friendship to those who have helped me with inspiration and ideas and encouragement during the many years the present study was in the making. By far my deepest gratitude in this regard is owed to two persons, Professor C. Hugh Holman and Mr. Owen Barfield. The former, long an advocate of the kind of William-Henry relationship found in these pages, first brought my attention over a decade ago to the need for such a study, guided me while it was in its initial stage at North Carolina, and has since followed its progress with sympathy, interest, and wise counsel. The latter, whose philosophic writings literally have retaught me Coleridge, among others, provided the aesthetic framework without which this study could not have been completed. His friendship has been as indispensable to me as his writings, and I would like to thank him for his thoughtful reading of an early version of this manuscript, a version which did not incorporate his work and formulations on polarity now so prominent in the argument.

As these remarks suggest, this book has gone through many phases and rethinkings. Thanks are due to several friends and colleagues at the University of Missouri who read, listened, or assisted me in various ways during various drafts—especially to Professor Roger Meiners, now of Michigan State University, who gave generously of his time and mind over the greater part of a summer to the consideration of the Jameses; Professor J. Donald Crowley, whose invaluable assistance and advice during the final stages of preparing the manuscript went far beyond the requirements of friendship and intellectual companionship; and Professor Howard W. Fulweiler, who has encouraged me in this work over the years both as department chairman and friend. I wish also to acknowledge my debt to Professor William

Bauer, of the University of New Brunswick, who has followed this project with keen interest from its inception and whose grasp and understanding of William James has found its way into this book on many occasions.

The frontispiece is from *Alvin Langdon Coburn, Photographer: An Autobiography*, edited by H. and A. Gernsheim. © Alvin Langdon Coburn 1966. Reprinted by permission of Praeger Publishers, Inc., New York. The portrait and the snapshot appearing in the text are used by permission of the Harvard College Library.

I am grateful as well to Mrs. Lynette Ballard, who typed the final version of the manuscript and remained cheerful throughout a hard, laborious task; to Mr. Albert Von Frank, whose proofreading of the work was meticulous and led to several helpful suggestions; and to the Research Council of the University of Missouri, who provided me with a summer research grant to do preliminary study.

Finally, I am immeasurably grateful to my wife, Elaine, whose unfailing support of and enthusiasm for this book over so many long years causes me pleasure and wonderment.

Part One

William and Henry James

The Nature of the Relationship

I. Perspective, Method, and Aesthetic Assumptions

> *There may be times when what is most needed is, not so much a new discovery or a new idea as a different "slant"; I mean a comparatively slight readjustment in our way of looking at the things and ideas on which attention is already fixed.*
>
> OWEN BARFIELD, *Saving the Appearances*

In the final volume, recently published, of what is now the definitive biography of Henry James, Professor Leon Edel quotes from a hitherto unpublished letter by William James in which the philosopher declines membership in the Academy of Arts and Letters, because, in part, "my younger and shallower and vainer brother is already in the Academy."[1] Edel maintains that such an "irrational" gesture by William James constitutes the surfacing of a "hidden animus" for Henry James that was lifelong and indeed became most fully expressed in the philosopher's antagonism toward his brother's late style.

Almost immediately Edel was challenged by Jacques Barzun, who, as current president of the Academy, has access to the letter in question. Barzun contends that Edel has distorted the tone of William James's remarks, totally overlooked his comic irony, and needlessly de-emphasized the various other reasons given explicitly in the letter for not joining the organization.[2] It is the sort of debate which gives little promise of being resolved to everyone's satisfaction. Edel is Henry James's definitive biographer, and his case has the authority of a *Life* which has taken five volumes and twenty-one years to write, and which in turn culminates his lifelong study of Henry James. On the other hand, no student of either of the famous brothers has ever previously failed to be impressed by the warm relations that seemed, at least, to exist between them, however different the directions of their respective intellectual lives or their distinctive temperaments. The portrait drawn of their relationship in Gay Wilson Allen's *William James* (1967) is as close and fundamentally affectionate, as lacking in psychic hostility and "rivalry," as it had been earlier in Ralph Barton Perry's monumental *Thought and Character of William James* (1935), where the discussion was of course more on the side of intellectual rather than personal biography.[3]

In the pages that follow I shall be presenting a case the implications of which can be shown, I believe, to be *ultimately* compatible with both positions; a case, that is, which may be said to clarify them both by suggesting the actual relationship between them. More immediately and directly, however, my allegiances belong with and my argument derives from the older position, although I am not at all embarking here on a biographical study. This book, then, attempts to present the only case left, the only one which has not as yet received its extensive treatment, although it has certainly been many times suggested and talked about. William James's growing impatience with Henry's work of the "major phase" has long been known, and it has now been given a prominent psychological foundation in the Edel biography. But the obverse view—namely, Henry James's growing affirmation of and identity with William's philosophical thought during the same period of time—has been correspondingly ignored or else (as in Perry's work) fully cited and promptly dismissed. Leon Edel, for one, does not quote Henry's extensive claims of apposition with William's "later thought"; neither does Gay Wilson Allen, however, even though his view of the personal relationship might perhaps have prompted it. Only Ralph Barton Perry and F. O. Matthiessen have to my knowledge cited the full range of Henry's remarks and then chosen to discard them—Perry unhesitatingly, Matthiessen more thoughtfully.[4]

I am proposing essentially that William James's pragmatistic thought is literally *actualized* as the literary art and idiom of his brother Henry James, especially so in the later work. I would suggest that, whereas William is the pragmatist, Henry is, so to speak, the pragmatism; that is, he possesses the very mode of thinking that William characteristically expounds. To embody so fully William's thought, I would further contend, is to be

"Jamesian" in just those ways that have long been the subject of literary criticism. In other words I do not propose a radically new and different interpretation as such of Henry James, either of his themes or of his distinctive method: he has probably received, all in all, about the best critical exegesis of any American writer. At the same time I would argue that his later work, at least, can be literally and positively *reinterpreted* by way of this perspective: the difference between a *reinterpretation* and a new one is that expressed in the epigraph to this chapter. Nevertheless, my aim remains primarily that of demonstrating the remarkable congruity between William's philosophical thought and the Jamesian idiom much perceived by the literary criticism. It is a relationship something like that between "vitamin C" and the orange.

For this reason the reader should not anticipate an argument from "influence" which, even if there were some evidence for it, does not truly clarify the nature of the relationship between their respective work. Nor should he expect an argument in any way analogous to Quentin Anderson's thesis, that James's three late novels—*The Ambassadors, The Wings of the Dove,* and *The Golden Bowl*—form a unified allegory of his father's Swedenborgian religious thought.[5] A Henry James who embodies William's pragmatistic thought is certainly no allegorist, but a psychological realist who possesses as well a prevailing measure or characteristic tendency toward ethical idealism.[6] The Henry James of this study can be shown, above all, to have "unconsciously pragmatised," which is what the novelist himself unquestionably believed and which he never conceived to have extended to his father's thought. That there is an overtone, an idealistic resonance, from Henry Senior present in *both* William's and Henry's work is a more reasonable and persuasive hypothesis; and it is one which was given its hearing ten years before Quentin Anderson by F. O. Matthiessen in *The James Family.*[7]

I have said that the relationship that obtains between William and Henry James might perhaps be imaged as that between "vitamin C" and the orange. The demands of demonstrating such a conjunction are often different from those of presenting conventional "influence"; they are even different—not entirely, but at certain key points—from presenting an extended series of internal parallels. The reader should keep in mind that Henry James does not merely express William's views or "doctrine" in his work, but that William in his thought effectively "names" or "tells" what Henry characteristically portrays or dramatizes. William's famous subtitle for *Pragmatism—A New Name for Some Old Ways of Thinking*—is therefore the appropriate key signature for the kind of relationship to be found in this study. It is also the relationship perceived by Henry himself, particularly in his reference to "M. Jourdain."[8] It is perhaps worth recalling in this general context the remarks made by one of James's better critics, Dorothea Krook, at the conclusion of her study of his later work—*The Ordeal of Consciousness in Henry James*. "There remains," she writes, "the question of the sources of James's view of reality and its essential logic as these have been outlined here. It will be evident that it has affinities with the so-called idealist philosophies of the nineteenth century; and it is even possible that James was aware of the connexion." Krook then continues:

I have thought it safer, however, to proceed on the hypothesis that he did not take it from anywhere, or anybody, in particular: neither from Hegel, nor F. H. Bradley, nor from his brother William's Pragmatism, nor (least of all) from his father's Swedenborgian system. I have supposed he took it from the ambient air of nineteenth-century speculation, whose main current was the preoccupation with the phenomenon of self-consciousness. To this air he had been exposed from his earliest years; and the animating intellectual atmosphere of his remarkable home, created by his father and the circle of gifted friends and relations commemorated in the pages of *Notes of a Son and Brother*, made perhaps the heaviest contribution to Henry James's philosophical development.[9]

Krook does acknowledge in a footnote the fact of Henry's claims of identity with "William's Pragmatism." Her general conclusion, however, as it is here expressed, is both representative and significant. It is representative in its wish to avoid tying James down to anyone's philosophical "system"; it is significant because Krook's view of James is a good deal more explicitly philosophical in its implications than that of the overwhelming majority of Jacobite critics, for whom James is preeminently an artist and not a philosopher.

My own view is perhaps more "cordial"—to use one of

William's favorite pragmatistic terms—to Krook's remarks than may at first appear. Indeed I hope my view can be shown to be equally "cordial" to any number of critics for whom Krook's own approach makes James too much of a "thinker."[10] The key to the whole issue, really, is the precise quality of that "ambient air of nineteenth-century speculation . . . the preoccupation with the phenomenon of self-consciousness"; that is to say, how, first, to identify the main currents of that "ambient air"; and how, second, to put ourselves back—if indeed it is possible to do so—into something like an internal or "existential" relationship with it. The answer to the first problem involves us with William James, both because he articulated the "new" psychology in his famous "stream of consciousness" argument and because his pragmatism, itself an organic development from his psychology, was, as he said, "A New Name for Some Old Ways of Thinking." The answer to the second question is more difficult, obviously, and involves in the most fundamental way our views of what constitutes proper "historiography." The relationship here proposed between William and Henry James is one which merits, at least in part, the sort of approach to the materials of the past outlined by Owen Barfield in his book *Speaker's Meaning*, or found in the following passage from *Saving the Appearances*, where he concludes his chapter on "The Texture of Medieval Thought":

It will be well to point out here that, if I have concentrated on one particular medieval philosopher [Thomas Aquinas], rather than attempted a conspectus of the whole field of medieval philosophy or theories of knowledge, it is because that is the method which a history of consciousness, as distinct from a history of ideas, must adopt. It must attempt to penetrate into the very texture and activity of thought, rather than to collate conclusions. It is concerned, semantically, with the way in which words are used rather than with the product of discourse. Expressed in terms of logic, its business is more with the proposition than with the syllogism and more with the term than with the proposition. Therefore it must particularize. It must choose some one, or at best a few points, for its penetration.[11]

The method here called for by Barfield is one that Henry James throughout his career naturally adopted, his "sense of the past," although James characteristically limited its scope to his own "cultivated consciousness," as in the late autobiographical volumes, or to the more immediate past of his central fictional characters, as in Lambert Strether's memories of Woollett and of Mrs. Newsome in *The Ambassadors*. It assumes increasing importance, moreover, in his very late "ghostly" tales, such as "The Jolly Corner" or the unfinished *Sense of the Past*, where it only begins to approach a conscious theory or *Weltanschauung* proper, having earlier and throughout most of his career been a matter of subordinating all historical and ideological "background" materials to the dramatic presentation of character and individual consciousness. It is not so important, however, that we subscribe to the notion that James's methodology anticipated the viability of a history of consciousness, as distinct from a history of ideas. In his case we happen to be confronted with the appropriate sensibility, much as we speak of those writers, James included, who "anticipated" Freud. What *is* important is the pertinence of such a methodology and the assumptions on which it is based to our ever "penetrating" that "ambient air" referred to by Dorothea Krook. The William-Henry relationship simply forces us to attempt such an exploration, because it is the most appropriate way to test the proposition—Henry James's proposition—that "all [his] life" he had "unconsciously pragmatised." Although the issue is not one of influence, it is one of a "family consciousness"; beyond that, however, it is a situation which extends to and bespeaks the brothers' fundamental and similar participation in the inner working of the later nineteenth century.

The adoption of such a method as the one just outlined is not, however, so pervasive in this study as to present any real difficulties in comprehension or clarification. It is more in the way of a guiding presupposition and only surfaces as an obvious "strategy" in Part 2, the rather unusual "explication" there given a well-known letter by James to Henry Adams. This segment rather unabashedly utilizes the letter to Adams as a convenient "locus" for an extended foray into the Jamesian mind or—more properly—mode of thinking. The letter is, really, an "excuse," a point of departure, a way to move into and eventually to come out of the Jamesian mind. It provides purely artificial boundaries for my examination, but that examination has—as will quickly become apparent—a far more ambitious subject and scope. It examines the main lines of Henry James's later fiction and criticism and its counterpart in the philosophical thought of his brother. This use of a "moment" or "locus" in the Adams letter simply means that I have taken seriously Kant's famous adage that "concepts without percepts are blind," and extended it to the William Jamesian position that experience is always conjunctive and continuous, and that within its ongoing circular movement ideas have their role to play: they are "transitional," i.e., generated *by* an experience in order to terminate back *in* the experience. The letter may thus be thought of as a "chosen" experience; whereas my discussion, via it, of James's writings and of William's thought, together with my ranging over the mid and late nineteenth century—these may be conceived of as a series of "transitional" ideas, both generated by the "moment" (the letter) and then terminated in it again and again. Let me add that since this is a study of the Jameses and not a lyric poem I have taken pains to remember, especially in this same section, the rest of Kant's adage: "percepts without concepts are dumb." For most readers the main value of Part 2 will lie in the demonstration of the surprisingly total identity of William's thought with Henry's idiom; at the same time the continual occasion for it, the continued and persistent presence of the letter, may appear puzzling—as though the weight of importance has been reversed and matters big and broad are needlessly made as if to "depend" on the less significant letter. Of course the argument does not, obviously, depend on the letter to Adams. My making it appear to do so merely simulates—and at a distance—the distinctively Jamesian mode of thinking I am at the same time writing about. The philosophical name for this procedure, in any case, is William's doctrine of "ambulation," the subject of the last chapter of Part 1. A more familiar term from Henry James for the very same process is that of a "germ"—I have used the letter to Adams as a germ.

It is my hope nevertheless that the section just spoken of may serve to reinforce the general proposal that the William-Henry relationship is one that yields additional understanding from the sort of penetration that occurs at the level of history of consciousness rather than that of the history of ideas. As we have seen Barfield point out, the former approach "must particularize . . . must choose some one, or at best a few points, for its penetration." The same necessity duly explains, I hope, my not covering anything like James's entire corpus in this book. I trust however that I have sufficiently visited his work to claim legitimate representation.

Having spent these last several pages attempting to distinguish between a history of consciousness and a history of ideas, I think it might be helpful now to bring them back closer together; that is, to suggest their positive relationship to each other. Only in this fashion can I hope to keep my overall perspective before the reader and indicate as well my general views of James as a literary artist—a matter I have yet to address. A history of consciousness perspective is merely the capacity at a given moment to penetrate to the "soil" out of which grow the selfsame ideas which, when we do "collate" them, give us our more familiar history of ideas approach. The relationship between the two methods is therefore not really disjunctive at all—quite the opposite. At its best it resembles the following relationship James depicts in a famous and oft-cited passage from the "Preface" to *The Portrait of a Lady*:

There is, I think, no more nutritive or suggestive truth . . . than that of the perfect dependence of the "moral" sense of a work of art on the amount of felt life concerned in producing it. The question comes back thus, obviously, to the kind and the degree of the artist's prime sensibility, which is the soil out of which his subject springs. The quality and capacity of that soil, its ability to "grow" with due freshness and straightness any vision of life, represents, strongly or weakly, the projected morality.[12]

To suggest the aforementioned parallel between James's central aesthetic proposal above and the relationship that obtains between a history of consciousness and a history of ideas may at first appear rather heady and presumptuous; but it is really not a radical analogy at all. The aesthetic tradition James is affirming is preeminently Coleridgean, a fact much recognized by his critics.[13] It is actually Coleridge himself who, as Barfield has recently demonstrated, first contended that a history of "thought"—or consciousness—is not an essentially different activity from that of the creative imagination, for which he is so much better known. For Coleridge, in fact, the two historical methods in question stood in pretty much the same relationship to each other as that of the imagination to the fancy.[14] In any event, James's indisputable ties with the aesthetic tradition of

Coleridge—and one can hardly deny them in the literary theory, however much one may attempt to ignore them in the fiction— can be said in a curious and roundabout way to validate anew Barfield's proposals, derived in most instances both from his philosophical engagement with Coleridge and with the scientific theories of Goethe—whose "metamorphic" principles of the "trained imagination" then in turn reappear inadvertently all but paraphrased in Henry James's literary criticism.[15]

Perhaps these last comments will have begun to anticipate the obvious question that a study with the thesis of this one raises: namely, if Henry James "unconsciously pragmatised," does it ultimately account for his having been the great literary artist he was. The answer is no: his genius alone must account for that. William's pragmatistic thought does, however, both account for and illuminate just those qualities we would call "Jamesian." The clarification resides, once again, in the conception of the creative act as Coleridge best understood and articulated it. Pragmatistic thought is for James's fiction the equivalent, roughly, of the faculty of the fancy. In using this analogy, however, let me stress in the strongest way that fancy is not for Coleridge a faculty "separated" from imagination by dint of being less important. He points out repeatedly that, in proposing such aesthetic categories, "distinction is not division."[16] It would be as impossible to "divide" fancy from imagination in the work of a given artist as it would, say, the ramifying buds of a plant from the vital "sap" which realizes and expresses itself in these very metamorphic forms. Fancy is thus to the imagination as the history of ideas is to the history of consciousness, and as James's "vision of life" is to the artist's "prime sensibility" in the passage quoted before. They can none of them be divided, although we must, for purposes of understanding, distinguish between them: for taken together they are (much like the contents of a photographic plate in the electron microscope) "dynamic forces in momentary arrest."[17]

But suppose we were forced for the moment, however, to consider the question of just what does constitute James's genius—that primary agency he shares with other great imaginative writers, but which in his case expressed itself in the "Jamesian" mode mirrored by William's pragmatistic thought. The most persuasive explanation at present seems to me to reside in the following thoughtful and creative reinterpretation of Coleridge's famous "reconciliation of opposites":

A polarity of contraries is not quite the same as the *coincidentia oppositorum*, which has been stressed by some philosophers, or as the "paradox" which (whether for the purposes of irony or for other reasons) is beloved by some contemporary writers and critics. A paradox is the violent union of two opposites that simply contradict each other, so that reason assures us that we can have one *or* the other but not both at the same time. Whereas polar contraries (as is illustrated by the use of the term in electricity) exist by virtue of each other *as well as* at each other's expense. For that very reason the concept of polarity cannot be subsumed under the logical principle of identity; in fact, it is not really a logical concept at all, but one which requires an act of imagination to grasp it. . . . Unlike the logical principles of identity and contradiction, it is not only a form of thought, but also the form of life.[18]

This formulation, again by Owen Barfield, is altogether different from our usual way of thinking about polarity—as when we speak of society becoming "polarized." What is notable here is the insistence on the life-creating relationship present in all authentic cases of polarity. We should therefore try to distinguish it from our more familiar notions of dichotomy—"dialectic," "tension," "irony," "ambiguity," and the like. The important difference is that, whereas a dichotomy involves a relationship of *juxtaposition*, polarity involves *interpenetration*. Thus Keats (for example) does not actually "incorporate," as we might say, the ideal and real realms in his "Eve of St. Agnes," nor does he "juxtapose" them; "they" are instead *a* polarity, the opposing poles existing by virtue of each other as well as at each other's expense. It is the same relationship to be found in Thoreau's *Walden*, Whitman's "Song of Myself," or indeed any work of art that we conceive to be organically unified through "paradox," "tension," and the like. Polarity therefore really refers to the very relationship we strive to comprehend and articulate by these other terms. Nevertheless, a life-endowing relationship—literally brought into being and sustained through opposition—is not the same as these various concepts of dichotomy: to say that James, for example, "balances" the legitimate requirements of the romantic and realistic views of life in *The Portrait of a Lady*, or those of "experience" and "imagination" in *The Ambassadors*, is not quite the same as to perceive that such contraries are each other's source of life and meaning in the first place and literally the cause of aesthetic unity in these works. At the same time, such approaches, no less than others that are concerned with his "irony," "dialectic," or "ambiguity," are for the most part genuine attempts to grasp and explicate this essential activity of his genius. They perhaps only go astray when the critic, imbued too much with the thinking of dichotomy rather than polarity, wishes to conclude that James should have affirmed or chosen one particular "side" over the other in his novels.[19]

If we refer this issue back to the matter of James's embodiment of William's thought, it simply means that the novelist characteristically "empiricizes" polarity in his fiction; he transforms it from a level of transcendence and exhibits it dramatically at the level of psychological consciousness. Put another way, we could say that it attaches itself in his work entirely to "the deeper psychology." It therefore does not call attention to itself with explicit references to larger categories of intellectual generalization, which is why James remains predominantly an American Realist, despite the aesthetic ties in his literary criticism to the tradition of Coleridge. In this connection it cannot be said of William's thought that it ever affirms the principle of polarity. As a devoted pluralist his closest doctrine to anything like organic unity is to be found in his principles of "confluence," "conjunction," "concatenation"—all terms which insist on locating unity in the flux of experience itself, without, that is, resorting to some transcendent unity to solve the problem of "The One and the Many" at the expense of the living particular nuances of things. It is a view of and devotion to experience most heartily endorsed by the novelist and given dramatic life by his fiction. And if it does not address those very last aesthetic questions raised by his best work, it does something at least as important: it addresses Henry James where we first and foremost encounter him—in the ongoing reading experience. The fact of polarity as such in Henry James, it should be said once again, is not what is distinctive about his work, but is the assurance we have of the genius he shares with other great imaginative writers. The fact that it occurs in his work at a dramatically empirical level—a level of psychological consciousness, that he too insists on locating his unity within the perimeter of immediately "felt life"—is what is properly "Jamesian."[20] William's thought will invariably answer to his brother's distinctive mode and idiom.

Nevertheless—and finally—the fact that William's pragmatistic thought may be said to correspond vis-à-vis the aesthetic act to the fancy in James's literary art need not preclude the possibility of a relationship very much like that of polarity between the brothers themselves personally; and one given expression in their personal views of each other's work—William stressing opposition, Henry maintaining identity.

II. The Brothers:
On Each Other's Work

Your methods and my ideals seem the reverse, the one of the other.
Letter from WILLIAM to HENRY, 1904

Then I was lost in the wonder of the extent to which all my life I have (like M. Jourdain) unconsciously pragmatised. You are immensely and universally right.
Letter from HENRY to WILLIAM, 1907

It was said at the beginning of the preceding chapter that the view proffered by Leon Edel's *Life*—that there existed a lifelong psychic "antagonism" between the two brothers, so that, for example, "both relapsed into petty illnesses when they had to be together for too long a time"[1]—is one that seems diametrically at odds with previous biographers of the family. Similarly, the two assertions above by William and Henry James are in diametric opposition. It is quite possible that these two sets of findings may derive ultimately from a fundamental relationship between William and Henry in their personal lives. It is a relationship of polarity—but polarity as proposed in the preceding chapter, not as generally understood. Such a relationship would be genuinely life-endowing and for that reason mutually defining. I do not, however, absolutely insist on this in the personal relationship, which is not in any event the central subject of this study; I only propose it as a way of apprehending and responding to the evidence that appears in their correspondence both to and about each other. If they were in any sense enemies, they were surely "sweet enemies." The story of their last trip together on the occasion of William's death is both memorable and touching, and seems both the appropriate conclusion to their life together as well as the starting point for Henry's eventual encomium to William in *Notes of a Son and Brother.*

With respect to the intellectual relationship—the one, that is, which obtains between their respective work—it is a matter above all of our seeking its positive identity rather than assuming juxtaposition. For this reason Henry's avowal above is a preferable starting point to William's, even for the sake of eventually clarifying William's. In any case it is at least required that we attempt to see what the novelist had in mind by his claim, rather than to assume—as has generally been the case—that William was correct, since he was the philosopher and Henry was not.

If Henry James does unconsciously pragmatize, it does not necessarily follow that he is a pragmat*ist*; nor that, like George Eliot and August Comte, or Melville and Thomas Carlyle, he sets about to use and incorporate certain philosophical doctrines voiced by his brother. Nor must it follow that there is a mysterious, hitherto unexplored, side to the novelist where the "pragmatising" takes place. The proper perspective lies in James's own allusion to "M. Jourdain"—which scholars have generally preferred to omit when quoting the remark. It is assuredly genial in spirit, but it is not to be taken lightly. The titular hero of Moliere's play, *Le Bourgeois Gentilhomme,* Jourdain comes to discover from the "Philosophy Master" that for forty years he has without knowing it been speaking "prose." What James is saying is that William's thought identifies his own idiom—his prose. He is not saying however that William's philosophy in any way causes or determines his own idiom, which would be the case in a situation bespeaking influence or conscious appropriation. William in *Pragmatism*—like the "Philosophy Master" with "M. Jourdain"—effectively articulates, or *names,* Henry James's distinctive prose style, a style in 1907 having long since originated in the spoken word. What makes the allusion especially stunning and appropriate is that William's own title reads: *Pragmatism: A New Name for Some Old Ways of Thinking.* To name the prose is thus by implication to name the "way of thinking."

It may be argued, of course, that James is being ironic and that we ought not therefore to take him seriously. It seems a great deal to ask, however, that we find in the "operative irony" of his fiction a great deal of meaning only to close the valves of our attention here. It is just not the same thing to recognize that there is surely no solemnity in James's reference to "Jourdain" as to say the allusion does not mean anything—especially if it can be shown to mean a great deal. In my judgment James is in fact participating in irony, a fact which will emerge shortly when we look more closely into the context out of which this letter came to be written: William had maintained that James's later manner was a mistake, and the novelist discovered in William's thought what he took to be the rationale for the later manner. In the meantime it should be stressed as a general principle that any presupposition of irony in James which argues for and designates a meaning *only* the opposite of what is said invariably begs the question—and is one of the more obvious cases of misconstruing polarity for dichotomy.[2] As it happens, a considerable amount of the genuine irony present in James's fiction issues from a spirit not unlike that here in the reference to "Jourdain." In other words, the discovery from the novelist's perspective that he *had* "unconsciously pragmatised" was in all likelihood a remarkable, delightful, unlooked-for occurrence—and not without its comic side.

And yet we have also just seen that William James voices the opposing position, that his ideals and Henry's method "seem the reverse, the one of the other." To a great extent, then, our understanding of the possible insight contained in Henry's counterclaim involves a thoughtful and engaged examination of William's thought. It is obviously impossible to demonstrate convincingly that Henry James realizes William's thought, unless it can be shown just how much and in what sense William's thought is "realizable"—even to an extent that William himself did not appear to comprehend. His thought is, of course, a philosophical doctrine; or rather, it is a complex of doctrines: pluralism, radical empiricism, the pragmatic method, the "new" psychology. Still, it hardly need be said that philosophical systems even more abstruse than William's purport to refer to the affairs and conditions of life—to go beyond speculation per se.

William James in particular seems almost deliberately to have constructed his doctrines out of this contention: that philosophy is continually "happening" in other places, is continually "an event." Thus, once again—the title of his most famous book is *Pragmatism: A New Name for Some Old Ways of Thinking.* "Old" in several respects: because of its affinities with earlier empiricisms and even in certain aspects with older idealisms; "old," furthermore, because he along with others had been espousing pragmatic thinking (he maintains) for over thirty years; but, most of all, because his doctrine *is* a way of thinking and can therefore be "old" in the colloquial sense of familiar, friendly, even humorous. These few considerations alone may begin to suggest to us just how broad a gamut the connotations of William James's thought can run: from the recondite world of radical empiricism, where a primordial, yet somehow also empirical, "world-flux" yields itself to the indeterminate "cuts" of the Self, to the plain old resonances of the Yankee ethic: democratic, optimistic, utilitarian, anti-intellectual.

In this latter connection especially, William James has not always fared well. He tends on occasion to be seen as an unwitting spokesman for a number of national disgraces, best summed up as Yankee individualism and optimism debased into the commercial rapacity of the robber-barons: an excuse for acquisitiveness, irresponsibility, even fascism. William's own role in all of this would appear to be summed up in the word "naïve." Now mine is of course a critical examination, and my own analysis of William's thought is (to borrow from Mark Twain) perhaps more on the "dandy" than on the "squatter" side. At the same time, it is just because Henry James usually connotes thoroughly "dandy" associations, whereas William by and large does not, that I cannot entirely divorce certain prevalent attitudes about the quality and import of William's pragmatism from the concerns and interests of this study. It is especially necessary by now, if only because Jacobite criticism has on occasion argued that Henry James's stature rests fully as much on his moral vision of the corrupting dimensions of a civilized and commercially energized society as on his devotion to a meticulous artistic form in which to present that vision.[3] The difficulty always in claiming that someone personifies someone else's thought (as distinct from the question of influence) is that, if the personifier is construed to be permanently ethical as well as aesthetic, then what he personifies had better not be superficial or irresponsible. All the "embodiment" in the world is only as pertinent as what is embodied: and if it happens to be pragmatism, with some of its

present connotations, an already challenging matter becomes an all round suspicious affair.

One does come back, of course, to the fact that the two were brothers; and if it is true that their being a year apart in age, their living away from each other most of their adult lives, and their mutual "illnesses" together point to psychic difficulties, it is nevertheless apparent that their prolific correspondence reveals an attachment only less intellectual for its being so personally warm. William's earlier statement to Henry, "I feel as if you were one of the two or three sole intellectual and moral companions I have,"[4] sets the predominant tone for what proceeds to pass between them over the years. As for Henry, his early admiring reference to his brother's "Williamcy of mind," seems of the same basic stitch with his statement to Thomas Sergeant Perry, upon William's death, that the older brother had been "my protector, my backer, my authority, and my pride."[5] As was said before— if they were in fact enemies, they were (like polarity itself) "sweet enemies." Their very attachment is for that matter Ralph Barton Perry's only explanation for what he deems Henry's obviously unfounded discipleship of William's pragmatism.[6]

William James did not, however, care for Henry's distinctive later manner, and he repeatedly said so; whereas I have already indicated that the same later manner is just the mode of presentation which most thoroughly embodies William's own views, and that Henry perceived it. There are, most certainly, some curious and even remarkable aspects to William's elaborations of his "dislike," as we are about to see. Nevertheless it is generally true that, as far as fiction was concerned, William always claimed to prefer what he once described to Henry as "the gushing system."[7] Here are his most elaborate statements on the subject. The first, in reference to *The Wings of the Dove* (1902), contains the same extraordinary blend of fascination and impatience—quite literally attraction and repulsion—that we shall see displayed in all of his major declarations on Henry's late style:

I have read *The Wings of the Dove* (for which all thanks!) but what shall I say of a book constructed on a method which so belies everything that *I* acknowledge as law? You've reversed every traditional canon of story-telling (especially the fundamental one of *telling* the story, which you carefully avoid) and have created a new *genre lit-*

téraire which I can't help thinking perverse, but in which you nevertheless *succeed*, for I read with interest to the end (many pages, and innumerable sentences twice over to see what the dickens they could possibly mean) and all with unflagging curiosity to know what the upshot might become.

William admits the book is "very *distingué* in its way" and concedes "touches unique and inimitable"; but he insists, "it's a 'rum' way; and the worst of it is that I don't know whether it's fatal and inevitable with you, or deliberate and possible to put off and on." The philosopher thereupon tells his brother to send along his additional new works—"whether in this line or not"— and clearly appears to have brought his remarks on the subject to an end. Then suddenly he is compelled to add below: "'In its way' the book is most *beautiful*—the great thing is the way—I went fizzling about concerning it, and expressing my wonder all the while I was reading it."[8]

The next of William's extended criticisms of the late style is in reference to *The Golden Bowl* (1904):

It put me, as most of your recenter long stories have put me, in a very puzzled state of mind. I don't enjoy the kind of "problem," especially when, as in this case, it is treated as problematic (*viz.*, the adulterous relations between Charlotte and the Prince), and the method of narration by interminable elaboration of suggestive reference (I don't know what to call it, but you know what I mean) goes agin the grain of all my impulses in writing; and yet in spite of it all, there is a brilliancy and cleanness of effect, and in this book especially a high-toned social atmosphere that are unique and extraordinary. Your methods and my ideals seem the reverse, the one of the other—and yet I have to admit your extreme success in this book. But why won't you, just to please Brother, sit down and write a new book, with no twilight or mustiness in the plot, with great vigor and decisiveness in the action, no fencing in the dialogue, no psychological commentaries, and absolute straightness in the style? Publish it in my name, I will acknowledge it, and give you half the proceeds. Seriously, I wish you *would*, for you.*can*; and I should think it would tempt you, to embark on a "fourth manner." You of course know these feelings of mine without my writing them down, but I'm "nothing if not" outspoken. Meanwhile you can despise me and fall back on such opposite emotions as Howells's, who seems to admire you without restriction. . . .[9]

Henry's response to all this is a most eloquent defense of his entire aesthetic ideal. He chides William for his popular taste in fiction and asserts: "I *will* write you your book, on that two-and-two-make-four system on which all the awful truck that surrounds us is produced, and *then* descend to my dishonoured grave." He laments not seeing "done or dreamed of the things that alone for me constitute the *interest*" of novelistic art, whereas William's suggestion is "a sacrifice of them on their very own ground." He says furthermore that he is "always sorry when I hear of your reading anything of mine . . . [since William is] so condemned to look at it from a point of view remotely alien to mine in writing it." And he reflects: "It shows how far apart and to what different ends we have had to work out (very naturally and properly!) our respective intellectual lives."[10]

Henry thereupon takes the occasion to inform his brother-critic in a lovely turnabout: "And yet I can read *you* with rapture"; he even maintains that "philosophically, in short, I am 'with' you, almost completely, and you ought to take account of this and get me over altogether."[11] He does not appear to mean anything much by this, however—certainly nothing with respect to his own work, as the letter taken whole makes altogether clear. Nor will he grasp the full implications of being "with" William philosophically until three years later after reading *Pragmatism*, the main reason being that he is presently reading William's argument piecemeal and has yet to see it put together as a whole "way of thinking."

William's third and final extended critique is by far the most remarkable of his letters on the late style. The reference now is to *The American Scene* (1907), and we are about to see the extent to which the philosopher has finally managed to solve the problem, voiced in his previous letter, of just "what to call" Henry's late manner. He begins, characteristically, by pronouncing the book *"supremely great"* in its "peculiar way." But this time he continues:

You know how opposed your whole "third manner" of execution is to the literary ideals which animate my crude and Orson-like breast, mine being to say a thing in one sentence as straight and explicit as it can be made, and then to drop it forever; yours being to avoid naming it straight, but by dint of breathing and sighing all round and round it, to arouse in the reader who may have had a similar perception already (Heaven help him if he hasn't!) the illusion of a solid object, made (like the "ghost" at the Polytechnic) wholly out of impalpable materials, air, and the prismatic interferences of light, ingeniously focused by mirrors upon empty space. But you *do* it, that's the queerness! And the complication of innuendo and associative reference on the enormous scale to which you give way to it does so *build out* the matter for the reader that the result is to solidify, by the mere bulk of the process, the like perception from which *he* has to start. As air, by dint of its volume, will weigh like a corporeal body; so his own poor little initial perception, swathed in this gigantic envelopment of suggestive atmosphere, grows like a germ into something vastly bigger and more substantial. . . . but the *core* of literature is solid. Give it to us *once* again! The bare perfume of things will not support existence, and the effect of solidity you reach is but perfume and simulacrum.[12]

I have already called attention to the singular degree of simultaneous attraction and repulsion present in all of these letters by William. But here in this final one we have something else in addition: we have what is simply one of the most beautifully exact descriptions of the late "Jamesian" method anywhere to be found. What is even more astonishing, we have William apparently reaching out and pulling from the air the concept of Henry's entire method as resembling an expanding "germ"— Henry's own private aesthetic terminology! Henry, it should be remembered, had hitherto virtually confined his formulations on the "germ" to his *Notebooks*, but was now, even when this letter from William arrived, in the process of writing his *Prefaces*.

The result of this remarkable letter is a response from Henry that is at once altogether different from the extended apologia following the earlier letter and also mysteriously coy. "You shall have," he writes, "after a little more patience, a reply to your so rich and luminous reflections on my book—a reply almost as interesting as, and far more illuminating than, your letter itself."[13] I should imagine anyone who is taken with Henry James's "operative" and "applied" irony might well ponder what "reply" he deems "almost as interesting as, and far more illuminating than" William's own "so rich and luminous" letter. It seems altogether likely that Henry, soon to make public his most ambitious and intricately woven set of documents on his aesthetics, a series of *Prefaces* which were by precept and example his views of the organically expanding "germs" governing his novels and tales, perceived immediately the remarkable parallel between what

William was saying about his procedure and his own understanding and justification for it. The unending irony was of course that William's formulation was, as usual, in the context of his own disapproval of the later manner. The "reply" James intended may well have been the *Prefaces* themselves. They would be "almost as interesting" as William's letter because less of a surprise. Yet they would be "far more illuminating" than William's "rich and luminous" letter because they would fully articulate the entire rationale and prove it more than the "perfume and simulacrum" William maintained to be the upshot of the method. Henry, in any case, no longer feels obliged in his reaction to lament William's taste in fiction, to speak of his opposing aesthetic requirements, or to reflect on his and William's different intellectual lives.

But suppose Henry's "reply" did not refer to the *Prefaces*, but to a private revelation in a subsequent letter. He appears never to have written such a reply. The absence of such a letter seems most unexpected given the circumstances. On the other hand, there is still one more consideration that must be taken into account. In this very same letter by William he goes on to tell Henry of having finished "the proofs of a little book called 'Pragmatism' which even you *may* enjoy reading." What happens next in the correspondence perhaps compensates in abundance for the "reply" that did not materialize: for Henry's next letter to William, after an interval of several months, records the novelist's shock of recognition from reading William's "little book":

Why the devil I didn't write to you after reading your *Pragmatism*— how I kept from it—I can't now explain save by the very fact of the spell itself (of interest and enthralment) that the book cast upon me; I simply sank down, under it, into such depths of submission and assimilation that *any* reaction, very nearly, even that of acknowledgment, would have had almost the taint of dissent or escape. Then I was lost in the wonder of the extent to which all my life I have (like M. Jourdain) unconsciously pragmatised. You are immensely and universally *right*, and I have been absorbing a number more of your followings-up of the matter in the American (Journal of Psychology?) which your devouring devotee Manton Marble . . . plied, and always on invitation does ply, me with. I feel the reading of the book, at all events to have been really the event of my summer.[14]

What appears in retrospect to have occurred is that Henry, spurred by William's astounding "naming" of his own germ method, then read *Pragmatism* as soon as it appeared with greater interest than he had read William previously, although (as we have seen) he was already headed in the direction of William's thought and becoming increasingly sympathetic with it. When he read William's book, however, and discovered what he took to be the intimate ties between pragmatism and his own work, then the surprise and irony deriving from William's earlier letter was probably both diminished and simultaneously clarified by the newer discovery which was also the newer surprise. There would have been more "irony" in one sense if Henry had not soon come upon the connection between William's philosophy and his own work, and there would have been more point to his fulfilling his rather sly promise of a rejoinder. As it was, there was irony enough built into the sum of discoveries, and it is most accurately and perceptively distilled into his allusion to "M. Jourdain"—the implications of which have already been touched on.[15]

It may be well to point out at this juncture that, apart from the ambience surrounding Henry's letter above, there are, certainly, various ways one could interpret its substance. One can regard it, as F. O. Matthiessen and Ralph Barton Perry have done, as Henry's belief that he had "embraced pragmatism," had claimed "discipleship." And, I suppose, if we begin to think only in those terms, we are already on the way to what we will conclude: he exhibits no real grasp of the *doctrine*, and therefore his discipleship is not to be taken seriously. And yet, must his statements comprise a *philosophical* expression of his understanding of William before we can say there *is* any understanding of the philosophy? Is not the task more one of trying to discern what he may have had in mind, rather than evaluating his remarks primarily by what we have in mind? Or again—if he had given out just this one picture of himself sinking under William's philosophic spell, and let it go at that, then perhaps it might be well to limit or even discount its importance. But we find instead that he is persisting, after the successive publications of William's other two major works, *A Pluralistic Universe* and *The Meaning of Truth*, in exactly the same sort of identification with the philosopher's thought. And he makes even more explicit his belief in its rich appropriateness to his own artistic life:

All this time I'm not thanking you in the competent way for your *Pluralistic* volume—which now I can effusively do. I read it, while in town, with a more thrilled interest than I can say; with enchantment, with pride, and almost with comprehension. It may sustain and inspire you a little to know that I'm *with* you, all along the line—and can conceive of no sense in any philosophy that is not yours! As an artist and a "creator" I can catch on, hold on, to pragmatism and can work in the light of it and apply it; finding, in comparison, everything else (so far as I know the same!) utterly irrelevant and useless—vainly and coldly parallel![16]

Finally, we have his response to William's now much neglected work, *The Meaning of Truth*, a work which provides an important bridge from William's pragmatism to his subsequent radical empiricism. Henry's enthusiasm is without bounds, although more than two years have elapsed since his self portrait of sinking down into "depths of submission and assimilation" from *Pragmatism*. He declares:

I find it [*The Meaning of Truth*] of thrilling interest, triumphant and brilliant, and am lost in admiration of your wealth and power. I palpitate as you make out your case (since it seems to me you so utterly do,) as I under no romantic spell ever palpitate now; and into that case I enter intensely, unreservedly, and I think you would allow almost intelligently. I find you nowhere as difficult as you surely make everything for your critics. Clearly you are winning a great battle and great will be your fame. . . . You surely make philosophy more interesting and living than anyone has *ever* made it before, and by a real creative and undemolishable making; whereby all you write plays into *my* poor "creative" consciousness and artistic vision and pretension with the most extraordinary suggestiveness and force of application and inspiration. Thank the powers—that is thank *yours!*—for a relevant and assimilable and *referable* philosophy, which is related to the rest of one's intellectual life otherwise and more conveniently than a fowl is related to a fish. In short, dearest William, the effect of these collected papers of your present volume—which I had read all individually before—seems to me exquisitely and adorably cumulative and, so to speak, consecrating; so that I, for my part feel Pragmatic invulnerability constituted.[17]

When we look back over the entire sequence of William and Henry's responses to each other's work during their mutual "major phases" and become aware of the complexity and indeed "operative irony" that obtains in the situation, it is possible to overlook one rather simple but perhaps most significant fact about these exchanges taken as a whole. It is noteworthy that William's claims of opposition end abruptly as soon as Henry's claims of apposition begin: William was never again to criticize the later style or method; the reiterating voice now belongs to Henry.

What is necessary to understand about all three of Henry James's assertions of identity with William's thought is that they are neither mystical, arcane, nor eccentric. They are rather a very natural, although greatly enthusiastic, apprehension of a fundamental affinity. His intellectual encounters with *Pragmatism* and *The Meaning of Truth* in particular have the shock of recognition about them; but it is unlikely that the shock qua shock lasted very long or remained intense from one reading to another. It is doubtful in fact that Henry James thought a great deal, or needed to, about "applying" William's philosophy; his sentiments of "application" are rather repeated recognitions of the prior affinity. Thus, when Henry says he "unconsciously pragmatised," and that William's views are predominantly "creative," he divines a relationship between his own mind and pragmatistic thought which is at once so natural and so deep that it is unnecessary for him to make a continuous fanfare about it; alternatively, there is indeed some fanfare to be made when he is reminded of it in reading William's books. It is perhaps analogous in spirit to the exuberance and delight expressed by William James himself in response to Bergson's *L'Évolution Créatrice*:

O my Bergson, you are a magician, and your book is a marvel, a real wonder in the history of philosophy, making, if I mistake not, an entirely new era in respect of matter, but unlike the works of genius of the "transcendentalist" movement (which are so obscurely and abominably and inaccessibly written), a pure classic in point of form. You may be amused at the comparison, but in finishing it I found the same after-taste remaining as after finishing "Madame Bovary," such a flavor of persistent *euphony*, as of a rich river that never foamed or ran thin, but steadily and firmly proceeded with its banks full to the brim. . . . Oh, indeed you are a magician! And if your next book proves to be as great an advance on this one as this is on its two predecessors, your name will surely go down as one of the great creative names in philosophy.[18]

The sum and substance of the Jameses, then, is this: Henry James belongs to the late nineteenth century in a particular and important way. He has its inner "mind," or mental set. And if Henry has that mind, William probably *expresses*—or "names"—it more consciously and clearly than anyone else in the Anglo-American sphere. I think what Henry remembered when he read William, or rather what he would not have needed to remember, is that pragmatism is itself a continuous and concatenated mentality—a way of thinking; it was not for him simply another "ism"; in no case was it a justification for our various national ills, or the "symbol" of a moral inertia eventually brought to fruition by the world wars. It was instead for him a consciousness *of* consciousness—an awareness that philosophical speculation, hitherto forbidding and remote, was suddenly a justification for the imaginative act of the mind operating on the produce of the common day. It was therefore more "relevant, assimilable, and *referable*" to the rest of one's intellectual life than "a fowl is related to a fish," because Truth, the ancient mountaintop, was suddenly presented somewhat like the realistic novel as occurring from moment to moment; and "Being," that rather frightening metaphysical concept, was suddenly to be apprehended "in the making," the poetry of alternatives in the actual world. The sense of possibility and delight which Henry feels on behalf of William, and William on behalf of Bergson, issues quite naturally in Henry's expression of William's thought as "living" and William's allusion to the poetic novel *Madame Bovary*.

And yet, as I have already indicated, neither Ralph Barton Perry nor F. O. Matthiessen can be said to have taken Henry's response to William's philosophy as particularly meaningful. Perry especially sees almost nothing in it whatever. In his magnificent exposition and tribute to William's work, *The Thought and Character of William James*, his own quite different purpose and direction precludes a penetrating analysis of Henry's avowal. His comment is brief and decisive:

It is evident from these letters that Henry let William do his philosophizing for him. . . . I can only conclude, as might have been supposed, that his mind was quite naive on that side, and that his profession of pragmatism was an extension of that admiring pride with which he had from childhood viewed all of William's superior attainments. The relation was not symmetrical. As to Henry's work, William freely offered both advice and criticism; while as to William's, Henry could offer only an undiscriminating praise.[19]

For F. O. Matthiessen the matter is not nearly so cut and dried as this, although his conclusion could be described as similar to Perry's in the long run. In his classic study of James's later work, *Henry James: The Major Phase*, he gives the following assessment:

Henry was hardly more of a philosopher than he was a theologian, even though, as we have seen, he was concerned, particularly in the cases of Isabel Archer and of Strether, with what Strether called "the illusion of freedom." But, even though he continued to read his brother's works "with rapture," and declared, upon the appearance of *Pragmatism* (1907), that he was "lost in the wonder of the extent to which all my life I have (like M. Jourdain) unconsciously pragmatised," he had scarcely the trace of a system. Spectator rather than either doer or thinker, he had proceeded to compose and to frame the most glittering scenes.[20]

Three years later, in *The James Family*, Matthiessen again reiterates this position: "All their other discrepancies in thought and expression would seem to stem back to their contrasting conceptions of knowledge, since the knower as actor and the knower as spectator are bound to behold different worlds, and to shape them to different ends."[21]

Despite the similarity in these conclusions, however, Matthiessen makes, in *The James Family*, some very penetrating remarks pertaining to certain parallels in the brothers' work. He asserts that "no matter how wide the divergence between the directions taken by these brothers' minds, or between the curves of their reputations, they are held together by a solid core of values." Foremost among these values, he believes, is "the sacredness of the individual"; and, what is perhaps more striking still, their mutual "willingness to stand sympathetically inside other points of view"—which Matthiessen illustrates by comparing a passage from *A Pluralistic Universe* with Henry's famous "house of fiction" conceit from his "Preface" to *The Portrait of a Lady*.[22]

Nevertheless Matthiessen, as we have just seen, seems unable to reconcile Henry's lifelong commitment to observation and "composition" with William's activist, "doing" dimension. Thus, William's impatience with Henry's later manner would in that sense seem a logical extension of his philosophic thought: "To W[illiam] J[ames] such a world was far too static, far too attenuated in its aesthetic essences, for him to enter into it with much sympathy or even understanding." Alternatively, Matthiessen feels that Henry is certainly the one who justifies through his work the values of contemplation and reflection. In what seems to be a favorite locus of reference for those who have spoken to the subject, Matthiessen cites as example the "free spirit" of Fleda Vetch, heroine of *The Spoils of Poynton*; she is ultimately triumphant over the symbol of "will" embodied in Mona Brigstock. Matthiessen assures us, however, that "H[enry] J[ames] unquestionably had no thought there of giving a warning to W[illiam] J[ames], though some of the distorters of W[illiam] J[ames]'s philosophy have seized upon its danger point in its too unguarded exaltation of the will."[23]

Perhaps because of these assessments by F. O. Matthiessen and Ralph Barton Perry, two of the most penetrating and influential minds in American letters, there have been comparatively few scholars willing to posit a pervasive identity of mind between the work of the two brothers. Of these, Eliseo Vivas is to my mind the most important. Before turning to his argument, however, it will be helpful to glance at the assumptions contained in two propositions from Joseph Firebaugh and John Henry Raleigh. They are, I believe, illustrative of two sorts of pitfalls hard to avoid when arguing Henry's relationship with William or with any empiricist philosopher. In an article concerned with *The Awkward Age* Firebaugh asserts: "Henry James expressed fictionally . . . what his brother William James was expressing in the pragmatic philosophy: the discovery of truth in the market place of human life: truth as process rather than truth as absolute: truth for men, not Truth for Man."[24]

This is certainly in my judgment the proper stance, and yet its difficulty lies partly in its being primarily a "stance"; it inadvertently sidesteps the kind of situation we have with William and Henry. If the relationship is a truly viable one, then I am afraid both William and Henry must be *shown* together dovetailing, coalescing. If Henry James unconsciously pragmatizes or (as Firebaugh says) "expresses" something as vast as William's philosophy, William James must then be very much present in the demonstration. A capsule of pragmatic philosophy, however accurate as far as it goes, is not fully convincing.[25]

An essay by John Henry Raleigh, "Henry James: The Poetics of Empiricism," presents an argument which is even more unsatisfying. Raleigh's thesis is—again, quite inadvertently—about as misleading as his title is interesting and promising. His own statement of this thesis unfortunately contains its own best evaluation:

This perhaps sounds too simple to be true but James' beloved consciousness, the chief subject matter of his works, was nothing more than an artistic presentation of the idea of the tabula rasa being written upon by experience, or sense impressions. If the mind is a blank upon which experience writes, then it follows that personality itself is passive rather than active and that a person is more of an observer than anything else; consequently there is that thin red line of sad young men in the James novels who rise to life's battles only to renounce, and the archetypal figure, Isabel Archer or Strether, is the perfect observer upon whom nothing is lost.[26]

Henry James is actually precluded any true "poetics," empirical or otherwise, by virtue of this contention. It is a classic instance of inadvertently equating characteristics which may hold true of some fictional characters presented by an author with the author's own creative process by which he *makes* such characters. If James's "beloved consciousness" is really nothing more than an "artistic presentation" of the tabula rasa, then surely all the more need to address the active agency at work in the present*ing*. The "Henry James" of such a thesis thus stands in relation to the actual James of our reading, as do the associationism or "mind dust" theories of Locke and the older empiricists in relation to the post-Kantian empiricism of William James. The main difficulty is that ultimately Raleigh does not mislead for lacking knowledge of Henry James but for not being sufficiently concerned with philosophy.

This brings us now to a most important formulation for any discussion of William and Henry James. It is a short article by Eliseo Vivas, his contribution to the Henry James issue of *Kenyon Review* in 1943. It has the very deceptively modest title, "Henry and William: (Two Notes)." Although he does not concern himself with Henry's own responses to William's pragmatism, Vivas nevertheless wishes to propose what he calls "deep and complex spiritual affinities" between Henry and William. What he argues in his two notes is best summarized by Vivas himself: "while, on the one hand, in their moral conceptions they stand, as it were, back to back, there is a resemblance between them, on the other, in the way they conceive the mind's mode of apprehension, in which they conceive the process, that is, through which the mind enters into relations with its world."[27]

We have in other words a fundamental moral opposition and yet an equally fundamental epistemological identification. In his first note Vivas elucidates the moral opposition, and he is extremely hard on William James. He characterizes William's thought and entire theoretical view of life as a "morality of expedience," an "attenuated Darwinism." This, he believes, contrasts sharply with Henry's lifelong commitment to the principles of contemplation, ideal principle, and beauty: "Henry, in other words, repudiates the anti-intellectualism which underlies his brother's vision of the world, and which opposes life to thought, *real* living to theorizing, action to contemplation. He finds, as he puts it in *The Sacred Fount*, that 'for real excitement there are no . . . adventures as intellectual ones.' For some men at least, thinking is itself the most intense way of living."[28]

Such "opposing conceptions of what constitutes life," as Vivas speaks of them, give rise in turn to the brothers' conflicting ethical attitudes. He cites as illustration *The Spoils of Poynton*, because he believes that it "embodies clearly and fully [Henry James's] ethical vision": Fleda Vetch, the heroine, refuses Owen Gereth's proposal of marriage because she is, according to Vivas, "guided by a high ideal, [and] regards the claims of principle as higher than those of personal convenience"—this latter, Vivas insists, amounting to William's doctrine of "expedience." Hence: "The contrast between Henry's moral vision and William's moral theory is sharp and shocking. For the beauty of character, faithfulness to the pledged word, and scrupulous sensibility for the feelings and rights of others, which we have seen to be implicit in Henry's vision of life, we must now substitute a barely attenuated version of Darwinism in the moral life, which hardly conceals the doctrine that successful force is the right."[29]

Vivas, in what seems oftentimes a much too common inter-

pretation of William James, proceeds then to indict the philosopher's thought for standing but a step removed from aiding and
abetting some of the horrors of the present century. What I have
already quoted, however, sufficiently indicates his view of the
Jameses' opposing ethics.

His second note is so different it is difficult at first to believe
they are written by the same person:

There is one respect in which Henry and William are at one. I do not
know exactly how to refer to it, but I seem to see between William's
conception of consciousness and his philosophy of "pure experience"
which is based on this conception, on the one hand, and on the other the
mode of perception which became characteristically Henry's, an intimate relationship. It need not be, though it may be, a question of influence. But however it came about, each brother expresses in his own
domain something which, I suspect, is somehow essential to the last
half of the 19th Century, since it is not only found in pragmatism, and
in the novels of Henry James, but in Bergson and elsewhere in philosophy *. . . and also in the painting of the impressionists. In William it is
best to be seen in his analysis of "the mind from within," while in Henry
we must look for it in the way in which he apprehends his material.
. . . We might indeed say—though it can not be intended literally of
course—that Henry illustrates quite aptly his brother's doctrine of the
stream of consciousness and of "pure experience."

Vivas recognizes the implications in what he is suggesting as
well as the severe difficulties in actually demonstrating it: "If
this hunch," he writes, "could be made clear and plausible the results would, I am sure, amply reward the difficulties involved in
presenting a topic on which, I fear, I am not adequately clear."[30]
The rewards, he feels, would lie primarily in showing that
Henry's art is "a personal expression of a larger movement," an
intrinsic part of the late nineteenth century, and not just an
exotic or monastic affair of art. The difficulties he deals with in
the following way: he quotes to us a short passage from *The
Principles of Psychology*, in which William proposes his famous
conception, different from that of the earlier empiricists, that the
activity of the mind is essentially streamlike and fluid, rather
than an elaborate mechanism resembling an intricate set of
movable "containers." As William puts it: "The traditional psychology talks like one who should say a river consists of nothing
but pailsful, spoonsful, quartpotsful, and other moulded forms

of water. Even were the pails and the pots actually standing in the stream, still between them the free water would continue to flow."[31]

Vivas finds William's image of the human mind's continuum resembling that of successive "flights" and "perchings" to be an especially helpful analogy to Henry's fictional presentation (I might suggest here that the reader think of Henry's well-known "foreground," "panorama," or "picture" alternating with "scenic" rendition for William's "flights" and "perchings," but always as one dramatic continuity). The central point, and Vivas recognizes it, is that the flights are as real as the perchings, even though they are usually more difficult to speak of. He then makes the following application to James's fiction:

> Let us now attend to a man walking with his daughter on a Sunday afternoon in an old English garden. They go out of a gate and search for a bench under an oak, and sit down and talk. Our psychological information, if we have been convinced by William James, will make us aware that what we observe from our point of vantage—the garden, the man and woman, their talk, the quality of the day, its light and warmth and fragrance—comes to us enveloped in an affective light which fuses the elements intimately. . . .
>
> Our psychological knowledge, if we are not artists, would not be a blessing, but a positive hindrance. For under its influence the problem that presents itself to us is not merely that of noting down faithfully what we saw and heard. If what we want is the reality of the scene, it is in its sensational flux that we must look for its true shape. Our problem then is to capture what we saw and heard in such a way as not to lose the fluid affinity that the things that make up the episode had for one another.[32]

In short, it is the later manner of the later Henry James. Eliseo Vivas (in what, after long consideration of this subject, strikes me as a most pertinent statement arising from his astonishing second "note") chooses not to quote Henry James illustrating William's view of the mind. He says instead: "To see how [Henry] actually managed the scene in the old garden let the reader turn to the third and fourth chapters in *The Golden Bowl*. No short quotation can give the full impression of a scene from his pen."[33] The unwillingness here to quote from James's fiction in this context is not accidental or arbitrary. It results in part from the very implications of the William-Henry relationship, and is no minor consideration in any genuine attempt to demonstrate it. For to argue that Henry's fiction realizes William's fundamental view of the human mind is to be saddled with the inference that practically any passage, so long as it is from the late style and properly characteristic, could serve as illustration and paradigm. The commentator thus finds himself in the position (if I may appropriate William's imagery) of choosing arbitrarily from the continuous "flight" and fluidity of Henry's late prose. Denied, so to speak, the intellectual and ideological "perchings" built into most arguments of the scholarly sort, he is likely to say in effect, as Vivas does: well, you had just better go read Henry with all this in mind. If on the other hand Henry were only echoing the "Ideas" of William or even "expressing" them (as Firebaugh says), the ideological "perchings" would then become more discernible. I myself have attempted to deal with the same difficulty most directly in Part 2 of this book.

Nevertheless, Vivas's second note is clearly a most seminal grasp of the brothers' intellectual relationship. His very language, in saying that Henry's scene in *The Golden Bowl* comes to us "enveloped in an affective light which fuses the elements intimately," recalls to us William's own statement to Henry that the reader's perception is "swathed in this gigantic envelopment of suggestive atmosphere." And Henry's belief that the relationship was literally that of "M. Jourdain," and that William's philosophy is first and foremost a "creative" philosophy, is the clear analogue to Vivas's second note—though Vivas himself rather surprisingly observes that the entire matter "can not be intended literally of course."

For the very same reasons, however, it must be said that Vivas's first note, dealing with the moral opposition, is unfounded. The mistake lies in divorcing William's ethical viewpoint from his epistemology. In point of fact they are so thoroughly interdependent that it is always most unwise to consider him at any length and keep them apart. The very "continuity" which Vivas perceives in his second note is precisely what, on deeper examination and reflection, makes the first note specious. We have just seem him claim, for example, that Henry illustrates William's "doctrine of the stream of consciousness and of 'pure experience.' " There we have just the point: one has no sooner addressed the earlier psychology than he finds himself drawn into the later epistemology of radical empiricism. William James is of continuous esemplastic stitch that way, and what holds true of his psychology and epistemology holds true as well of his ethical view. That ethical view is no more aptly described as "attenuated Darwinism" than his view of consciousness as merely a sophisticated tabula rasa.

For the reader to see this in full perspective it is only necessary for him to recollect the heart of F. O. Matthiessen's argument and to compare it with Vivas's claim of moral opposition. He may be surprised to learn that they are quite identical. According to Vivas, Henry's ethical values proceed from his intellectualism, his devotion to the dramatic life of thought and contemplation, as opposed to William's "real living" and real action. For Matthiessen, likewise, "all their other discrepancies in thought and expression" stem from the fundamental distinction of "knower as actor" [William] from that of "knower as spectator" [Henry]. The surprise I speak of results from the fact that it was Matthiessen who found the brothers *epistemologically* at odds for the foregoing reasons while sharing otherwise "a solid core of values"! Thus Vivas's moral opposition argues for Matthiessen's epistemological opposition, whereas Matthiessen's moral equation of the brothers standing sympathetically "inside other points of view" is closely allied to Vivas's epistemological argument of "the mind from within." The very terms of one commentator's alpha view constitute the other's omega, and vice versa. It is a situation not unlike the "operative irony" of James's fiction and one often repeated in the reverse readings given individual stories by his commentators.

The immediate reason for this particular turn-of-the-screw is that William's thought is not an affair of ethics on the one hand and theory of knowledge on the other; and to compartmentalize them in that fashion is not to talk sufficiently about William James's thought.[34] As for Henry, he may or may not realize William's theory of knowledge; but if he does, there will be more involved ultimately than "flights" and "perchings," as crucial as these may be; or rather, it is just because they *are* so crucial that there *is* more involved. And the strongest external evidence that this is so lies in the meaning of Henry's own responses to William's philosophy. For what "part" of William James is, after all, "unconsciously pragmatised"? Those volumes by William which elicited the "undiscriminating praise" Ralph Barton Perry speaks of are distinguished by the thorough *conjunctiveness* of all that we are liable to pull out of its stream and treat as individual "things": his ethics, his individualism, his democracy, his psychology, his cognition, and so forth. It may be that in the end the biggest difficulty with William's doctrine lies in the sheer demand it makes that we think in the totally conjunctive manner it implies. Alternatively, if Henry's enthusiastic identification with it strikes for us a vague or "undiscriminating" note, that may be because he did have the conjunctive mind it implies to a far greater extent than do most of us. This is suggested in particular by the fact that Henry did not become truly excited by William's work *until* he read *Pragmatism*. It is reiterated when he points out, with reference to *The Meaning of Truth*, that the case there is so rich in its "cumulative" effect as compared with the individual papers. Continuity and conjunction, we should remember, are also what stare us in the face on every page of his mature fiction. It is primarily what we mean by "Jamesian."

It remains however to make an adequate response to Matthiessen's distinction between "knower as actor" and "knower as spectator"; or, since in his argument it comes to the same thing, Vivas's between "experience" and "intellectuality." I mean now a rejoinder apropos of William James's philosophy itself. It is most appropriately found in *The Meaning of Truth*. Speaking there of his famous (or infamous) "practical consequences," William James notes: "'Practical' in the sense of *particular*, of course, not in the sense that the consequences may not be *mental* as well as physical."[35]

It is quite astonishing that this essential element in William James's work has not been made more of in connection with his relationship to Henry, for his own writing is itself such a continual demonstration and example of it. Must it really be said that the famous pragmatic method is both by precept and example in William's philosophy primarily a way of making concepts come alive by projecting the dramatic particularities which would follow from them first in one direction, then in another—and one need not step off the platform except expressly with one's mind and imagination? The pragmatic method is about as much a justification for, let us say, Hitler, as his famous "Will to Believe" a set of criteria for choosing among brands at the supermarket.[36] If we really wish the tough-minded assumptions, let us attend to the various positivistic schools, which William in such essays as "The Dilemma of Determinism" almost made a life's work of deploring and contesting. And if we wish more the sort of destructive innocence of mind, let us look more to the transcendentalist mentality, which William likewise persisted in bringing down to cases.

In summary, it might be said that Henry James's relationship with pragmatistic thinking lies very much in the fact that he would have been the last person who needed to read William's note on the phrase "practical consequences." It may even be the case, though we can never know for certain, that the correspondence between the brothers on each other's work had a hand in William's clarifying note. In the same book William addresses what he calls the "misunderstanding" that his doctrine is primarily "an appeal of action" and retorts in language that echoes one of the most famous passages in his brother's writings:

This pragmatist doctrine, exhibiting our ideas as complemental factors of reality, throws open (since our ideas are instigators of our action) a wide window upon human action, as well as a wide license to originality in thought. But few things could be sillier than to ignore the prior epistemological edifice in which the window is built, or to talk as if pragmatism began and ended at the window. This, nevertheless, is what our critics do almost without exception. They ignore our primary step and its motive, and make the relation to action, which is our secondary achievement, primary.[37]

What would have made this clarification as unnecessary for Henry as the previous note is that both clarifications so unquestionably describe what William's own writings are "*known-as*"—to borrow his own terminology.[38] If Henry had been the unconscious pragmatist, William had been the unconscious Jacobite.

III. William James
and Ambulatory Relations

In the work of William James there is no more fundamental statement of his entire epistemological argument than in his discussion of what he calls "saltatory" and "ambulatory" relations.
This is to be found in *The Meaning of Truth* (1909), a book
which, as we have just seen, drew unqualified praise and enthusiasm from Henry James, who spoke of its "cumulative" effect
on him. The argument from William that follows will give us
that "cumulative" sense of a great portion of his thought.

Saltatory relations are defined by William as "pure acts of
the intellect coming upon the sensations from above, and of a
higher nature," so that one believes himself justified in "jumping
as it were immediately from one term to another." This is not the
case, however, if one's view of cognition is ambulatory or "made
out of intervening parts of experience through which we ambulate in succession." He then declares: "Now the most general
way of contrasting my view of knowledge with the popular view
(which is also the view of most epistemologists) is to call my
view ambulatory, and the other view saltatory; and the most
general way of characterizing the two views is by saying that my
view describes knowing as it exists concretely, while the other
view only describes its results abstractly taken."[1]

Even though he has yet to fully characterize the difference
between these two views, William James's direction is already
clearly apparent: it is toward the importance of affirming a concrete process, and away from affirming what that same process
is alleged to come to or mean in the abstract. As regards a literary work, it might be useful to express this same distinction as
the difference between what we regard to be the work's final

"theme" or "meaning," and something like the actual experience of reading it from point to point—how it *proceeds* to mean. This distinction, generally rather important for the explication of poetry, nevertheless points toward the method and the literary issues peculiarly associated with the novelist-brother. One thinks, for example, of such standard Jamesian critical expression and language as "the dramatic method," or what Joseph Warren Beach calls his "art of *representation*." What does such methodology imply, what do Beach's acute words, "manoeuvers," and the reader's "assist[ing] at the gradual process," depict, but the very relation William James has here named "ambulatory"?[2] The reader can begin to surmise the extent of the case if he now observes William James's fuller elaboration of his saltatory/ambulatory distinction. It is a remarkable argument and must be quoted rather extensively; for it inadvertently names and justifies that celebrated and illusive form of art known as the later manner of Henry James:

I fear that most of my recalcitrant readers fail to recognize that what is ambulatory in the concrete may be taken so abstractly as to appear saltatory. Distance, for example, is made abstract by emptying out whatever is particular in the concrete intervals—it is reduced thus to a sole "difference," a difference of "place," which is a logical or saltatory distinction, a so-called "pure relation."

The same is true of the relation called "knowing," which may connect an idea with a reality. My own account of this relation is ambulatory through and through. I say that we know an object by means of an idea, whenever we ambulate towards the object under the impulse which the idea communicates. If we believe in so-called "sensible" realities, the idea may not only send us towards its object, but may put the latter into our very hand, make it our immediate sensation. But, if, as most reflective people opine, sensible realities are not "real" realities, but only their appearances, our idea brings us at least so far, puts us in touch with reality's most authentic appearances and substitutes. . . .

The idea is thus, when functionally considered, an instrument for enabling us the better to *have to do* with the object and to act about it. But it and the object are both of them bits of the general sheet and tissue of reality at large; and when we say that the idea leads us towards the object, that only means that it carries us forward through intervening tracts of that reality into the object's closer neighborhood, into the midst of its associates at least, be these its physical neighbors, or be they its logical congeners only. Thus carried into closer quarters, we are in an improved situation as regards acquaintance and conduct; and we say that through the idea we now *know* the object better or more truly.

My thesis is that the knowing here is *made* by the ambulation through the intervening experiences. If the idea led us nowhere, or *from* that object instead of towards it, could we talk at all of its having any cognitive quality? Surely not, for it is only when taken in conjunction with the intermediate experiences that it gets related to *that particular object* rather than to any other part of nature. Those intermediaries determine what particular knowing function it exerts. The terminus they guide us to tells us what object it "means," the results they enrich us with "verify" or "refute" it. Intervening experiences are thus as indispensable foundations for a concrete relation of cognition as intervening space is for a relation of distance. Cognition, whenever we take it concretely, means determinate "ambulation," . . . [Therefore] there would appear to be nothing especially unique about the processes of knowing. They fall wholly within experience.[3]

It may seem odd to equate a theory of cognition here described as "nothing especially unique" with of all things the renowned and "unique" later manner of Henry James. And yet the very nexus for all of the basic features of that late style are provided by William's formulation. What he has done above all is to make knowing continually dramatic, a "happening" if you will. Similarly to *Pragmatism*, where truth is "itself an event," he now conceives the knowing process as a continual event, for intervening experiences, like "intervening space" in distance relationships, must be mentally grasped as real "territory" and thus made living and present, the sacredness of each "intermediary" as important as Henry's nuances and "shades" of meaning. William furthermore presents us with a theory of knowledge in which all that we ordinarily think of as the means, the method, or the instrumentation become radically reversed—the what-we-know itself the activity of know*ing*. Hence the fundamental open-endedness of William's thought—and of Henry's novels. Henry James, it is well recognized, spent his life perfecting the art of the novel, and has therefore been adjudged by many until recent years to be a master craftsman, the novelist's novelist. But now, owing both to extensive study of his work as well as more comprehensive aesthetic assumptions, it is virtually commonplace to point out that in James's work one should not separate his form from his content, his craft from his meaning, his aesthetic from his ethic. Indeed James himself in "The Art of Fiction," perhaps the singular argument in English criticism for the values of execution, nevertheless argues that it cannot be separated from plot or story anymore than one can separate character from incident, and either of these from picture or novel.[4] William and Henry came to maturity at a time when both the rigidity in prevailing philosophy and literary practice called for innovation and renovation, which each attempted in his own field. The sense of the world as actual process was for them such a liberating conception that it issued in writings which proclaim consciousness "functionally"—construing it in reciprocal relation with the abounding flux and content of mental life, while yet operating in this fashion apart from fixed transcendent principles.

For what has William James said: not that his view of knowledge gives merely more importance to intervening experiences, but—"My thesis is that knowing here is *made* by the ambulation through intervening experiences." Let the reader imagine a literary work which corresponds to this assumption, and he will quickly come upon a unique situation: what is asserted by many commentators to be the fusion of craft with meaning, art with morality, method with value, may at the same time evoke readings and meanings by the same commentators quite antithetical to one another. In that way Henry's fiction is certainly "cordial" or open-ended in the William Jamesian sense.

These considerations may be further clarified if we return once more to William's exposition of ambulation. Having defined his own position on the matter, he now goes on to tell how and why it is we often confuse the actual knowing situation with a "saltatory" explanation of it:

But there exist no processes which we cannot also consider abstractly, eviscerating them down to their essential skeletons or outlines; and when we have treated the processes of knowing thus, we are easily led to regard them as something altogether unparalleled in nature. For we first empty idea, object and intermediaries of all their particularities, in order to retain only a general scheme, and then we consider the latter only in its function of giving a result, and not in its character of being a process. In this treatment the intermediaries shrivel into the form of a mere space of separation, while the idea and object retain only the logical distinctness of being the end-terms that

are separated. In other words, the intermediaries which in their concrete particularity form a bridge, evaporate ideally into an empty interval to cross, and then, the relation of the end-terms having become
saltatory, the whole hocus-pocus of *erkenntnisstheorie* begins, and
goes on unrestrained by further concrete considerations. The idea, in
"meaning" an object separated by an "epistemological chasm" from itself, now executes . . . a *"salto mortale"*; in knowing the object's nature, it now "transcends" its own. The object in turn becomes "present"
where it is really absent, etc.; until a scheme remains upon our hands,
the sublime paradoxes of which some of us think that nothing short of
an "absolute" can explain.

The relation between idea and object, thus made abstract and saltatory, is thenceforward opposed, as being more essential and previous, to its own ambulatory self, and the more concrete description is
branded as either false or insufficient. The bridge of intermediaries,
actual or possible, which in every real case is what carries and defines
the knowing, gets treated as an episodic complication which need not
even potentially be there.[5]

This passage is perhaps even more remarkable than the preceding one. In so many ways it inadvertently both raises and
clarifies a number of basic issues surrounding Henry's fiction
which have persisted ever since he began to develop the late style,
shortly after his failure as a playwright. These issues have on
occasion been dealt with in such a piece as "The First Paragraph
of *The Ambassadors*: An Explication," by Ian Watt.[6] But there
remains no better touchstone for the same issue of the late James
style than the memorable exchange the novelist had with H. G.
Wells in 1915, the year before his death. Let us revisit that exchange with William's ambulation in mind.

Wells, it will be remembered, wrote *Boon*, less a book than
a frenetic collection of odds and ends on various topics, but
which nevertheless included a lengthy attack on James and the
theory of literature he represented. Wells calls him "the culmi-
nation of the Superficial type," who "pick[s] the straws out of
the hair of Life before he paints her." He goes on to compare
James's work (in an enduring image) to a beautifully lit church
without a congregation, and with an altar containing "a dead
kitten, an egg-shell, a bit of string." James, he says, is "leviathan
retrieving pebbles." He is "a magnificent but painful hippopotamus resolved at any cost . . . upon picking up a pea."[7]

All of this represents of course a view towards James's work which is now generally repudiated, the view that he expends enormous manner and pyrotechnics on little or no matter. What *is* significant in this context, however, is that whenever one responds to James along the lines of Wells (such as the student introduced to his work for the first time), he invariably refuses not merely, as we say with James, to grant the author his donnée, but to conceive of meaning as in fact the process, the proceeding-to-mean. If he is our young student, he may even be imbued with such contemporary dogma as that "the medium is the message," or that meaningful life is "a happening," or even that "all values are relative"; but he nevertheless disjoins process from content in the late work of James. He has without knowing it the saltatory mind. For in Henry James the "hippopotamus" is one and the same *as* the "pea" for precisely and distinctly the same reason why William James's "idea" and "object" are made confluent by the actual ambulation which takes place between them. Conversely, William's explanation of how the saltatory theorists begin by "eviscerating" the actual knowing process down to its "skeleton" or "outline" by eliminating its "particularities," and thus subsequently come to imagine that the "bridge of intermediaries" is not even "potentially there," is precisely the same mentality and viewpoint which can find Henry so radically disproportionate in manner to meaning that he gives us "tales of nothingness"—as Wells wrote.

The point is that all human thinking is to some extent "ambulatory" and to some extent "saltatory," with the latter tending, in most intellectual areas, at least, to predominate. The professor's age-old insistence that his students demonstrate their generalizations "from the text," or even the caveat of the (now old) new criticism about the "heresy of paraphrase" in the case of lyric poems, constitute examples of an ambulatory predominance. Conversely, a "history of ideas" approach, whereby one can get from the Puritan mind in seventeenth-century America to the Enlightenment period without too much difficulty; or, say, the famous "Edwards to Emerson" link—would illustrate a saltatory predominance. But a "history of consciousness" method such as that discussed in my opening chapter would tend back in the direction of ambulation. The reason is that such a method arises in turn from the assumption that a Cartesian dualism of subject-object disjunction and division is not the actual state of affairs—in cognition, perception, or indeed any of the fundamental relationships which comprise the human condition. The whole issue is that of the "fox" and the "hedgehog." William's view of ambulation is itself an intermediary "bridge" from his pragmatism to his radical empiricism, for it so clearly expresses his own desired attempt to undermine that same Cartesian dualism. Ultimately, in his last and most "radical" empiricism, he was to reject Cartesian dualism altogether by positing as given and prior a world-life itself of "pure experience," anterior even to human consciousness which participates in it.

But if William's *view* is "ambulatory through and through," as he says, William himself is for the most part saltatory, even when he is expounding ambulation or other various pragmatistic doctrines allied to it! Henry, on the other hand, is a "natural" ambulator. William is the fox, Henry the hedgehog. In answering H. G. Wells, for example, Henry James is ever so characteristic in the refusal of his "later mind" simply to treat the younger novelist's antagonistic ideas as "other," or *dis*joined from the continuity and process of his own conscious experience. By attempting to embrace even Well's harsh attack as *not*, in William's terms, "an empty interval" between their two minds, and *not* therefore "unparalleled in nature," Henry James makes that attack a genuine "interval"—"democratically" equal to his own beliefs—on the vector of his continuing sensibility. He refuses in short to jump over any "bridge of intermediaries." Let us see:

It is difficult of course for a writer to put himself *fully* in the place of another writer who finds him extraordinarily futile and void, and who is moved to publish that to the world—and I think the case isn't easier when he happens to have enjoyed the other writer enormously, from far back; because there has then grown up the habit of taking some common meeting-ground between them for granted, and the falling away of this is like the collapse of a bridge which made communication possible. But I am by nature more in dread of any fool's paradise, or at least of any bad misguidedness, than in love with the idea of a security proved, and the fact that a mind as brilliant as yours *can* resolve me into such an unmitigated mistake, can't enjoy me in anything like the degree in which I like to think I may be enjoyed, makes me greatly want to fix myself, for as long as my nerves will stand it, with such a pair of eyes.[8]

It will be understood, of course, that James does not agree with Wells's evaluation of him. We are speaking of how he characteristically sees an issue, and how this seeing is given utterance in the late style. It makes us appreciate, I think, the real sincerity with which he held time and again that the whole interest of the novel derives from its variety of form and execution, its freedom to embrace the most multiple and "unlikely" of practitioners. Henry is, in other words, a thoroughgoing pluralist, which follows in turn from his being an ambulator. He articulates this pluralism repeatedly in his responses to Wells: "The fine thing about the fictional form to me is that it opens such widely different windows of attention; but that is just why I like the window so to frame the play and the process!" And again: "But I *have* no view of life and literature, I maintain, other than that our form of the latter in especial is admirable exactly by its range and variety, its plasticity and liberality, its fairly living on the sincere and shifting experience of the individual practitioner."[9]

What is preeminently "Jamesian" in this matter of pluralism is that for him variety and difference do not merely constitute his tolerance and lip service. They are close to an *élan vital* for him. The fact that Wells thinks his sense of life "doesn't exist" can even make the novelist call into question his own assumption "of the various appreciability of our addiction to the novel and of all the personal and intellectual history, sympathy and curiosity, behind the given example of it." Nevertheless, for his own part: "It is when that history and curiosity have been determined in the way most different from my own that I want to get at them— precisely *for* the extension of life, which is the novel's best gift."[10]

Nothing could be more expressive of the pluralistic ideal. James's late ambulating mind is so genuinely devoted to this way of thinking that on more than one occasion he raises it to something like the level of a lyric hymn; and when he does, it should not surprise us that such utterances make up the best known and already most widely attended of his poetic statements. Such an instance is this, from the "Preface" to *The Portrait of a Lady*:

Here we get exactly the high price of the novel as a literary form—its power not only, while preserving that form with closeness, to range through all the differences of the individual relation to its general subject-matter, all the varieties of outlook on life, of disposition to reflect and project, created by conditions that are never the same from man to man . . . but positively to appear more true to its character in proportion as it strains, or tends to burst, with a latent extravagance, its mould.[11]

This is, to repeat, on the order of a hymn to pluralism—and pluralism rightly grasped and understood. That is, James provides here in the context of fiction the pluralist's fundamental viewpoint on the ancient problem of the One and the Many. What is so remarkable is that he chooses, after already introducing his series of qualifications on behalf of individual particularities and differences (the many), to then assert his unity only by virtue of its own tendency to "burst . . . its mould"! We have precisely the same way of thinking in the celebrated passage that immediately follows this one and seeks to image it:

The house of fiction has in short not one window, but a million—a number of possible windows not to be reckoned, rather; every one of which has been pierced, or is still pierceable, in its vast front, by the need of the individual vision and by the pressure of the individual will. These apertures, of dissimilar shape and size, hang so, all together, over the human scene that we might have expected of them a greater sameness of report than we find. They are but windows at the best, mere holes in a dead wall, disconnected, perched aloft; they are not hinged doors opening straight upon life. But they have this mark of their own that at each of them stands a figure with a pair of eyes, or at least with a field-glass, which forms, again and again, for observation, a unique instrument, insuring to the person making use of it an impression distinct from every other. He and his neighbours are watching the same show, but one seeing more where the other sees less, one seeing black where the other sees white, one seeing big where the other sees small, one seeing coarse where the other sees fine. And so on, and so on; there is fortunately no saying on what, for the particular pair of eyes, the window may *not* open; "fortunately" by reason, precisely, of this incalculability of range.[12]

It is of course a truism by now to point out the parallel in this lovely passage with James's characteristic method in the late fiction, not to mention that of the passage itself with the imagery of that fiction. But both arise in turn from the positive affiliations with the pluralistic ideal ("'fortunately' by reason, precisely, of this incalculability of range"). That his later method so arises has been in effect the point of this brief chapter. That the poetic imagery also so arises will require more elucidation and more examination of the work of Henry and William put together side by side, overlaid and alternating. The implications of the relationship this study seeks to bring to light are even indicated by the fact that in the foregoing passages Henry is explicitly addressing the question of where his "moral reference" comes from. Thus, the pluralistic ideal is at once the moral ideal, and vice versa. Because of such continual interconnectedness, Part 2 of this study will enter more closely still into the texture of the William-Henry relationship, hopefully penetrating down from the level of a history of ideas in the direction, at least, toward a history of consciousness.

``Confluent,'' ``Conjoined,'' ``Concatenated'':

A Letter to Henry Adams

IV. The "Jourdain" Relationship (I)

The Later Manner an Habitual Mode of Thinking

Most often cited as an eloquent defense of his artistic life is a letter which Henry James addressed to his close friend, Henry Adams, in March 1914. This letter was apparently prompted by Adams's displeasure, expressed in a letter to James, with *Notes of a Son and Brother*, a copy of which the novelist had sent him. The letter from Adams is now lost, but it appears the book distressed and irritated him, prompting him to lament his and James's mutual plight in outliving their time and to insist it was pointless to dwell upon a past no longer viable. It is possible that his very criticism of James's autobiographical volume proceeded from much the same point of view earlier given shape and expression in his own—*The Education of Henry Adams*. We know he wrote this to Elizabeth Cameron the day after writing the now lost letter to James:

I've read Henry James's last bundle of memories which have reduced me to a pulp. Why did we live? Was that all? Why was I not born in Central Africa and died young. Poor Henry James thinks it all real, I believe, and actually still lives in that dreamy, stuffy, Newport and Cambridge, with papa James and Charles Norton—and me! Yet, why!

It is a terrible dream, but not so weird as this here which is quite loony.[1]

I intend using at length the text of James's return letter as the locus of an extended argument which, while it aims primarily at demonstrating the William-Henry relationship, may also bring us into communion with something of the inner life of the nineteenth century. I would therefore make it clear that this letter is not offered here mainly for its supreme "defense of his life as an artist,"[2] nor for its rebuttal to Henry Adams. Its interest derives not even from its remarkable qualities as such but from a number of characteristic ones contained within a reasonable space. By dwelling upon these, and by searching out and inquiring into their implications, we may perhaps continue to grasp what *is* rather remarkable about James. Here is the letter:

My Dear Henry [Adams], I have your melancholy outpouring of the 7th, and I know not how better to acknowledge it than by the full recognition of its unmitigated blackness. *Of course* we are lone survivors, of course the past that was our lives is at the bottom of an abyss—if the abyss *has* any bottom; of course, too, there's no use talking unless one particularly *wants* to. But the purpose, almost, of my printed divagations was to show you that one *can*, strange to say, still want to—or at least can behave as if one did. Behold me therefore so behaving—and apparently capable of continuing to do so. I still find my consciousness interesting—under *cultivation* of the interest. Cultivate it *with* me, dear Henry—that's what I hoped to make you do—to cultivate yours for all that it has in common with mine. *Why* mine yields an interest I don't know that I can tell you, but I don't challenge or quarrel with it—I encourage it with a ghastly grin. You see I still, in the presence of life (or of what you deny to be such,) have reactions—as many as possible —and the book I sent you is a proof of them. It's, I suppose, because I am that queer monster, the artist, an obstinate finality, an inexhaustible sensibility. Hence the reactions—appearances, memories, many things, go on playing upon it with consequences that I note and "enjoy" (grim word!) noting. It all takes doing—and I *do*. I believe I shall do yet again—it is still an act of life. But you perform them still yourself—and I don't know what keeps me from calling your letter a charming one! There we are, and it's a blessing that you understand—I admit indeed alone—your all-faithful [Signed] Henry James.[3]

Some few readers might find this piece of writing neither particularly eloquent nor remarkable, but no one familiar with James would deny it is characteristic. If unsigned, its authorship would, I expect, prompt little confusion. More pointedly, it illustrates his later prose of somewhat elaborate syntax, much qualification, underlinings, and dashes. His manner is· in fact so intrinsic to the letter, and to any decent judgment about its import, that we might properly begin with that subject.

One by-product of the great critical interest in James over the past thirty years is that even the disagreement over the merits of his late style is now time-honored. This is seen in the fact that both the principal spokesmen within the disagreement and the main directions of it have on occasion become as much the subject of Jacobite scholarship as James himself.[4] Let us instead attend to a feature of the Jamesian discussion which never has been controversial: our predisposition toward such designations as "the later manner," "the late style," "the later James," and so on. This may appear to focus only on what is obvious and trivial. And yet, these designations do have the virtue of familiarity. Their ubiquity is in fact their importance. James is usually taught in connection with American Realism, so we can perhaps do worse than entertain the realist's notion that what is ordinary may be for that reason of interest. Actually, it is not a very ordinary practice apart from Henry James. We are apt to speak of Shakespeare's later plays, Yeats's late poetry, Hemingway's late work. But not even Joyce appears to have a "later manner," although each one of his major volumes has far more pyrotechnic display than its predecessor. To insist, of course, that such locutions themselves comprise a special terminology is both to make too much of them and to overlook what significance they have. It is probably easier in one sense to address the supreme "nuances" of the later manner than to clarify the simple phrase itself, in the sense that typicality is often more troublesome to deal with than speciality. The problem is analogous to Hawthorne's confession, in *The Custom-House*, that he was unable to "fathom" the "deeper import" of the "petty" and "opaque" ordinary world, though he admits it would have provided "something new in literature," if he had.[5] Hawthorne there voices the very task which challenged James and William Dean Howells, and the "something new in literature" became their achievement, what we call The Rise of Realism. But, also, some small part of the challenge remains to the literary historian, for it is his task to explore the presuppositions on which their achievement is based.

What is then the deeper import of our petty and opaque habit of using "later manner," "late style," "later James"? Must they only refer to a host of specialities—refinements, delicacies, techniques? Do they not simultaneously call to mind an habitual presentation, the ordinary, the normal thing we can expect from James? I hope to suggest that by stressing typicality we need not minimize James's real distinctiveness but in fact apprehend it all the better.

The correlative point is, of course, that we can approach the later "mind" or "mode of thought" in the same way. There is nothing untoward, therefore, in supposing that James's language—his choice of words, his syntax, even his punctuation— may be useful in determining, not just what he "thinks" about a matter, but how he is think*ing*. If, on the other hand, these expressions are employed to pertain only to his views or opinions, they may then end up labels and share the limitations attendant upon all labeling. While recognizing that James is far from the only writer of merit in the English language, I suspect that there is no one quite so poorly served by the label as he; and there seems no one more continually destined to attract them. Yet, his is the presentation perhaps least conducive to the standard critical disquisition, in which one proposes his label—realist, fabulist, melodramatist, aesthetic critic; or point of view, dramatic method, panoramic method, foreshortening—and proceeds to extract from the writings enough instances to buttress the label. This does not mean that James has to be something "else" from any or all of these—pragmatist, for example. Rather, I am suggesting that it is the peculiar character of his later manner with its circumambience, its qualification, its enormous sense of the provisional, to do battle with those very intellectual foundations which inhere in our "extracting from." With him the gap after such extracting tends to be too wide from term to phenomenon, from "principle" or "method" to reading experience, from "moral values" to the unfolding language. Put another way, there is the same basic difference, if not the same extent, between James's various "principles" and his *Prefaces* in which they are presumed to reside, as between "Lambert Strether journeys to Europe on behalf of Mrs. Newsome" and the opening chapters of *The Ambassadors.*

If it is then reasonable to consider James's later manner the extension of an habitual mode of thinking, and that we do him justice by attempting to explore the nature of that thinking, the letter to Adams can serve a useful purpose. Through it we can investigate the very disposition of the mind which produced the late writings, while allowing it in turn to impose an altogether arbitrary frame to our investigation. As we shall presently learn from William James, in all matters which pertain to the mind there are really no beginnings or ends except as we conceive of and artificially impose them.

The Pragmatic Mind

The letter begins: "My Dear Henry, I have your melancholy outpouring of the 7th, and I know not how better to acknowledge it than by the full recognition of its unmitigated blackness."

This has, immediately, the Jamesian "note," but how do we best describe it? Is it one of compassion? Is it of concession? Does anything about it take issue with Adams? Perhaps the so-called uninitiated reader might see here only the sympathy. The more initiated reader might wish to point out James's "irony." The inclusive reader might speak of its "elements" both of sympathy and irony. Of consequence is not the naïveté of the first reader, the shrewdness of the second, nor necessarily even the wisdom of the third (since his division into "elements" does not really provide much illumination); of consequence, rather, is the way that James's articulation can engender such various responses. These readers are of course imaginary, but they become quite real when one thinks of the essentially different or opposite ways that James's fiction is so often read and understood.[6] His statement above can in fact grow more enigmatic the longer we look at it.

How in that case does his manner here express his mind? To begin with, he calls Adams's letter a "melancholy outpouring," which by itself sounds a little more like patronage than it does sympathy. But to "acknowledge it," which soon follows, seems a little more sympathetic and less patronizing. "Acknowledge" can mean either to agree with or to answer someone. But what is the precise sense here, when the "it" is a "melancholy outpouring"? Similarly, his syntactical pairing of the phrases "full recognition" with "unmitigated blackness." "Recognize" can mean either to see or to agree: does he "agree" with the blackness, or does he "see" an unmitigatedness about it?

The particular quality of mind found here is in my judgment what William James calls the "unstiffening" one, which we shall see the philosopher depict again and again in his writings. It is a mind thoroughly at odds with fixed values or meanings. Henry's mind, in selecting such counterpoising diction to express itself, is at the farthest remove from a priori certitude. It is not so much a case of not knowing as of knowing that one can never know prescriptively.

Any question involving Henry James and the idea of prescriptiveness properly brings to mind "The Art of Fiction,"

famous for its refutation of the literary prescriptions of Walter
Besant: "I should not have affixed so comprehensive a title to
these few remarks, necessarily wanting in any completeness
upon a subject the full consideration of which would carry us
far, did I not seem to discover a pretext for my temerity in the interesting pamphlet lately published under this name by Mr.
Walter Besant."[7]

Although this passage begins what most consider James's
best single presentation of his artistic views and those of the
post-Civil War realism, it already implies a bit of skepticism
toward its own title, "The Art of Fiction," and of the *concept* to
which it refers. That James felt the actual *practice* of writing to
be artful is beyond dispute. That is just the point, both of his disagreement with Besant's prescriptions and of the thinking with
which he came more and more to be imbued: concepts are
meaningful only in so far as they describe an experience which
results from them; rules for fiction are only as valid as they point
to the particular experience one has of them: "Mr. Besant does
not, to my sense, light up the subject by intimating that a story
must, under penalty of not being a story, consist of 'adventures.'
Why of adventures more than of green spectacles? . . . And
what *is* adventure, when it comes to that, and by what sign is the
listening pupil to recognize it? It is an adventure—an immense
one—for me to write this little article."[8]

I have just said that James came more and more to be imbued with a certain thinking, for it is clear that there is a difference between the character of his utterance here in "The Art of
Fiction" and in that of his letter to Adams. The difference is that
the letter to Adams is itself more like the mode of thinking which
"The Art of Fiction" tells or informs us of. Put another way, to
the extent that his irony in "The Art of Fiction" is more directed
away from himself and at Besant, to that extent James is himself
more "prescriptive" than he is in the letter to Adams when he
writes:

Of course we are lone survivors, of course the past that was our lives is
at the bottom of an abyss—if the abyss *has* any bottom; of course, too,
there's no use talking unless one particularly *wants* to. But the purpose,
almost, of my printed divagations was to show you that one *can*,
strange to say, still want to—or at least can behave as if one did. Behold
me therefore so behaving—and apparently capable of continuing to do
so.

It is difficult to imagine anything more late-Jamesian than this; at the same time, we must always do more than label it his fine sensibility and respect for nuance, as accurate as that may be. Presumably Adams argued that James's sort of labored exploration of their mutual past in his book was pointless, apart from just the "hankering" to do it. Such an argument would bespeak more than a contrary view of the past; it would involve as well an assumption about what is significant activity. To clarify more precisely, then, what is occurring in James's "mannered" response (and as a way of introducing William James's thought into the picture) let us conceive for a moment how the novelist might have otherwise reacted here to Adams's challenge. He might have insisted that his labor was very significant, since the past is never really dead in the sense his friend suggests. He might then have developed this counterargument along the lines of how past and present are, after all, a continuity, the values obtaining in the one illuminating and often accounting for those we find in the other. I project this argument partly because it represents a genuine Jamesian "view"—that is, a view which a reader could legitimately insist the entire letter *does* express. Perhaps so, but what is equally Jamesian is that it is *proceeding* to express something more. He is saying, first of all, that Adams is right: the past is at the bottom of an abyss, if there is any bottom, and there is, to be sure, no use talking about it aside from a personal wish; still, the wish seems to persist, and the admittedly curious behavior resulting from the wish looks as though it will probably continue.

After hearing this paraphrase, the reader who would prefer to see James's views expounded may be tempted to echo, with Henry Adams: "Was that all?" The "all," however, may be said to promise its own kind of significance, for it does take some account of how James's views, whatever they may be, are in the process of unfolding. In fact, if we will allow ourselves to have a particular stake in how James is proceeding to think, and make that our primary perspective for determining what are his "views," we can begin to perceive an entire cognitive process as if breathed into life through the later manner. He is responding to the issues raised by Adams in the way William James responds to the argument about the squirrel and the tree in his famous definition and illustration of the pragmatic method; or in William's discussion of such knotty questions as free will or design in the world, in "Some Metaphysical Problems Pragmatically Considered." This does not mean merely that Henry James looks to the "consequences" of the question, or that he exhibits its "practical" considerations. It does mean that, but it also means a great deal more. It means that he *sees* the question in a certain way. It takes an intellectualist (or saltatory) cast of mind to decide out and out about a matter as vast as whether the past is dead or not, just as it takes a variation of the same mentality to prescribe, as Walter Besant does, a set of rules for the art of fiction. Henry James instinctively cuts the question down in this instance to what he *can* know, the "wanting to talk." This is what the question means to him, for it is fundamentally what he knows about it empirically. The claims in such a position are limited and local, but the evidence, such as it is, is at hand.⁹ And even *that* evidence, we see, must be provisional—"or at least can behave as if one did." William James says in *Pragmatism:* "Grossness is what grossness *does*—we now know *that*,"¹⁰ and Henry's "wanting to talk" here is what it does; all the more because the past, in any sense of a fixed thing, really is at the bottom of an abyss—if the abyss has any bottom. William asserts:

The pragmatic method is primarily a method of settling metaphysical disputes that otherwise might be interminable. Is the world one or many?—fated or free?—material or spiritual?—here are notions either of which may or may not hold good of the world; and disputes over such notions are unending. The pragmatic method in such cases is to try to interpret each notion by tracing its respective practical consequences. What difference would it practically make to any one if this notion rather than the other notion were true? If no practical difference whatever can be traced, then the alternatives mean practically the same thing, and all dispute is idle. Whenever a dispute is serious, we ought to be able to show some practical difference that must follow from one side or the other's being right.¹¹

As we continue to observe the unfolding of Henry James's mind we will find that he does indeed "unconsciously pragmatise." But this involves as well doing the fullest justice to the thought of William James. The reader is assuredly familiar with the definition of the pragmatic method just quoted. Yet, pragmatism, or rather pragmatistic thought, for that is really what Henry James embodies, involves many "ways of thinking"; and the famous definition of the pragmatic method is but the point of departure for them. Thus, for example, Henry's remark, "Behold me therefore so behaving—and apparently capable of continuing to do so," may be set against the following passage by William concerning the respective importance of the past, the present, and the future in assessing a profound question; the reader may find it helpful to substitute for William's references to matter and to spirit something like the past is dead, the past is alive:

What do we *mean* by matter? What practical difference can it make *now* that the world should be run by matter or by spirit? I think we find that the problem takes with this a rather different character.

And first of all I call your attention to a rather curious fact. It makes not a single jot of difference so far as the *past* of the world goes, whether we deem it to have been the work of matter or whether we think a divine spirit was its author.

Imagine, in fact, the entire contents of the world to be once for all irrevocably given. Imagine it to end this very moment, and to have no future; and then let a theist and a materialist apply their rival explanations to its history. . . . Then let the pragmatist be asked to choose between their theories. How can he apply his test if a world is already completed? *Concepts for him are things to come back into experience with*, things to make us look for differences.[12]

Henry's phrase, "continuing to do so," gives us exactly the same prospective and ongoing sense of mind ascribed above by William to the pragmatist. Since concepts are, as William says, "things to come back into experience with," they are by extension themselves ultimately part and parcel of experience itself.[13] Furthermore, when Henry says "apparently capable," we can become increasingly attuned to William's "metaphysics," actually an anti-metaphysics amounting to an epistemology: one knows only what an older metaphysic might call "the apparent," not the so-called "real" presumed to cause it, and which the apparent is said to reveal. If the real past is down the abyss, then it is indeed pointless to grope after it with printed divagations. But if the past is not a matter apart from its present "appearance" in the mind, but in fact the continual unfolding of the mind about it, then the significance of the activity is primarily whether one's "appearance" can be articulated. That Henry James will go on to defend his work by an appeal to consciousness, and that his only "evidence" comes down to the existence of his book, which created the argument in the first place, only avoids the issue or is obvious to an intellectualist mind. The conjunctive argument of the pragmatist is almost invariably a circular one in a special sense.

Willing and Wishing

In addition to its conveying the pragmatic openness of mind, Henry James's self-styled "apparent behavior" of "wanting to talk" suggests an attitude about belief which is at one with William's, and which relates to the philosopher's thought generally. William James approached the matter of belief empirically: one has free will primarily in his actual desire to have it, and also in his actual illusion (the apparent) that he does have it. "Willing" and "wishing" in the matter of belief are continually interrelated in his thought against any position assumed purely from logic and so-called hard evidence: "Free-will and simple wishing do seem, in the matter of our credences, to be only fifth wheels to the coach. Yet if any one should thereupon assume that intellectual insight is what remains after wish and will and sentimental preference have taken wing, or that pure reason is what then settles our opinions, he would fly quite as directly in the teeth of the facts. . . . We want to have a truth; we want to believe that our experiments and studies and discussions must put us in a continually better and better position towards it."[14]

Furthermore, Henry's "wanting" must in turn be considered itself but provisional evidence—if one is imbued with William Jamesian thinking: "But practically one's conviction that the evidence one goes by is of the real objective brand, is only one more subjective opinion added to the lot."[15] Hence, Henry's "—or at least can behave as if one did," if it is a "nuance," is a particular kind of nuance.

Pragmatism is an attitude at odds with assuming knowledge from concepts apart from their unfolding consequence in sensory and perceptual life. To know the object free will is to know more than we can; but to know there is no such thing because we cannot prove it as a concept is to be just as prescriptive and dogmatic: " 'What would be better for us to believe'! This sounds very like a definition of truth. It comes very near to saying 'what we *ought* to believe': and in *that* definition none of you would find any oddity. Ought we ever not to believe what it is *better for us* to believe? And can we then keep the notion of what is better for us, and what is true for us, permanently apart? Pragmatism says no, and I fully agree with her."[16]

It is not difficult from these passages to understand why William James constantly called pragmatism the "mediating" philosophy. That Henry James has the mediating mind described by that philosophy is implicit in the way his later work constantly evokes what he called "the possible other case."[17] Perhaps the most memorable instance of the novelist's mediating, pragmatic mind realized as art is the speech by Lambert Strether in *The Ambassadors* which grows out of the "germ" of the novel: "Live all you can; it's a mistake not to." Strether declares:

The affair—I mean the affair of life—couldn't, no doubt, have been different for me; for it's at the best a tin mould, either fluted and embossed, with ornamental excrescences, or else smooth and dreadfully plain, into which, a helpless jelly, one's consciousness is poured—so that one "takes" the form, as the great cook says, and is more or less compactly held by it: one lives in fine as one can. Still, one has the illusion of freedom; therefore don't be, like me, without the memory of that illusion.[18]

This is the certainly not out-of-the-way James, any more than the Adams letter is out-of-the-way James. The novelist himself called this statement of Strether's the "whole case" and "the essence of 'The Ambassadors,'" and he called the book itself, as we know, "frankly, quite the best, 'all round,' of my productions."[19] It would of course be possible to spend as long with these words of Strether's as with the letter to Henry Adams, exploring fully the intellectual presuppositions involved in them. The following commentary on them comes from Leon Edel: "Strether," he tells us, "is, at bottom, a romantic of romantics. . . . But he is at the same time someone who has been touched by the scientific thought of the mid-century, and he tugs, with his delicate psychological understanding, at Darwinian 'determinism' when he offers Little Bilham his image of man as a creature molded and formed—and even 'conditioned' as we might say today—and therefore bereft of free will." And Edel continues:

Strether believes nevertheless in one kind of free will: "Still, one has the illusion of freedom," he says, and he adds to Little Bilham, "don't be, like me, without the memory of that illusion." There is, perhaps, in such a pronouncement that *penchant a la tristesse* which Turgenev discerned in James; but what is explicit in the way James has shaped Strether's magnificent utterance is the absence of any hint of resignation. The answer is active and positive: "Live all you can." In effect he argues that whatever bonds fate places upon man, he still has his ears and should therefore listen; he has eyes and should therefore *see*.[20]

These comments by Edel are exactly right in the perspective they offer, with Strether both touched by and yet distinct from Darwinian determinism, and with his taking an "active and positive" response to his conditioning, such as it is. What is noteworthy, therefore, is that Edel, who quite correctly has just said that James "was not a philosopher," nevertheless proceeded to describe (indirectly to be sure) something of the matrix of pragmatistic thought in his commentary. First, there is the mediating stance between the "romantic" and the "scientific" views, precisely the line William James threads between what he called "tender-" and "tough-" mindedness. Then, there is the notion that Strether's "bonds of fate" need not prevent his "hearing" and "seeing," which is only one step removed from the William Jamesian doctrine that the bonds of fate are themselves the consequential perceptions one continually has of them. That added step is however an important one, especially if we are thinking of Henry James's art in *The Ambassadors*: for Strether's own sentiments at that moment in Gloriani's garden are themselves rendering such "bonds of fate" as do encompass Lambert Strether. That is, his constantly awakening experiences of life are the terms, the primary terms, of his statements about "life." To say this is of course to say what the entire novel is about: for Strether's continually unfolding perceptions are inseparable from his ideological reflections, and these inseparable from his succeeding perceptions. This entire process *is The Ambassadors*. That process told, as I have just told it and as we shall see William James tell it, is the doctrine of radical empiricism and the transitional nature of ideas.

In the same speech to Little Bilham, Strether conceives of himself as someone who has missed a train, a train which "had fairly waited at the station for me without my having the gumption to know it was there." Late in the book he will actually board a train and go to the country, and there get the surprise of his life in discovering by chance the sexual intimacy of Chad Newsome and Madame de Vionnet. James's impressive rhetoric in using the two "trains" is not the main point, however; nor even that train-one occurs in the context of "determinism" and train-two then inaugurates the disclosure of Jamesian "fate." The point is, rather, that *both* the imagined train he has missed and the actual train he rides out on (and returns on with Chad and Marie de Vionnet) are confluent points on the vector of his ongoing experience, and that *is* what fate or chance comes to. Strether's lament, or rather how he proceeds to lament, is the "truth happening to" his idea.[21] His trip to the country is the same truth continuing to happen. For the most salient feature of the country recognition scene, and one not always sufficiently featured by James's critics, is that Strether actively and radically meets the discovery; he enters into a reciprocal relation with it, grafting meaning while receiving in kind; he empties every possible insight about himself, his previous assumptions, the thoughts of the two lovers in having to deal with *him*, and even the imagined responses of those back at Paris, into it. It is a recognition scene only in that sense, but in that sense it is recognition with a vengeance.

It will be recalled that James presents the entire episode as Strether's remembered construction back in his hotel room the same evening of his return on the train. In speaking of a book like *The Ambassadors*, we always find ourselves speaking about what *it* is that Strether learns or discovers. The fact is that Strether's "encounter" of Chad and Marie de Vionnet stands in much the same relation to his creative faculty as James's little "germ" stands in relation to the novel which includes that encounter. That is what it means to apprehend fate, chance, or truth itself pragmatistically. It means that these matters are what they can become, which is all the possibilities of realizing them.

A "Radically" Empirical Mind

Returning now to where we left off in James's letter to Henry Adams, we find the following remarkable utterance:

I still find my consciousness interesting—under *cultivation* of the interest. Cultivate it *with* me, dear Henry—that's what I hoped to make you do—to cultivate yours for all that it has in common with mine. *Why* mine yields an interest I don't know that I can tell you, but I don't challenge or quarrel with it—I encourage it with a ghastly grin.

If his previous remarks have suggested that James is unwilling, even on behalf of his work, to assume an assertive posture which is not grounded in the best even if most modest of empirical evidence, these remarks give us the kind of generalization his temperament permits him to make. He is speaking of his literary endeavor in so natural and intimate a connection with his personal consciousness as to imply that they are one and the same. This identification is one which we in our more modern era might incline to view suspiciously, all the more for coming from James. For, although our aesthetic theory persists in describing as "organic" the relation of mind to material, it is just such fiction as James's and that of the post-Jamesian tradition in particular which has taught us to distinguish the personal consciousness of a writer from his work of art. This paradox is not resolved, but I believe it is better understood by our recourse to William James. If for pragmatistic thought the bounds of knowledge are "appearances"—perceptual effects which continually emerge, waxing and waning in their reciprocal relation with an active mind—then "*cultivated* consciousness" becomes the heart of what is eventful and "interesting" at the very same time that it points to the limitations of knowledge, thereby implying the necessity for something like aesthetic distance to "keep things honest."

Since we are concerned in this question with an author's personal relationship to his subject, it might be useful to approach it here in terms of irony, especially since James's invitation to Adams to "cultivate [consciousness] *with* me, dear Henry—that's what I hoped to make you do"—has the character of irony: Adams had in fact already "joined" him eight years before by writing *The Education of Henry Adams*. At the same time that we are duly appreciative of James's ironic strain here and generally, perhaps we ought not emphasize it without attending to its particular quality. This is occasionally done by his critics, and in a time when irony is highly valued it would seem a good service to the novelist. But "irony" can have its way, too, of oversimplifying things: to call James's later work "ironic" or the product of a comprehensive "ironic vision" can sometimes close off many of the apertures to his house of fiction; an "ironic" approach may even end up fixing his values just as rigidly as the straightforwardness it claims to complicate. Thus, for example, we have the issue of James's so-called "unreliable narrators." Wayne C. Booth in *The Rhetoric of Fiction* uses this concept for discussing not only such narrators as that of James's story, "The Liar," but what he deems to be James's own later increasingly unreliable mode of narration.[22] The main point about unreliable narrators, as opposed to unreliable narration, is that we may think they reveal to us what is "reliable" in reverse—only too well. While fully cognizant of James's wit and urbanity, I believe it is better described as "mediating" or "cordial," in William's use of those terms. That this quality in James's later writings becomes then "unreliable," because it proceeds from a mind which increasingly refuses to perceive values as fixed but is, rather, constantly imbued with "possible other case[s]," is another question.[23] It is in fact the question which, hopefully, the present book has been addressing.

James exhibits the quality in point, the cordiality, when he concedes to Adams: "Why mine [my consciousness] yields an interest I don't know that I can tell you, but I don't challenge or quarrel with it—I encourage it with a ghastly grin." This is of course one of his celebrated "caught images." Our understanding of his singular imagery, no less than his irony or his refinement of technique, is again a matter well advanced by our having a stake in the particular thought processes in which they occur. Here we find that having just described his personal consciousness and his written work as much the same thing, he has now proceeded to picture consciousness as a "someone" other than himself, one whom he "encourages" and with whom he does not "quarrel."

With respect to William's thought, Henry's remarks here continue to express the pragmatic state of mind: i.e., there is no comprehending the "*why*" of the "interest" of consciousness except in terms of what it seems to come down to. But even the imagery itself, which arises quite easily and naturally in the context, has its analogue in William's radical empiricism. William James defines the doctrine as follows: "I give the name of 'radical empiricism' to my *Weltanschauung.* . . .To be radical, an empiricism must neither admit into its constructions any element that is not directly experienced, nor exclude from them any element that is directly experienced. For such a philosophy, *the relations that connect experiences must themselves be experienced relations, and any kind of relation experienced must be accounted as 'real' as anything else in the system.*"[24]

This is perhaps at first not the easiest *Weltanschauung* to grasp; *Weltanschauungs* of any kind rarely are. The following statements, proposing the living continuity of the pluralist's world, give us another formulation of the same doctrine:

You see also that it stands or falls with the notion I have taken such pains to defend, of the through-and-through union of adjacent minima of experience, of the confluence of every passing moment of concretely felt experience with its immediately next neighbors. The recognition of this fact of coalescence of next with next in concrete experience, so that all the insulating cuts we make there are artificial products of the conceptualizing faculty, is what distinguishes the empiricism which I call radical, from the bugaboo empiricism of the traditional rationalist critics. . . .[25]

William's "felt experience" here recalls Henry's oft-quoted "felt life." This is of course what Henry is referring to in his image of a consciousness he does not "quarrel" with but encourages with a "ghastly grin." Henry's striking image furthermore gets at just those crucial aspects of William's doctrine which part company with its "bugaboo" predecessors. For Henry's image denies in effect that his consciousness is a mere "entity" and makes it in William's words an "experienced relation." For Henry that becomes tantamount to endowing the activity with a "life of its own" and making the relation between himself and it a *situation.* Thus, the novelist has simultaneously detached his consciousness from, and reattached it to, himself. He expressed much the same viewpoint in his exchange with H. G. Wells, when he eventually wrote: "It is art that *makes* life, makes interest, makes importance, . . . and I know of no substitute whatever for the force and beauty of its process." Wells's retort should not be overlooked: "I can only read sense into it by assuming that you are using 'art' for every conscious human activity."[26]

If Henry's assertion that "art makes life" sounds at first like Walter Pater's Aestheticism, let us recall that Aestheticism too in its way comes out of the philosophic thought of the late nineteenth century, and that Pater in his "Conclusion" to *The Renaissance* argues for his impressionism on the scientific basis of the impermanence of matter.[27] We are often reminded by his commentators that Henry James was no Walter Pater, because of the strong demands of his "ethical" as well as his aesthetic sensibility; but we can forget, for example, that something may be mutually operative in prose styles as similar as Pater's and James's later manner. That "something" has to do with an epistemological disposition of mind. The real difference between Henry James and Walter Pater can be seen as the difference of Pater's argument in his famous "Conclusion," from the thought of William James. Pater embraces flux as an end in itself, whereas William James embraces it as a means for making it yield something workable while, in his more prospective view, never denying the *possibility* of some final goal toward which the cosmos moves. That this kind of distinction can have artistic resonance is seen by the way Pater often tends to end his fictions like a mind which has closed down shop for the day, whereas the stories of the later Henry James have a quality of being projected beyond their conclusions: we often speak of what Lambert Strether will or will not do after he returns to America, as well as of Isabel Archer's future. And yet, despite all the differences we might want to cite between James and Pater (including James's ethical view), we ought never to forget that most fundamental difference between James, Pater, and William James on the one hand and, on the other, the kind of thinking found, for example, in Carlyle's *Sartor Resartus*, where Teufelsdröckh would have us gaze *through* the apparent, through the "trappings," and comprehend the Real.[28] To say that neither Carlyle's mind nor the two minds in America so like his, Melville's and Emerson's, would ever depict their consciousnesses as a "someone" not to "quarrel" with but to "encourage," is, in a certain way, to be involved with some of the most basic literary and intellectual presuppositions of the mid and late nineteenth century.

A Pragmatic Intellectual

When James says to Adams of his consciousness: "*Why* mine yields an interest I don't know that I can tell you, but I don't challenge or quarrel with it—," he exhibits that distrust, characteristic of the pragmatist, of assigning reasons apart from consequences. Just to *impose* reasons otherwise strikes the pragmatist as somehow too categorical, too prescriptive. We might describe his mental attitude as one not likely to construct "A Dynamic Theory of History," and not likely to present "The Dynamo and the Virgin" as encompassing symbols distinguishing the moral force of two epochs. He is, after a fashion, "anti-intellectual"; but that very fashion is from another angle his own kind of intellectuality.

It is often pointed out that Henry James had little intellectual life properly speaking. His admirers, however, tend on more than one occasion to view this as still greater evidence of his monastic dedication to art. That James was an artist, and conceived of himself as one, is hardly to be disputed. But to designate James a "total artist" or "complete novelist" as a sort of reverential response to all questions pertaining to his intellectual life is risky: one wonders if, say, Coleridge, Shelley, or Melville, who were intellectuals, were therefore nowhere near as serious about their art as was James. He once wrote: "Balzac's 'Comédie Humaine' is on the imaginative line very much what Comte's 'Positive Philosophy' is on the scientific. These great enterprises are equally characteristic of the French passion for completeness, for symmetry, for making a system as neat as an epigram — of its intolerance of the indefinite, the unformulated. The French mind likes better to squeeze things into a formula that mutilates them, if need be, than to leave them in the frigid vague."[29]

This reference to Auguste Comte, that he is characteristic of French symmetry and system, is equally characteristic of James. In his essays and reviews of fellow-realist George Eliot, whose work was greatly influenced by Comte, James repeatedly and admiringly speaks of her mind as "philosophic"; but there is nothing to speak of about the philosophy in question.[30] This case appears to repeat itself wherever we turn: not only is the thought of Kant, Locke, or Hegel noticeably absent from his writings, fiction or nonfiction, but, as Theodora Bosanquet relates: "He could let Huxley and Gladstone, the combatant champions of Darwinian and orthodox theology, enrich the pages of a single letter without any reference to their respective beliefs. . . . the personal impression [was] the thing sought."[31]

It will be recalled, too, that James was unable to embrace intellectually the Swedenborgian writings of his father. As he admitted to William: "I can't enter into it (much) myself—I can't be so theological nor grant his extraordinary premises, nor throw myself into conceptions of heavens and hells, nor be sure that the keynote of nature is humanity, etc. But I can enjoy greatly the spirit, the feeling and the manner of the whole thing . . . and feel really that poor Father, struggling so alone all his life, and so destitute of every worldly or literary ambition, was yet a great writer."[32]

James did name Lambert Strether after Balzac's Swedenborgian protagonist Lewis Lambert; but Strether's name is told of in *The Ambassadors* itself without any mention of the Swedenborgianism of Balzac's character:

"Mr. Lewis Lambert Strether"—[Maria Gostrey] sounded it almost as freely as for any stranger. She repeated however that she liked it—"particularly the Lewis Lambert. It's the name of a novel of Balzac's."

"Oh I know that!" said Strether.

"But the novel's an awfully bad one."

"I know that too," Strether smiled. To which he added with an irrelevance that was only superficial: "I come from Woollett Massachusetts." It made her for some reason—the irrelevance or whatever—laugh. Balzac had described many cities, but hadn't described Woollett Massachusetts.[33]

Why does James write that Strether's statement, that he comes from Woollett, is "only superficially irrelevant"? Apparently because Strether considers himself, like Balzac's "awfully bad" novel, as cutting something of a sorry figure here in the cosmopolitan atmosphere of a great European metropolis, especially when he is in company with a practiced cosmopolite like Maria Gostrey. And yet, Balzac, who has "described many cities," and is therefore cosmopolitan himself still has not managed, despite that "French passion for symmetry, for making a system as neat as an epigram," to include into it Woollett, Massachusetts. Besides, even *within* his vast symmetry and system, his French "intolerance of the indefinite and the unformulated," there is at least one "awfully bad" part—the novel *Lewis Lambert* itself. Would it not therefore be curious if the unlikely namesake, Strether, were to compensate for that single chink in the armor of Balzac's "system"? Would it not be even better if he eventually took the measure of his sophisticated European

friends just by dint of being from little Woollett, and especially
by having an "indefinite," "unformulated" quality of mind that
both allows him to learn and to make mistakes?

I hope it is clear that I am arguing for there being more than
one kind of intellectuality, and that when a critic says that
the "sacred fount of the philosophers was a mystery which
none of the passionately curious observers in his novels ever
explores," or that he was "quite naïve" in matters intellectual,
or "had scarcely the trace of a system," he has not necessarily
said the last word about James's intellectuality.[34]

Such remarks as he did make about contemporary thinkers
have at least this in common: he will speak of something "lesser" or more "local" about them than their ideas as such.
Whether it is how Comte's Positive Philosophy bespeaks a particular trait of the French; or, that his father's writings are the
spirit and manner of the man, and the man's rather sad plight;
or when, for example, he confesses that he does not know the
final "validity" of Taine's *race-milieu-moment* theory, and pre-
fers to dwell upon his "pictorial" quality of presentation—
James is invariably apprehending a theory first in terms of how
it is *proceeding* to be told, and then as motive (or "germ") for
whatever consequential perceptions or "experiences" he yields
from it.[35] He is thus sensing about systematic thought what
William James insists about any concept, that it is something
"to come back into experience with," that abstractions are
"only active in their re-directing function" of heading the individual back toward his "sea of sense."[36] Henry's "intellectuality,"
then, is that he tends to see someone's thought first as its procedure or happening, and eventually as a situation which involves himself.[37]

I suppose the one notable exception to this would be
Henry's responses to William's writings. There he insists upon
the validity of the views as views: "You are immensely and
universally *right*. . . . I palpitate as you make out your case
(since it seems to me you so utterly do,) . . . and into that case I
enter intensely, unreservedly. . . ." But this hardly constitutes
any demonstration that he comprehends all the "-ism" of pragmatism. Rather, these responses are very like those others cited
before, in that he makes William's views the point of departure
for his own consequential situation: "As an artist and a 'cre-

ator' I can catch on, hold on, to pragmatism and can work in the light of it and apply it." To put it another way, William's view *becomes* the "palpitating," the "spell," the "sinking down, under it," and even the "lost in the wonder" that one has unconsciously pragmatized. Apparently truth can happen even to William James's ideas.

At the risk of appearing to cultivate paradox, is not this precisely part of what makes Henry James the very personification of pragmatistic thought? If someone were the *embodiment* of William's thought, how else would he react to the "doctrine"? I really do not know which is the better evidence: that Henry for once comes out and insists he is a disciple of anyone's philosophy, or that he is unable to describe his discipleship of this particular philosophy except as the result of what happens to him.[38]

These are then the terms of Henry James's particular form of intellectuality. It has become the habit, whether one is a Jamesian or not, to cite as *point d'appui* for one's argument the statement by T. S. Eliot that James "had a mind so fine that no idea could violate it."[39] Whether one construes this as the supreme praise to be paid artistic detachment, or else the unwittingly uttered key to James's limitations, I know of no better brief description that could apply to pragmatistic thought: for the fundamental refusal to be violated by ideas undergirds and permeates all else.

The Rise of Realism to the Later Manner

The refusal to be violated by ideas, and thus to have an acute sense of the fallacy of profundity, is for the pragmatist the very reverse of his being silent and inarticulate. His task is, rather, to become involved with his little "percepts," to show how interesting *they* are, and how they can even have surprisingly broad dimension.

The belief that the "lesser" can be interesting and even at times exhilarating, is one that we associate with the earlier Henry James and William Dean Howells, and the literary movement of American Realism. The knotty question of whether James, in his own movement from early to middle to late, remained a realist or became something else, is not one I would presume to solve here; still, there is one angle to the question worthy of some consideration. From a pragmatistic standpoint, at least, the progression of James's literary career has a certain rationale. With articulate statements of intent and purpose such as Howells's *Harper's Essays* and James's own "Art of Fiction," it is common for us to describe American Realism as primarily a commitment in fiction of the post-Civil War period to portraying the ordinary, the everyday, the typical. And, with the same documents in mind, it is also common to understand these views of the realist as coming primarily from Europe. At the same time, our practice of relating the work of James and Howells to their various European models—Balzac, Flaubert, Tolstoy, and Turgenev, in particular—can have at least one unhappy side effect: the energy involved in our delineating these influences may then deflect us from the predispositions which made James and Howells value their continental masters. Cosmopolitanism, the "European Experience" in matters belletristic, is not only to come upon a new and bracing group of assumptions about fiction, but also to substantiate certain habits of mind one might already have.

The assumption, then, that the ordinary, the everyday world is somehow to be caught and rendered in all its drama is first to sense that these things *mean* without recourse to a higher form of understanding. This epistemological sense can be involved even in those more technical or properly artistic qualities one adopts. To say, for example, that Henry James's *The American* and Howells's *A Modern Instance* employ a Balzac-like multiplicity of events and characters drawn from the actual world, is also to recognize that such shaped and rendered multiplicity may proceed from a habit of mind which William James was eventually to describe as the pluralistic one. This is the habit of mind that "[t]here is no possible point of view from which the world can appear an absolutely single fact."[40]

To be aware, as well, that the earlier James renders "the sense of place" or "the sense of milieu," as do Flaubert and Turgenev, is also to recognize that such rendering puts a premium upon the imaginative faculty no less than, say, in the more obvious case of Melville. That is, James's *Washington Square* is as much a creative or "re-constructed" everyday, old New York as Melville's Spouter Inn is a creation in terms of the strange, the grotesque, the exotic—all the attributes Ruskin lists in connection with the Gothic. At the same time, James's imaginative city (or Howells's Boston in *A Modern Instance*) may suggest the William Jamesian notion of the constantly potential imaginativeness of the human mind as it acts and reacts with *its* quite everyday world: *"for rationalism,"* he declares, *"reality is ready-made and complete from all eternity, while for pragmatism it is still in the making. . . ."*[41] Similarly, the wit or ironic distance informing *Washington Square*, *The American*, or *A Modern Instance*, can certainly be said to compare with similar modes of irony in Flaubert or Turgenev. But this, too, is to recognize that such wit or irony may have epistemological foundation. The comparison with Flaubert is less pertinent, perhaps, since his irony is a bit more "tough" and moves in the direction toward someone like Stephen Crane.[42] But James, early Howells, and Turgenev all employ an irony which will *partially* undercut the seriousness of the portrayed incident or the fervid utterance by one of the characters. The reality which is rendered seems thereby more relative, the values more open-ended, and all somewhat "mediated" in the William Jamesian sense. Thus, if the realist's obligation to invest the produce of the common day with meaning and imagination can from one angle be said to adumbrate those later writings by William James (he calls them after all "old ways of thinking"), it is equally possible that Henry James's own progression is not so much a movement away from the realism of the 1870s and 1880s as it is a peculiarly apt extension of it.

In fact, one could call it the epistemological assumptions of realism pushed to their very limit: for that subject matter of the everyday which is at once common to all men while yet enormously flexible and individual as it pertains to any one man is the subject matter of individual human consciousness. James's commentators have always done full justice to the insight that he employs the most sensitive, delicate "registers" in the persons of his late characters. But James in defending his "super-subtle fry" insisted that they were *"signal* specimens."[43] It is therefore as important when thinking of the literary-historical genesis of James's later phase to emphasize the *typicality* of human consciousness as it is his "super-subtle" rendering of it. On his part he continued to think himself a realist, a "painter of life," right on through the later writings. If we say that his late characters are so special as not to be realistic, we would at least be overlooking something of what underlay American Realism to begin with. From the pragmatistic perspective, at least, the act of rendering a world in terms of the consciousness of its inhabitants is tantamount to portraying the nature of reality itself. For to present the actual world without recourse to a transcendent order apart from experience is eventually to project the shifting sands of perception operating in the typical and everyday affairs of life. The now minority opinion that the late James is much ado about nothing has in this connection a certain interest. His late fiction would have to presuppose that much *is* happening in what, to stand apart and *categorize* a "thing" or "entity," seems indeed very little; by the same token, I cannot think of a better way for the intellectualist thinker to so categorize the pragmatist. We are back, again, to what constitutes intellectuality. The pragmatist's passion for making his little "percepts" interesting ends up in his commitment to the unfolding of experience in local situations. This is in part how he compensates for the sort of profundity that he considers unverifiable.

Dupery for Dupery

When Henry James concedes to Henry Adams that he does not know why consciousness yields him an interest, but that he does not challenge or quarrel with it, he conveys the "cordial" acceptance of experience which is so central to the thought of William James. If this cordiality is for the philosopher's thought a key to there now being few "pure [William] Jamesians, in the sense of direct descent, [but many] mixed Jamesians, who acknowledge their common relationship to him without feeling any bond with one another,"[44] Henry James's cordiality has prompted something different. In his case there have tended to be pure Jamesians (Jacobites) and non-Jamesians, who feel little or no bond with one another. In part this arises from the particular comic dimension resulting from cordiality—or irony. If, for example, some of our most ironic readings of his work appear to cohere and hold together the more we avoid asking why the object of his irony appears, when viewed from another angle, perfectly and importantly valid, it may imply how much we ourselves (as interpreters of literature) are nonpragmatistic: we employ concepts not so much as "things to come back into experience with, things to look for differences," as for finding common directions, patterns, underlying ideas, and the like. This may also account in part for the alternative tendency to then interpret him as profoundly dark or tragic. If one is a non-Jamesian, the problem is more easily solved by denying any "importance" to his vision.

In the Adams letter, for example—is his phrase "ghastly grin" an ironic comment on his wanting to encourage consciousness? It seems that it is. But is he not "serious" about wanting to encourage consciousness? A small library of his writings is suffient answer. Cordiality is then William's "unstiffening" quality of mind precisely because it is not ultimately wedded to cynicism. Its natural bent is rather an optimistic one, and results from a remarkable combination of skeptcism, good humor, and hope. The thing about Henry's "possible other case" is that it can always be a better one, if only because on many occasions there could not possibly be a worse one. "The Art of Fiction" exemplifies this attitude. Its artistry does not lie in *the case* he makes out against Walter Besant but from his cordiality both of mind and presentation: that is, he takes up Besant's dictums, in fact his very words, and proceeds to recast them, make them "germs" for exploration, until Besant's words have eventually become James's own meaning for them; and that meaning is, specifically, that they can have *any possible* meaning. Alternatively, James's friend Robert Louis Stevenson wrote a good-humored but noncordial rebuttal to "The Art of Fiction" entitled "A Humble Remonstrance." If Stevenson's essay is now less celebrated than James's, it is primarily because he was simply unable to "unstiffen" in the William Jamesian sense: he had somehow to get across "Mr. James's kind of" fiction as a foil.[45] One can hardly blame him, for what else do you do when you confront a mind which is not itself really permeated by "kinds"? You must *impose* them on him, you must somehow point out what he "is-really-getting-at."

Our interpreting the later James as profoundly tragic or else deeply ironic can on occasion exhibit something of the same situation—at least in his work up to and including *The Ambassadors;* in *The Wings of the Dove, The Golden Bowl* and, say, the stories of *The Finer Grain* it seems to me far less a distortion. In these earlier cases we are not to be duped, not to be fooled, whether by the "seemingly tiny" segment of life he takes as his domain, or by that merely "apparent lightness," which in fact masks the troubled moralist pondering the complex problems of western civilization. One is always thankful for the Hawthorne influence—no question about going out far and in deep there! But even Hawthorne called himself a "genial consciousness," and there is a certain quality to James which this phrase hits at, just as there are correspondences between the Master's *Prefaces* and Hawthorne's "Custom-House" (which James thought so well of): [46] they are both explorations of the "artistic sensibility," no doubt, but what is their attitude and tone? Three of James's favorite words are "charm," "interest," and "enjoy," whether the context is Hawthorne, the novel, or even what a reader should experience reading him. Must we never be duped?

For my own part, I have also a horror of being duped; but I can believe that worse things than being duped may happen to a man in this world. . . . *Our errors are surely not such awfully solemn things.* In a world where we are so certain to incur them in spite of all our caution, a certain lightness of heart seems healthier than this excessive nervousness on their behalf. At any rate, it seems the fittest thing for the empiricist philosopher.[47]

Is William's attitude and spirit here so different from that of much of Henry's work? Is it not just the attitude imputed to Lambert Strether when, having traced out the implications of before "supposing nothing" about Chad Newsome and Madame de Vionnet, he now decides: "Verily, verily, his labour had been lost. He found himself supposing innumerable and wonderful things."[48] If William's attitude toward dupery does not, on the other hand, seem directly imputed to Isabel Archer, when at the end of *The Portrait of a Lady*, she decides that there is "a very straight path" back to Rome, what about James himself? "Dupery for dupery, what proof is there that dupery through hope is so much worse than dupery through fear?"[49]

The point about this statement, and the habit of mind it stands for, is that the question is *left open* as well as giving hope its due. One could put it this way: Henry James's "ghastly grin" encouraging consciousness is in the end an "optimistic" sentiment because he has the humor to realize what the divagating and laborious *Notes of a Son and Brother* must have been like to read, especially for a man like Henry Adams, who "thought that if anything he sat too much in the center of the whole world," rather than James himself, who "knew himself actually at the periphery, and therefore to make himself a center in invoked reality."[50]

I have just said that a profoundly "tragic" reading of James is far less of a distortion in his work after *The Ambassadors*. This does not mean, however, that the epistemological basis for his cordiality is diminished. It means that his vision is less humorous than before, but still retains a strong measure of idealism—his portraits of Milly Theale, Maggie Verver, and her father, for example. To say that the epistemological framework remains as before is only to say that his pictorial image of himself encouraging his "friend consciousness" is very typical imagery from his late period. One can compare it, for example, with Adam Verver's proposal of marriage to Charlotte Stant as burning his ships in *The Golden Bowl*; or his daughter Maggie's accumulation of thoughts as a room filling with objects; or her silence in the face of betrayal as a piping caravan. One can think too of James's metaphorical titles—Milly Theale's innocence and generosity imaged as a dove. All of this imagery is intended to give a pictorial interest to an actual world without recourse to a higher order of understanding. To clarify this, it is perhaps best to think of an occasion when James does employ what at first may appear symbolic imagery proper—the golden bowl. The differences of this from Melville's whale, let us say, are far greater than the similarities. Like the white whale, the golden bowl will elicit various "readings" or understandings by several of the characters. But unlike Melville's whale, the golden bowl is not conceived in terms of those spiritual realities which, as William James often puts it, purport by metaphysicians to stand stately and independently *behind* the concrete experience: no character who speaks of the golden bowl, nor James himself through his continual "comment," ever seeks to explore the *nature* of, let us say, domestic discord. Its "nature" is rather the full conjunctive experience of *The Golden Bowl*, the many particular and individual consequences of the idea. Thus, for example, when Fanny Assingham dashes the bowl to the floor and it splits into three fragments, even she (an interpreter of situations second to none!) never explores the *Idea* of alienation or isolation. And if the fact that Maggie Verver picks up the pieces of the broken bowl and reassembles them can be said to prefigure her ability to confront the break-up of her own marriage, this too is to describe a typical Jamesian metaphorical occurrence: it gives interest or, if we will, poetry to the actual; it brings out the meaning of the actual, rather than directing us to the greater Real. Such natures or "Kinds" belong, on the other hand, as William points out, to the order of "[philosophic] Common Sense" with which he disagrees. They do not have meaning apart from empirical situations, and these situations, continuing and ongoing, *are* their meaning. Henry James's presentation of Maggie proceeding to deal with the rift in her marriage is the ongoing meaning of her picking up the bowl. And if, after our experience with a late James novel, we are indeed prone to close his book and then describe him in these larger categories, it seems to me a tribute not to his ability to find some preexistent meaning *in* particulars as it is his making concepts concretely meaningful. But if we should then turn around and treat our own larger categories as the inward grace of his outward sign, we at least risk doing it at the expense of precisely what makes him "Jamesian." We should probably guard against this, even at the alternative risk of sometimes being duped.

The Central Intelligence
"You see I still, in the presence of life (or of what you deny to be such,) have reactions—as many as possible—and the book I sent you is a proof of them"—thus the letter to Adams continues.

Throughout his novels and tales, and his criticism as well, Henry James speaks constantly of "what it comes down to." He is of course expressing the same sentiment here. If it is a sentiment habitual to him, it issues from the pragmatic mind. In this case the existence of his book, *Notes of a Son and Brother*, is the "cash value of" the interest yielded him by consciousness, just as the ceaseless activity of consciousness itself has been in turn the cash value of "the past." When we put each of his statements one by one with each of its predecessors, whether here in the Adams letter, in Strether's recognition scene, or in a passage from his *Prefaces*, we get the living phenomenon of William's pragmatic method: "The pragmatic method in such cases is to try to interpret each notion by tracing its respective practical consequences." That is, Henry's mind performs the tracing itself. His later manner not only addresses process by precept, it is process. And because it is process, the predominant attitude expressed is what William calls pragmatism's "melioristic"—or hopeful—one. Henry James can take heart in his "reactions—as many as possible," because it is precisely the possible, which to his mind, and to William's thought, is a viable reality.

At the risk here of appearing as obtuse as James himself is sometimes alleged to be, I wish to call attention to his parenthetical statement, "or of what you deny to be such." It is the most prescriptive, categorical remark in the letter! I think it tells us something—syntactically, if we will—of the comparative status of the cryptically decisive statement and the tentatively provisional one in his thought process. It suggests as well his characteristic presentation in the late fiction: his habit, for example, of portraying the events of his literal plot largely through subordinating constructions and sometimes even in parentheses. The events proper thus get themselves told on the periphery of the projecting thrust of the articulating Mind or Intelligence, just as his celebrated "viewpoints" are themselves subsumed into the workings of this same Intelligence.

Now in one sense I am dangerously close here to making much ado about nothing, since it is hardly worth the pains involved in noting, as one critic puts it so well, "the obvious fact that the distinctiveness of any writer is apparent in anything he writes."[51] Still, if a great deal of talk about James's fictive "Intelligence" can almost sound as though other writers of distinction do not themselves present a "voice," or exhibit a mind shaping and permeating its materials, it is nevertheless true that no one before James exploited the situation quite as he did. His Intelligence or "Authority" is a central locus conjoining and interpenetrating, as one continuous procedure, perceptual materials that otherwise would have to occur in more disjunctive sequence—thus violating to that extent the sort of seamlessness that in real life we often experience between perceiving and thinking. It is not that James is less fictive or artificial for this, but only that his particular illusion of life does convey this conjunctive relationship (it does not especially convey robustness of sensation or of intellectualization). The following example will serve to illustrate:

He had seen in the papers, her brother-in-law, Mr. Monteith's arrival —Mr. Mark P. Monteith, wasn't it?—and where he was, and she had been with him, three days before, at the time; whereupon he had said, "Hullo, what can have brought old Mark back?" He seemed to have believed—Newton had seemed—that that shirker, as he called him, never *would* come; and she guessed that if she had known she was going to meet such a former friend ("Which he claims you are, sir," said the pretty girl) he would have asked her to find out what the trouble could be.[52]

The parenthetical dialogue by the "pretty girl" gives James away entirely. I challenge the reader to describe this "incident" to some acquaintance who does not know the story. Perhaps the most inadequate statement would be the most standard Jamesian one—that it is all told from Mark Monteith's viewpoint! If we then say that Monteith is "remembering" the incident, there is still not much progress made. Suppose we were to say that James makes a single, present "happening" out of: (a) an encounter of the pretty girl with her brother-in-law, Newton Winch; (b) that encounter being related by the girl to Mark Monteith; (c) both of these in terms of Monteith reflecting later on his encounter with the girl. We would then begin to describe what we have just read. One is only less sympathetic than intrigued by William's remark: "But you *do* it, that's the queerness!"

What Henry "does" is to present William's own "fields of consciousness" as simultaneously present out of a single reconstructing Intelligence which unifies them into a dramatic and continuing experience—the very nexus of William's pragmatistic doctrines which grow (like a "germ") from his innovative psychology. The only part of William's doctrine left would be his final, "pure," pristine, or "dumb" experience in which all conscious activity participates—the darkness which one turns up the gas to discover. But William was to postulate these "further" experiences in part to both unstiffen and to celebrate the sheer indeterminate "cuts" of consciousness in all its fluid variety of manner one *can* talk about; such "pure" experience enabled him also to avoid solipsism, which would prevent mutual understanding and even humane treatment between individuals.

Which brings us back to Henry's letter to Adams: if James's artistic reconstruction of experience in the passage above (from "A Round of Visits"—1910) serves the cause of open-endedness and possibility, his brief cryptic "construct" of Adams's sentiments (whatever they were) as amounting to a denial of life, is just the reverse. In other words, his little statement in the parenthesis considered by itself partakes of intellectualist thinking as much as the letter—which includes the sentence—partakes of pragmatistic thinking.

Much of this can be expressed in more familiar literary terms. In "A Round of Visits" James has as usual taken an initial experience—something directly overheard, or something told to him, or something which came to him while sitting at Lamb House or, say, walking in London—and made it the germ for his exploration of the various projections, or consequences, latent in it. That his mind was essentially this way is clearly shown not only in his *Notebooks*, but in something like his "Project of Novel," which lacks little of being itself a nouvelle.[53] In his letter to Adams, it was Adams's own letter which provided the germ. But had he sat down and written, simply, "I received your letter, and everything you say constitutes a denial of life," he would *not* have been using Adams's letter as a germ. Now what is most interesting is that an enthusiastic Jacobite commentator describing this letter to Adams might indeed describe it in just that way: that James is pointing out to Adams that he is denying life, by which James means the artistic life, and so forth. Perhaps he is saying that, in the long run; but the long run is precisely not what makes him Henry James, nor even the thought that by "life" he had a definite, if refined and specialized, meaning.

James has, of course, some palpable faults—passages on occasion of sometimes unforgiveable vagueness in the selfsame later manner, for one—and it is doubtful that all the "sensibility" and "craftsmanship" we can invoke will rescue and transform them into diamonds. Nevertheless, the particular faults he does have occur because his mind is imbued with at least one very decent as well as highly imaginative attribute: the peculiarly pragmatistic commitment to ideas, whether one's own or *someone else's*, as happening, unfolding, going on from point to point; in fact stitchlessly merging into your own, becoming part of your present experience. I call this a decent quality because at least its tendency is never to treat other person's sentiments as lumps of lead, or even as finished statues with the chips, as Melville once expressed it, "carted off a million years ago." If he had had a different mentality, one which did not, so to speak, consign prescriptive thinking to the parenthesis, he might well have exhibited more of that "exposition" or "trace of a system" which F. O. Matthiessen and Ralph Barton Perry seek as evidence for his espousals of William's thought. He has, instead, "Central Intelligence," which, if it is one of his "artistic principles" for the art of the novel, is also something with epistemological implication.

Between Nominalism and Phenomenalism

In the work published posthumously under the title, *Some Problems of Philosophy: A Beginning of an Introduction to Philosophy* (1911), William James had embarked on what he hoped would be a series of volumes comprising a tightly reasoned exposition of his entire system. He intended this as the kind of presentation which even a logician like Charles S. Peirce would have considered rigorous.[54] In this book he gives the following description of what is real, reiterating his views expressed elsewhere on the relationship of concepts to percepts. "What is it," he asks, "to be 'real' "?

The best definition I know is that which the pragmatist rule gives: "Anything is real of which we find ourselves obliged to take account in any way." Concepts are thus as real as percepts, for we cannot live a moment without taking account of them. But the "eternal" kind of being which they enjoy is inferior to the temporal kind, because it is so static and schematic and lacks so many characters which temporal reality possesses. Philosophy must thus recognize many realms of reality which mutually interpenetrate.[55]

In the course of clarifying this basic stance as empirical William rejects nominalism, the doctrine that all universals are reducible to names, since there is no authoritative evidence for them in the external world. William remained from first to last "Aristotelian," in the sense that he always considered sensation to be a true report of the external world distinct from the perceiver. Nevertheless, the initial or motivating insight in nominalism, if not the conclusions it had led the nominalists to embrace, is for William most promising: for it takes account of the tremendous *individuality* of phenomena themselves:

A concept, it was said above, means always the same thing: Change means always change, white always white, a circle always a circle. On this self-sameness of conceptual objects the static and "eternal" character of our systems of ideal truth is based; for a relation, once perceived to obtain, must obtain always, between terms that do not alter. But many persons find difficulty in admitting that a concept used in different contexts can be intrinsically the same. When we call both snow and paper "white" it is supposed by these thinkers that there must be two predicates in the field. As James Mill says: "Every colour is an individual colour, every size is an individual size, every shape is an individual shape. But things have no individual colour in common, no individual shape in common; no individual size in common; that is to say, they have neither shape, colour, nor size in common.

"'What, then, is it,'" William continues, quoting James Mill, "'which they have in common which the mind can take into view? Those who affirmed that it was something, could by no means tell. They substituted words for things; using vague and mystical phrases, which, when examined, meant nothing.' The truth, according to this nominalist author, is that the only thing that can be possessed in common by two objects is the same *name*." William thus concludes: "This physical difficulty (which all house painters know,) of matching two tints so exactly as to show no difference seems to be the sort of fact that nominalists have in mind when they say that our ideal meanings are never twice the same."[56] William James's mature view, radical empiricism, seems to be a sort of expansion of this nominalist insight toward something like the phenomenalism which developed in philosophy after him. That is, he attests to both the individuality and the authority of each and every situation where we are attaching names to things, by construing the basic, circumscribing reality as phenomenological—even our continuous naming itself an authentic and crucial instance of experienced phenomena. His reference to the house painter, for example, is striking not just because he has the homely flair (or that his was a hopelessly "middle class" view), but because it suggests the "true" individuality of the paint-phenomena *as well as* the phenomenal "difficulty" of the situation.

Looked at from a literary context, to believe that our concepts describe phenomena truly and give us an entirely unique and particular situation each time this occurs is to discover an entire "new world" in the everyday affairs of life; one that is no less challenging to depict in all its rhythms and nuances as it is an authoritative description of reality. And, by contrast, when the literary Naturalist Frank Norris dismisses the work of Howells as mere "surfaces," as "the drama of a broken teacup," or "the tragedy of a walk down the block,"[57] he is in a real sense dismissing the nominalist's contention that "every colour is an individual colour, every size is an individual size, every shape is an individual shape." But when Howells himself remarks that, "every now and then I read a book with perfect comfort and much exhilaration, whose scenes the average Englishman would gasp in. Nothing happens; that is, nobody murders or debauches anybody else. . . . Yet it is all alive with the keenest interest for those who enjoy the study of individual traits and general conditions as they make themselves known to American experience"[58]—he is affirming the nominalist's contention. The following famous remarks from "The Art of Fiction" do even more than affirm it; they practically breathe it in life:

The power to guess the unseen from the seen, to trace the implication of things, to judge the whole piece by the pattern, the condition of feeling life in general so completely that you are well on your way to knowing any particular corner of it—this cluster of gifts may almost be said to constitute experience, and they occur in country and in town, and in the most differing stages of education. If experience consists of impressions, it may be said that impressions *are* experience, just as (have we not seen it?) they are the very air we breathe.[59]

That is, our impressions are *authentic*, true reports; yet at the same time no one of them is the final word; in fact, to feel life "in general" *is* to know a "particular corner" of it. Suppose, therefore, we were then to push the nominalist insight one step farther, to where the relationship of the mind with the individual color and shape it seeks to represent is itself one, concrete, living experience—authoritative, but not final. We would have entered the realm of William's radical empiricism. And, were we Frank Norris, we should then have to dismiss this as the mere drama of the mind itself in the act of portraying the implications of a broken teacup—or a golden bowl.

The same point may be better seen, perhaps, if we recollect for a moment Melville's "whiteness of the whale" from *Moby-Dick*, perhaps the peak of his art. In that presentation he marshals together a host of illustrations, the first group conveying the benign associations of whiteness, the second group its terrifying associations. All of these illustrations from the past, all of these particulars, if you will, body forth the reality of the single entity, Whiteness. It is a supreme example of Coleridge's secondary imagination, consciously reconciling as art the opposition of benignity and terror into a unified whole. The utilitarian school, or, broadly speaking, the empirical school deriving from Locke, moves in the opposing direction of implying that "whiteness" cannot really be said to expand its meaning the more particulars one attaches to it; rather, it is primarily meaningful in each occurrence, or particular. Furthermore, each occurrence is, as it were, a "whiteness" distinct from each and every other. Hence, the sum of these occurrences would comprise a sort of confederation of "whitenesses," whose society would look individualistic, democratic, pluralistic. Thus, in *The Golden Bowl*, Prince Amerigo recalls the dazzling whiteness at the end of Edgar Allan Poe's *Arthur Gordon Pym* and thinks to himself "what imagination Americans *could* have."[60] The difference between James and Melville here is not only that James is the essential novelist and must invariably "illustrate character,"[61] though that is true enough; it means also that his mind somehow senses what every house painter knows about trying to match tints of color. Experience is always unique, and concepts such as whiteness have indeed a part to play *within* its flux.

V. The "Jourdain" Relationship (II)

> *You see I still, in the presence of life (or of what you deny to be such,) have reactions—as many as possible—and the book I sent you is a proof of them.*

The Same Returns Not, Save to Bring the Different

Like William James's "poor reader" in his letter to Henry on *The American Scene*, the reader of this study has unquestionably come to discover that at the heart of the "Jourdain" relationship is the fact that pragmatistic thought is essentially circular in mode. Henry's statement above, which before provided us a point of departure for examining his "Central Intelligence," returns to us again. It was said of the novelist by Allen Tate, "he had that kind of intelligence which refuses to break its head against history."[1] William's thought likewise does not break its head against philosophical history. It is for this reason that he is philosophically a bit of everything: rationalist (concepts have a role), idealist (prevailing sentiment is optimistic), realist (external reality is "there" with or without us), empiricist (scientific verification is needed), and even phenomenologist (a world of pure experience). Much of this is summed up by William himself in a way which can facilitate both our understanding of pragmatistic thought and, indirectly, our recognition of why Henry's letter to Adams is somehow inexhaustible. It is the philosopher's favorite aphorism: "The same returns not, save to bring the different." It is the habit of mind which denotes the pluralist.

We can then keep returning to one letter, one locus, and find something which because it is the same is also different. This occurs because Henry James embodies that confluence between fields of experience that William continually celebrated. And the more we begin to see him in this way, the more we find ourselves within a circular pattern by which practically anything will take us out, only to bring us back where we begin. It is the difference, among other things, between addressing ourselves to "the other case" in James's work, and constantly confronting "the possible other case" of James's mind. For example: we could say that his having "reactions—as many as possible" is the same notion as that of finding his consciousness interesting; and that notion, we could say, is the same as his wanting to talk about the past; and his wanting to talk is the same notion (that is, he made it the same notion) as his being with Henry Adams a lone survivor. But what makes all these the same is precisely the continuity of a mind imbued with individual particulars or differences—a pluralistic mind. The difference, for example, between the belief that one carries on *despite* the abyss, and that one carries on precisely *because* of the abyss, is the difference between the more disjunctive thinking of intellectualism and the more conjunctive thinking of William's pluralism. "Reactions—as many as possible"—is pluralistic by virtue of its emphasis on additive possibility, and by its optimistic tenor, quite as much as by its literal expression of the many. For William's pluralism is primarily the view that conscious life is crammed with additive novelty:

When perceptible amounts of new phenomenal being come to birth, must we hold them to be in all points predetermined and necessary outgrowths of the being already there, or shall we rather admit the possibility that originality may thus instil itself into reality?

If we take concrete perceptual experience, the question can be answered in only one way. *"The same returns not, save to bring the different." Time keeps budding into new moments, every one of which presents a content which in its individuality never was before and will never come again. . . .*

The everlasting coming of concrete novelty into being is so obvious that the rationalizing intellect, bent ever on explaining what it is by what was, and having no logical principle but identity to explain by, treats the perceptual flux as a phenomenal illusion, resulting from the unceasing re-combination in new forms of mixture, of unalterable elements, coeval with the world.[2]

Does not this stunning passage from William characterize our reading experience of Henry's later manner? Constant perceptual novelty addresses both the unforeseeable implications of our broken teacup and, at the same time, the unwillingness by the author to impose from above an ideology which the perceptual flux must adhere to. If he did, the flux would not be

novel. The pluralistic view in its rejection of predetermined being is no more at home with Emerson's over-soul, within which
all concrete particulars derive their single meaning, than it is
with that "responsible" world of Frank Norris and the Natural-
ists—responsible because there too one must impose a single,
underlying force which all perceptual materials describe. William confronts this issue:

It is hard to imagine that "really" our own subjective experiences are
only molecular arrangements, even though the molecules be conceived
as beings of a psychic kind. A material fact may indeed be different
from what we feel it to be, but what sense is there in saying that a feeling, which has no other nature than to be felt, is not what it *is* felt? Psychologically considered, our experiences resist conceptual reduction,
and our fields of consciousness, taken simply as such, remain just what
they appear, even though facts of a molecular order should prove to be
the signals of the appearance. Biography is the concrete form in which
all that is is immediately given; the perceptual flux is the authenic stuff
of each of our biographies, and yields a perfect effervescence of novelty
all the time.[3]

It may be asked (it has certainly been asked before) whether
all of this provides a normative ethic. Frank Norris, for one, is
asking it in his idea of the novelist's responsibility. If all conscious life is ultimately sensational, even though in the broadest
terms, and if it is characterized by sheer undetermined novelty of
being—pure chance, in other words, though optimistically considered—then are there no norms, no standards? It is all friendly,
perhaps, but not serious. As for Henry James, if he embodies
this, what does it make him? What about his fine ethical sensibility? William responds:

When Berkeley had explained what people meant by matter, people
thought that he denied matter's existence. When Messrs. Schiller and
Dewey now explain what people mean by truth, they are accused of
denying *its* existence. These pragmatists destroy all objective standards, critics say, and put foolishness and wisdom on one level. . . .
[and yet] Pent in, as the pragmatist more than any one else sees himself
to be, between the whole body of funded truths squeezed from the past
and the coercions of the world of sense about him, who so well as he
feels the immense pressure of objective control under which our minds
perform their operations? If any one imagines that this law is lax, let
him keep its commandment one day, says Emerson.[4]

When the pragmatist gives up his absolutes and his fixed values, it means that he cannot ever take moral holidays: ethics become a continual matter, a matter of his constant readjustment in the light of whatever new turn-of-the-screw he finds himself obliged to take account of. In short, he becomes one of Henry's late protagonists, pent in by the norms of his past while coerced by the world of perceptual sense about him. The law is anything but lax, because the same is always returning as the different.

Pluralism and "Interest"
What Henry James has called "reactions—as many as possible," is, as we have just seen, his sense of constant perceptual novelty which distinctly characterizes William's pluralistic world. The following passage from William describing that world is perhaps his most arresting:

We are like fishes swimming in the sea of sense, bounded above by the superior element, but unable to breathe it pure or penetrate it. We get our oxygen from it, however, we touch it incessantly, now in this part, now in that, and every time we touch it, we turn back into the water with our course re-determined and re-energized. The abstract ideas of which the air consists are indispensable for life, but irrespirable by themselves, as it were, and only active in their re-directing function. All similes are halting, but this one rather takes my fancy. It shows how something, not sufficient for life in itself, may nevertheless be an effective determinant of life elsewhere.[5]

This must have been the sort of passage Henry had in mind when he wrote that he "simply sank down, under it, into such depths of submission and assimilation that *any* reaction, very nearly, even that of acknowledgment, would have had almost the taint of dissent or escape." For William's remarks are simply a cameo of Henry's later method. The fundamental realm or locus of life is the perceptual "sea of sense," continuously enveloping us as we swim. But we are still "bounded above" by the "superior element" of ideas—though not really, it is to be noted, in a "dualistic" relationship. William's entire effort here, with his oxygen metaphor, is to avoid such dualism, while still locating the center of our activity in experience. Without ideas we cannot swim, without the "sea of sense" we have nowhere to swim. The relationship is thus not catalytic, in which our ideas remain neutral or unaffected while creating "life elsewhere" (for they really and only begin to live *in* the "elsewhere," since "our course" is constantly "re-determined and re-energized" by them).

William's conceit evokes Henry's fictive mode so perfectly that it is at once astounding and yet appropriate (like William's naming Henry's "germ" method) to recall that the novelist had already conceived precisely William's "fish" imagery to describe the dramatic ambience of the world in which his characters circulate around one another. F. O. Matthiessen has called attention to this "odd variant of James's water-images," as he calls it: "In all three of his great final novels he conceives on occasion his social group as being 'like fishes in a crystal pool,' held together in 'a fathomless medium.'"[6] Henry's preponderant use of water imagery generally in this period, his "floatings," "currents," and such, are, of course, as familiar to his readers as "point of view." William's conceit insists on locating the center of our life dramatically in consciousness, while pointing to the fact that our ideas become living only as they occur in consciousness. The philosopher's quite delicate relationship parallels not only the "registers" in Henry's fiction but his narrative consciousness as well. This is why his most important "symbols," such as the dove or the golden bowl, are always most "active in their re-directing function": that is, they *accrue* meaning through context and character viewpoint, are dramatically *felt* by different individuals, and are modified—"re-determined and re-energized"—from episode to episode. They do not point to a single generic realm of transcendent meaning that such clusters of moments compositely symbolize. It is the same with any key idea or concept within the narrative framework, like "independent" in *The Portrait of a Lady* or "virtuous attachment" in *The Ambassadors*. And it is also of course what T. S. Eliot was addressing in his remark about James's refusal to be violated by ideas. One of the novelist's more recent commentators, Peter Garrett, has in this regard inadvertently put his finger almost at the center of William's thought—and at its distinctive point vis-à-vis William's predecessors—with this perceptive observation about Henry's late work: "The creations of consciousness constitute the essence of James's meaning; what lies beyond serves only to reinforce or extend that significance."[7]

The unusual appropriateness of Garrett's statement leads me to observe that in one respect, at least, I have often found

James's many admiring commentators no more pertinent for the "Jourdain" relationship as such than the opposition. There is however a certain logic in this. If our task as Jacobites is to point up James's supremacy in fiction, it perhaps follows that in expounding his ideas and insights we will not find the notion of ideas as mere "transitions" (i.e., "re-directors") particularly helpful. Our task in such instances is rather to stress the vision and the values which obtain because his elaborate stream of discourse or "sea of sense" symbolizes *them*. Thus we will probably operate on a principle the reverse of William James's. Whereas for him it is the ideas which "not sufficient for life in [themselves]," nevertheless determine "life elsewhere," for us it is the distinctive Jamesian methodology which helps determine its "life elsewhere"—his profundity of vision. It has been said earlier in this book that all thinking must be to some extent saltatory and to some extent ambulatory. All I am saying here is that with most favorable criticisms of Henry James the saltatory approach tends to predominate.

On the other hand, an objecting critic quite as much concerned with profundity, but who does *not* ascribe to James's supremacy, may often in a negative context point to a characteristic which is cognate to the interests, if not the assumptions, of the present study.[8] The difficulty with something which is genuinely *mediated*, as William's thought and Henry's mind both are, is that in grasping it we are always involved in a perplexing and sometimes agonizing activity: to find a discourse adequate to the experience. It is something like the difference between a teacher who informs his colleague how he presented Chaucer to his class, and one who represents his Chaucer lecture as "transitional" between his earlier encounter with his colleague and his present one: not just by mentioning where he has been in the meantime, and what he said to his class, but using his "intervening" lecture as the terms themselves for taking up again the present discussion; making his class lecture no "lecture" at all, but a point which like any other (including even the previous conversation) impinges on the present moment.

Pluralism's passion for novelty (the "present moment") is what opposes it to the more traditional metaphysical view (i.e., what have our "new" interests and sensations in *common* with their predecessors). Our Henry Jamesian teacher above considers his present encounter with his colleague unparalleled in his experience, which is why both his previous encounter with him and his class lecture as well (which at their times were also unparalleled) must all coalesce and tumble into the present moment. I hope it can be seen why the "mediated" view of reality *is* in a real sense challenging to discourse: in my own faulty analogy I must halt—turn off an imaginary switch which makes the waters of experience move—and treat the entire matter not as an event continuous and new, but as just another "episode" contributive to the whole, that "whole" in the present case being that Henry James continues to realize William's thought.

One can see nevertheless why the mentality which truly embodies William's pluralism would become more and more drawn to little things, tiny matters. Nothing is ever finished in the usual sense, the smallest matter yielding almost unlimited possibilities of meaning. William gives the rationale for this:

In many familiar objects every one will recognize the human element. We conceive a given reality in this way or in that, to suit our purpose, and the reality passively submits to the conception. You can take the number 27 as the cube of 3, or as the product of 3 and 9, or as 26 *plus* 1, or 100 *minus* 73, or in countless other ways, of which one will be just as true as another. You can take a chess-board as black squares on a white ground, or as white squares on a black ground, and neither conception is a false one.[9]

These various conceptions *about* the number twenty-seven are what give more meaning *to* the number twenty-seven. Twenty-seven is novel by virtue of all the points of view, actual or possible, that one can take toward it. Hence, when Henry in his "Preface" designates a set of "lamps" to light up the situation in *The Awkward Age,* or when he constructs *The Spoils of Poynton* around those practically disembodied "objects," or whenever he engaged in what he repeatedly called "happy points of view," he is realizing William's pluralism. William in the passage above speaks of its "human element" to distinguish it from anything philosophically ideal, and also because he believes everyday, familiar life to be robust in this sense. Similarly, Henry's continual reference to the "interest" of the novel, and in that context its "faithful illusion" of life, is for him much the same notion. When William speaks of reality "submit[ing] to our conception," we can be mindful of the creative orientation of his philosophy and can recollect once again Henry's "art that *makes* life, makes interest . . . " which so perplexed H. G. Wells. Pluralism is really, then, a habit of mind which accounts diversity as both novel and interesting: "The result is innumerable little hangings-together of the world's parts within the larger hangings-together, little worlds, not only of discourse but of operation, within the wider universe. . . . [T]he pragmatic value of the world's unity is that all these definite networks actually and practically exist. Some are more enveloping and extensive, some less so."[10]

But the "great point," William insists, "is to notice that the oneness and the manyness are absolutely co-ordinate here." Conjunction once again, we see, is his emphasis. Nevertheless, the pragmatist, as these remarks clearly indicate, sees unity only as it continually comes forth at us, so to speak, in particularity. His "interest" therefore has to be with that continual "lesser": "It follows that whoever says that the whole world tells one story utters another of those monistic dogmas that a man believes at his risk. It is easy to see the world's history pluralistically, as a rope of which each fibre tells a separate tale."[11]

Let us imagine the literary artist who sees the world in just this way, with "each fibre" telling its separate tale. Not only would he find significance and interest in the minute particulars of the world, but he might well describe the nature of experience itself in the following way:

Experience is never limited, and it is never complete; it is an immense sensibility, a kind of huge spider-web of the finest silken threads suspended in the chamber of consciousness, and catching every air-borne particle in its tissue. It is the very atmosphere of the mind; and when the mind is imaginative—much more when it happens to be that of a man of genius—it takes to itself the faintest hints of life, it converts the very pulses of the air into revelations.[12]

This famous passage stands in relation to William's thought not unlike William's conceit of the "fishes" to Henry's method. That is, Henry is first and foremost affirming William's open-ended world of experience, "in the making," as William always liked to say of it. Furthermore, when the novelist conceives of the "tissue" and "web" of sensibility having "the finest silken threads," he senses what William James says is the actual existence in its own right of "each fibre" of the world's history.

Those fibers in turn become one with the *act* of experiencing them, and thus one with each other; or, as William puts it just after his own image of the rope: "'The world is One,' therefore, just so far as we experience it to be concatenated."[13] Henry's "atmosphere of the mind" performs the same function as a part-maker of experience, not just a receptacle—in fact its making job is quite as indispensable as its receiving. "Air-borne particles" do not in themselves constitute "revelations." It is that "converting" process he speaks of which differentiates what he hears at a dinner party from *The Spoils of Poynton*, or a reported incident about William Dean Howells from *The Ambassadors*. And sometimes even his germs are themselves the result of his "atmosphere of the mind," as when he thinks of a young girl "affronting her destiny" (Isabel Archer). Being one on whom nothing is lost is then quite as much a matter of the mind's active role in not losing the possible meanings it can make from airborne particles.

We might wonder, then, how the pluralist conceives of a progression within his "rope" of history, from one point of time to another. William tells us: "Men and nations start with a vague notion of being rich, or great, or good. Each step they make brings unforeseen chances into sight, and shuts out older vistas, and the specifications of the general purpose have to be daily changed. *What is reached in the end may be better or worse than what was proposed, but it is always more complex and different.*"[14]

There is no more appropriate description than this of the mental journey in a late Henry James novel or tale. Whether the initial concern involves the "objects" at Poynton Park, an errant young man in Paris, a wealthy but dying American girl in London, a marriage of convenience by an impoverished Italian prince to an American heiress; or, even if what William here has called a "vague notion," is itself, "the sense of being kept for something rare and strange, possibly prodigious and terrible, that [is] sooner or later to happen"[15]—what is reached in the end may be better or worse than what was proposed, but it is always "more complex and different." These are, then, some of the considerations which relate to William James's pluralism and Henry's "interest." The novelist's remark to Adams affirming "reactions—as many as possible" bespeaks therefore what William liked to call the "democratic" spirit of his thought, by which he meant its open-endedness, its cordiality with various beliefs and assumptions that may appear otherwise at odds with one another—in short its pluralism. It amounts to a continual existential engagement with actual alternatives, like the number twenty-seven.

The "Democracy" of Henry James

When using the word "democratic" to describe Henry James, I should perhaps take particular pains to clarify its meaning. The assumption that Henry's work, particularly his later work, is a precious, delicate affair and most at home with an elite or "aristocratic" audience has probably been modified if not altogether dispelled by the amount of critical attention he has received by teacher, scholar, and student. Still, there are a number of issues, at least some paradoxical connotations, involved always in speaking of Henry James as democratic, even apart from William. Bringing William into the picture may even appear to compound them. The novelist lived abroad, does not "sound" or "seem" American (while admitting the hopelessness of knowing what "American" means). His models were mostly French or, as in the case of Turgenev, Russian-French. He likes to use French words and phrases (William likes German). His characters and subjects are too attenuated by comparison with those of most of his countrymen of equal literary stature—Melville, Twain, and Faulkner, for example.

In William's case the connotations are apparently just the reverse. He is more "masculine," and he reads that way. He "stayed" here, loved this country, and often said so (Henry does not speak too well of it early in his career, in his *Hawthorne*, or late, in *The American Scene*). What is most important, perhaps, William's philosophy is conventionally construed as "the inevitable American philosophy": it is everything from protestantism, to the cranky (but lovable) common man, to the cockeyed optimist, to the robber barons, to the smart Jonathan who distrusts the speculative perfume of Old Worldish abstraction. And yet, despite his criticism of Henry's later manner (itself a far different and more complicated affair than is usually made out, as we have seen already), it was not William's contention that Henry's "certain want of blood" in his fiction proceeded as such from his having become a European, as opposed to an American, writer. Clearly, it did not occur to Henry that William's philosophical views were too bloody or too narrowly practical for him.

I would certainly agree that the personal, temperamental differences between them find expression, for example, in William's 1889 letter to his wife, in which he speaks of Henry's "strange heavy alien manners and customs."[16] But I am only contending right now that when William characteristically speaks of his pragmatistic doctrine as "democratic," in that it remains open-minded and mediating, he is not expressing for his body of ideas a different sentiment from what Henry continually expresses for his artistic perspective. They are in fact remarkably similar sentiments and can be shown to be so. To illustrate this, let me cite Henry at his most "delicate" point, his *Prefaces*: I am choosing furthermore an utterance from them which to my knowledge all his commentators consider nothing less than a touchstone for our grasp of his artistic purpose at all points. He writes:.

There is, I think, no more nutritive or suggestive truth in this connexion than that of the perfect dependence of the "moral" sense of a work of art on the amount of felt life concerned in producing it. The question comes back thus, obviously, to the kind and the degree of the artist's prime sensibility, which is the soil out of which his subject springs. The quality and capacity of that soil, its ability to "grow" with due freshness and straightness any vision of life, represents, strongly or weakly, the projected morality.[17]

R. P. Blackmur, the most knowledgeable of James's aesthetic critics, says of these statements: "These sentences represent, I think, the genius and intention of James the novelist, and ought to explain the seriousness and critical devotion with which he made his Prefaces a *vade-mecum*—both for himself as the solace of achievement, and for others as a guide and exemplification."[18] The same sentences can be shown to embody fully the thinking which William calls democratic. If Henry is here expressing his belief that the novel should convey the most sensitively felt life, let us first note that he speaks initially of its "amount," not its quality or its integrity, which we might have anticipated, particularly since the context is that of the "moral sense." Still, he does go on to speak of "kind" and "degree" in connection with the artist's "prime sensibility," and likewise the "quality" of and "capacity" for the soil (a metaphor for the sensibility). It could be asked, what difference does it make whether James says "amount" of felt life·initially or not, since he obviously *is* concerned with the quality of the sensibility; after all, the felt life is itself the organic projection of the sensibility. .

There may be no difference whatever with respect to the moral content of a particular piece of writing—that is exactly what we cannot know about in advance, which is James's point. The question remains: what is James *proceeding to say* about the issue? Blackmur again has written that these same remarks illustrate "the relation which James again and again made eloquently plain between the value or morality of his art and the form in which it appears,"[19] and certainly they do exactly that; but no relation, not even one eloquently plain, becomes plainer for its being entitled a "relation." At least not if we conceive of the relation as itself a real process. That Henry so conceived of it is indicated by his choice of image, in which the "soil" (sensibility) proceeds to grow its "life." He senses moreover even the "proceedingness" of his own remarks about the question, for he calls all of this a ·"truth" which is "suggestive" and "nutritive": his mind is so totally imbued with process that when he conceives of a truth as "the process," it immediately begins to conjoin with his present sense of thinking about it! When I focus, therefore, on something like "amount" of felt life (or, the phrase "any vision" of life would do as well), I am simply emphasizing the openness or democracy of James's view of the whole question.

But, it is precisely because he *is* imbued with a real sense of process, that he *can* be open and democratic about these matters. Thus, he speaks of "kind," "character," and "quality," not as products of the fixed artistic mind, but of its operating; he speaks too of the entire matter as "the question" of it, not the answer. And the best indication that he truly means "the question" is to be found in our continuing the passage. It turns out that the predicates of James's "kind," "character," and "quality" are the following: "a varying element," "differences of the individual relation to its general subject matter," "varieties of outlook on life," and "never the same from man to man."[20]

It should not surprise us, therefore, if even this lovely aesthetic utterance can upon reflection start to resemble the very epistemology of pragmatism. The mind is active; it "grows" its vision; it is "any" vision which arises from the seed, and will be "strongly or weakly" (depending upon its quality of the growing) a "*projected* morality" of life: the mind continually projects ethical reality, then, and does not simply copy or agree with a preexistent one. And, because the individual vision of life and morality is projected out by the author's mind, the "truth" of his vision no less than its "moral sense" is to be understood as prospective and consequential. The full upshot is that when James in "The Art of Fiction" insists, and in his *Prefaces* almost poetizes, the view that one cannot speak of matters like *the* morality or *the* house of fiction except as all of their dramatic and projected possibilities, he is giving life to the following conviction: "This thesis is what I have to defend. The truth of an idea is not a stagnant property inherent in it. Truth *happens* to an idea. It *becomes* true, is *made* true by events. Its verity *is* in fact an event, a process: the process namely of its verifying itself, its veri-*fication*. Its validity is the process of its valid-*ation*."[21]

Operative Irony

If we return once again to Henry James's letter to Henry Adams, just after the notation of his "reactions—as many as possible," we find him now affirming: "It's, I suppose, because I am that queer monster, the artist, an obstinate finality, an inexhaustible sensibility."

This arresting declaration is certainly broad in its implications, but no more so than was the question of the past, the bringing down of which to cases has now enabled James to ambulate back into realms of "finality." What is once again Jamesian, therefore, is that he invariably makes his conceptualizations play a "transitional" role within his depicted experience. Put less philosophically, his mind cannot help but take account in some way of the pretension involved in his own generalizations, however deeply and seriously held, and so he puts things in a way that will allow for this sense. Thus, he designates himself the artist, but he precedes the designation by his image, "queer monster." Or rather, it is one designation, the syntax curiously making artist clarify monster, rather than the reverse. Were it the other way around, we would have more conventional syntax, and "artist" would be amplified by the queer monster, the obstinate finality, and the inexhaustible sensibility. This way, "artist" seems to mediate between being a predication of what he essentially "is" (surrounded by its amplifications), and being one of three equal ways of talking about the queer monster.

Now the "queer monster" refers in turn to his present empirical situation and is therefore related to process (he encourages consciousness with a "ghastly grin"). Which, then, is meant to have priority here, the nature of being an artist, or its consequential, resulting "monstrous" process—obstinate, final, and inexhaustible? Nor are his phrases, "obstinate finality" and "inexhaustible sensibility" any less unstiffened, even when considered by themselves apart from his context. "Finality" is certainly conclusive and profound enough, but I think it will be granted that the full possibilities of meaning that a self-styled "obstinate" finality might open up could resemble, say, the "unmitigated blackness" attributed by James to Adams at the opening of the letter. As for "inexhaustible" sensibility—surely James has included within his "varieties of outlook" and "happy points of view," the acute awareness that reading the very late Henry James of *Notes of a Son and Brother* can be an extremely laborious affair (remember his earlier choice of the word "divagations"). Such, too, is one more of his "reactions—as many as possible." It is also pragmatistic open-endedness, whether the issue in question is the number twenty-seven or even one's own aesthetic ideal. Operative irony, the quality being exhibited here, is a disposition of the mind, and it literally survives and is nourished on a view of reality which is prospective, or made of the possible. That same world of the possible is peculiarly the actual and authentic pluralistic world of William's thought. William proclaims this viewpoint in "The Will to Believe":

But please observe, now, that when as empiricists we give up the doctrine of objective certitude, we do not thereby give up the quest or hope of truth itself. . . .

. . . .

It is like a general informing his soldiers that it is better to keep out of battle forever than to risk a single wound. Not so are victories either over enemies or over nature gained. Our errors are surely not such awfully solemn things. In a world where we are so certain to incur them in spite of all our caution, a certain lightness of heart seems healthier than this excessive nervousness on their behalf.[22]

William's language and comparison of the empiricist to a general in a military campaign may seem out of step with Henry's sensibility and artistry. And yet, the novelist's definition of his operative irony captures William's spirit perfectly, and is not even altogether removed from William's expression of that spirit. He writes: "When it's not a campaign, of a sort, on behalf of the something better (better than the obnoxious, the provoking object) that blessedly, as is assumed, *might* be, it's not worth speaking of. But this is exactly what we mean by operative irony. It implies and projects the possible other case, the case rich and edifying where the actuality is pretentious and vain."[23]

I suspect that if this particular conception of irony were a little more operative in Henry's occasional detractors, such as Maxwell Geismar, there would be more of a genuine meeting ground between Jacobites and those who, like Geismar, are nettled by the indisputable fact that a little late James goes an awfully long way.[24] It does—in all of the meanings. There is not always that much difference between what makes the letter to Adams go a long way and the itch lodged just beyond reach which activates an anti-Jamesian. The terms of the one are the terms of the other. It is precisely what can happen when one is committed to a reality of process and unending possibility—and really means it, as Henry does. In one sense William was saved from this, in that he only had to tell of it. In another sense he has, of course, been anything but saved: for pragmatism, so often construed as "practical" not in William's sense of accounting every possible nuance of behavior (i.e., "practice"), but as expedient, moneymaking, or physical activity, is really as overwhelming in its continual demands at attending to actual process (no "moral holidays") as it is susceptible to derision if misapprehended. The same is true for Henry's fiction.

Henry chooses to emphasize the "something better" in his conception of operative irony in order to stress William's prospective sense and notion of reality. But the same something better always "*might* be," he says, to stress, like William, the inveterate fact of human fallibility. It is always a "possible other case" because, again like William, possibility itself is embraced and mediates with human error. And the irony is "operative," because the fundamental orientation and disposition of mind is to process. What always characterizes Henry's possible other case, in short, is William's sheer "indeterminable" number of them, and the way each one must be given its due. If each case were not novel and authentic, as William's pluralistic doctrine insists it is, then the springs of Henry's particular illusion of life ("interest") would begin to dry up.

This entire conception and practice of irony arises naturally and gets itself expressed in Henry's allusion to himself as "M. Jourdain" after reading William. But it is most beautifully sustained and articulated in his fiction, and exemplified extremely well in "The Art of Fiction." It is the difference there between contending, as he did, that the *value* of Besant's a priori "beautiful and vague" injunctions lies entirely in the meaning one attaches to them, and contending, as so many of his commentators do, that this was the very trouble with Besant's rules. In both instances we would have irony, but only in the first the operative irony described above by the novelist. And, again, if we are not to be duped (since he "really" means the trouble and not the value of those injunctions), what is it he actually proceeds to do for the remainder of the essay—show how troublesome they are, or how valuable? The trouble has, of course, been Besant's a priori claim about them, exactly the same trouble the pragmatist has with the claims of the rationalist schools: that one's a priori conceptions actually supersede phenomenal reality or "felt" life, so that these conceptions, because they are not seen as "transitional," are raised to the level of static Law or Absolute and are no longer allowed to yield their own indeterminant possibilities. Even so, Henry's fundamental point in "The Art of Fiction" is that a rule no less than the appropriate genre itself (fiction) is most valuable precisely in so far as it allows for the unexpected variation, not in how it embodies the fixed norms which all practitioners share and which can therefore be both codified and predicted. That is always the foundation for his well-known views on the novel's freedom.

The novelist denied least of all that there is prodigious art involved always in the writing of fiction; neither did he deny that a writer must constantly seek the most rigorous control in pursuing his objectives. But what he never propounded—and one is thinking now of the *Prefaces* as well as "The Art of Fiction" —is what those controls and those objectives are except as they become consequences in a particular story written by himself or another. Apart from this concrete, individual orientation, all he will say, as we have seen again and again, is just how different, and various, and "never the same" they are from one writer to another. If the value of Besant's injunctions lies wholly in the meaning to be grafted upon them, perhaps the only trouble with William's mediating view, which Henry's operatively ironic response to Besant parallels, is that, being located in the mind's reciprocal relationship with actuality which comprises the dramatic process of the world, it all but defies our efforts to conceptualize its landscape. William James is as post-Kantian in his commitment to the projecting thrust of the creative mind (Bergson, especially, realized this) as he is plain "old" empiricist and philosophical realist in his belief that the same visiting mind catches hold of real phenomena, real particles from the indeterminable flux. That is what his mediating view is like, if once we can get over the thought that to be "between" things is not to possess vitality and dynamically actual territory. A gentle push to pragmatistic thought ends up as Wallace Stevens, a gentle pull on it as William Dean Howells. But the pushing and pulling at once which William himself expresses ends up as Henry's late fiction, an idiom "between" realism and romance, a most unusually imaginative realism or a most empirical romance.

Mores and Lesses—as Real as Anything Else in the System
In the hope of bringing to light more fully the implications of William's mediated viewpoint—the actual territory in-between things—it may be helpful to conduct now a modest experiment. Let us look at a fairly sizable passage from *Pragmatism,* in which the philosopher addresses the question of salvation. It will provide us, I think, a rather unusual touchstone for grasping hold of that elusive territory proclaimed by a truly mediated view. It may also bring to light the grounds for the intellectualistic complaint that the pragmatist makes a great to-do over nothing, or very little (in precisely the way the anti-Jamesian might say of Henry):

One sees at this point that the great religious difference lies between the men who insist that the world *must and shall be,* and those who are contented with believing that the world *may be,* saved. The whole clash of rationalistic and empiricist religion is thus over the validity of possibility. It is necessary therefore to begin by focusing upon that word. What may the word "possible" definitely mean? To unreflecting men it means a sort of third estate of being, less real than existence, more real than non-existence, a twilight realm, a hybrid status, a limbo into which and out of which realities ever and anon are made to pass.

Such a conception is of course too vague and nondescript to satisfy us. Here, as elsewhere, the only way to extract a term's meaning is to use the pragmatic method on it. When you say that a thing is possible, what difference does it make? It makes at least this difference that if any one calls it impossible you can contradict him, if any one calls it actual you can contradict *him*, and if any one calls it necessary you can contradict him too.

But these privileges of contradiction don't amount to much. When you say a thing is possible, does not that make some farther difference in terms of actual fact?

It makes at least this negative difference that if the statement be true, it follows that *there is nothing extant capable of preventing* the possible thing. . . .

What does this mean pragmatically? It means not only that there are no preventive conditions present, but that some of the conditions of production of the possible thing actually are here. . . .

Let us apply this notion to the salvation of the world. What does it pragmatically mean to say that this is possible? It means that some of the conditions of the world's deliverance do actually exist. The more of them there are existent, the fewer preventing conditions you can find, the better-grounded is the salvation's possibility, the more *probable* does the fact of the deliverance become.[25]

I hope it will be agreed that there is something rather remarkable about this passage. Despite all of William's characteristic vigor and decisiveness of tone, it has nevertheless a slight Henry Jamesian cast to it, a something reminiscent of his later manner. The similarity may perhaps not strike the reader at once, but it begins to grow (if it does at all) just a little past midway through the selection. There is, let us say, almost a momentary suspension—a "momentary stay," as Robert Frost would say—between our more familiar intellectual shores of the real and the nonreal. These intervening realms of experience—from less possible, to possible, to more possible, to probable—are of course also what William is talking about in the passage, and we have already seen him expressing this viewpoint before in various other connections. But this particular utterance appeared momentarily to "resemble" what William was saying as we ambulated with him. We moved, that is, from who it was, at least, we could "contradict," to the "negative" difference that "there is nothing extant capable of," to "some conditions"; and then on to the "fewer preventing conditions," toward "the more probable," fact of salvation. This occurred because William paused for a moment in his remarks about salvation proper, and decided to take us through the various authentic consequences ("practices") of the word "possible." We saw him earlier describe the real as "anything . . . of which we find ourselves obliged to take account" and that definition *tells* much the same notion as the passage above. But the passage above almost simulated or personified its own notion.

Henry's late work continually personifies what William is talking about here; and William while talking about it has just grazed Henry's later manner. If the reader were to look again at the passage (or better still at the entire passage in *Pragmatism*, a few portions of which I have omitted), he might try this experiment. Let him think first of the following words from William to Henry: "interminable elaboration . . . succeeded *in getting there* after a fashion. . . . 'Say it *out*, for God's sake.' " Then let him read William's passage again. This results not from William's having a discourse like Henry's later manner. It results from the occasional pressure, imposed upon him by his doctrine, to "sound" like what he is expounding, a common enough occurrence for anyone with a prolonged association with some particular subject or network of ideas (the present writer not excepted). What is of interest, then, is what the doctrine itself "sounds" like, when it does begin to sound. It sounds like Henry James. And there is every good reason that it might, because William is here insisting upon the authentic reality—coequal and indispensable—of all those in-between areas of experience which Henry conveys by his provisionalness and circumambience. In the indetermined world of the pluralist, all those nuances, those "mores" and "lesses" of things, are legitimately as real and worthy of account as anything else in the system. These so-called marginal areas of life are in fact what the pluralist passionately insists be allowed equal status. We can go right back to William's same discussion of salvation and see him insisting upon this point (though no longer sounding like Henry):

Take, for example, any one of us in this room with the ideals which he cherishes and is willing to live and work for. Every such ideal realized will be one moment in the world's salvation. . . .

Does our act then *create* the world's salvation so far as it makes room for itself, so far as it leaps into the gap? Does it create, not the whole world's salvation of course, but just so much of this as itself covers of the world's extent?

Here I take the bull by the horns, and in spite of the whole crew of rationalists and monists, of whatever brand they be, I ask *why not?* Our acts, our turning-places, where we seem to ourselves to make ourselves and grow, are the parts of the world to which we are closest, the parts of which our knowledge is the most intimate and complete. Why should we not take them at their face-value? Why may they not be the actual turning-places and growing-places which they seem to be, of the world—why not the workshop of being, where we catch fact in the making, so that nowhere may the world grow in any other kind of way than this.[26]

This would seem to lay to rest any possibility of Henry's "naïveté" in his insistence that William's philosophy is so "creative." The doctrine here is well nigh "fictive," and almost in the Wallace Stevens sense of that word. William's entire passage is about making and creating moments; his notion and image of "the workshop of being" is a superb evocation of the authentic creative process. More to the point, it is fictive in precisely the Henry Jamesian way. That is, William's "salvation," like Henry's "past" in the Adams letter, or like the "whiteness" in *The Golden Bowl*, or like a girl affronting her "destiny"—is something to project back into experience and to make moments of; tiny moments which perhaps do not claim to explain the entire cosmos, but which may be "rich," as Henry said of William's book, *The Meaning of Truth*, "in their cumulative effect." William's striking metaphor of "growing-places" to describe our life as we feel it, is not just accidentally the same image for Henry's "growing" of "felt life" in his aesthetic theory.

An Act of Life
We may now return again to the letter to Henry Adams and see how the novelist begins to bring his argument to a close. Having conceded the "inexhaustible sensibility" of the artist, he continues: "Hence the reactions—appearances, memories, many

things, go on playing upon it [consciousness] with consequences that I note and 'enjoy' (grim word!) noting. It all takes doing—and I *do*. I believe I shall do yet again—it is still an act of life."

It would appear that we have at long last come in this letter to "orthodox" pragmatism, complete with explicit consequences and action, results and doing, just the way a pragmatist is supposed to speak. One might, of course, have presented a Henry James from a series of such orthodoxies as this. He would be James the pragmatist, brother of James the pragmatist; and not, I think, particularly Jamesian for that. But I am obviously thinking of the quality of William James's thought as well. Thus, for example, the novelist's unusual locution, "I note and 'enjoy' (grim word!) noting," is at the very heart of Henry James, both because no one else would write such a phrase and because it manages in its uniqueness to accomplish the pragmatistic un-stiffening of a single point of view. For the minute one steps within William's epistemology, he simply must begin to ask: what do these words "possible," or "past," or "notation," or even "enjoy" come to in one's continuing experience. The possible other case, or cases, for each of them allows for the sensibility of operative irony.

The novelist's most lasting way of asking them is his fiction itself, in the sense that, for example, *The Portrait of a Lady* asks: what does it mean to say that a girl affronts her destiny? Or the revised versions of *Daisy Miller* and *Madame de Mauves* ask: what does it mean to speak of innocence? Or *The Ambassadors* asks: what does it mean to say that a man should live, live all he can? More particularly, James does this asking by his distinctive mode of presentation; his way, for instance, of having dialogue occur as an element within someone's consciousness. We saw this earlier in "A Round of Visits," but we may now go to what some would consider the epitome of his work, the recognition scene in *The Ambassadors*. Here is how he concludes it:

[Strether] foresaw that Miss Gostrey would come again into requisition on the morrow; though it wasn't to be denied that he was already afraid of her "What on earth—that's what I want to know now—had you then supposed?" He recognized at last that he had really been trying all along to suppose nothing. Verily, verily, his labour had been lost. He found himself supposing innumerable and wonderful things.[27]

There is an intriguing question here for critics and aestheti-

cians: precisely what "actual" world does Miss Gostrey's imputed remark belong to? Or—since we do make a good deal over
Jamesian point of view—how is it that Strether allows the
imagined word from Miss Gostrey, "suppose[d]," to activate his
own response via the same word, "supposing"? These are not
always matters we address when we discuss James's point of view
or even his dramatic method, nor do we address them just by reminding ourselves that James is "really there" behind his character. What is rendered here, and uniquely Jamesian for doing
so, is that *conjunctively* experienced relationship, indispensable
for operative irony, between Miss Gostrey's imagined words and
Strether's ascribed present thoughts. That is, the notion of
Strether's "trying to suppose nothing" about Chad and Madame
de Vionnet does not come round to "supposing innumerable
and wonderful things," simply because James is witty. To begin
with, it is inconceivable that anyone who knows *The Ambassadors* would subscribe to the proposition that Strether has, until
this moment late in the story, "supposed nothing." The book has
been a symphony of his supposition. Nevertheless, it is certainly
true what he is now acknowledging about himself having "supposed nothing." Equally true, however, is the fact that Strether's
"supposing" propensities are expressly what have made the boat
scene yield so much to him.

The fundamental point here as elsewhere about Strether is
that he does not, intellectualist fashion, tend to prescribe—
which in turn means that he is continually open to supposition—
"supposing." Jim Pocock needs no boat scene to surmise the
"truth"; Mrs. Newsome does not even need to leave Massachusetts to know it. Such people are not "supposers"—they already
know. And therefore they could not be more wrong for being
right. If we think of Miss Gostrey's imagined remark, "What on
earth . . . had you then supposed?"—we have there indeed the
disjunction of mere supposition from truth. But Strether cannot
think in that way. He is too conjunctive, too ambulatory. Thus,
for him supposing nothing and supposing innumerable things
are confluent. He can for that reason be duped. Strether can be
duped because he can, ultimately, cope with being fooled. Conspicuously unlike the determinists William James addresses in
"The Dilemma of Determinism," or the tough-minded whom he
addresses in "The Will to Believe," Lambert Strether has not that

mental cast in which the stars go topsy-turvy when one discovers he has made an error. Strether will in fact be fooled again.
Just when he has determined to throw his wholehearted support
to Chad and Madame de Vionnet, he recognizes even more
clearly that Chad has tired of the lady and is extremely anxious
to return to Woollett, his mother, and his expectations in the
family industry. Does all this then mean that Strether is now
wrong? Was he therefore right in the original presupposition
brought with him across the Atlantic? The fact is, of course, that
James in this book has proceeded to unstiffen our prescribed expectations of right and wrong, true and false, by asking what we
mean by them in the flowing stream of consciousness and experience operative in the world of the actual. He has *not* thrown them
out for this, any more than William throws out truth for asking
what we mean by it. What Henry "means" by them in *The
Ambassadors* is what William means by truth in his thought:
they unfold, they happen, and there are just no moral holidays
to be taken in connection with them. The importance of Lambert
Strether as a character is not so much what he decides in a given
instance as what he can bring to any and all given instances. He is
an imaginative person in the pragmatistic way, and, therefore,
of all James's characters most closely approximates the pragmatist as such. It is the clearest instance in James of protagonist and
author sharing the pragmatistic mentality. Their minds are both
the unstiffening ones.

Conclusion—"Neither Out Far Nor In Deep"

And greatly unstiffening, too, are James's final remarks to
Henry Adams, by which he brings his letter to an end: "But you
perform them [reactions] still yourself—and I don't know what
keeps me from calling your letter a charming one! There we are,
and it's a blessing that you understand—I admit indeed alone—
your all-faithful [signed] Henry James."

What, in fact, is it that does *not* prevent James from calling
Adams's letter a charming one? Adams's own "reactions" do not
prevent it: that is to say, his own performances of consciousness. James has accomplished it once again: he has so thoroughly
unstiffened the terms of the context that he has made Adams's
performances in exploring the past now totally conjoined with

his present reaction against James in exploring the past! James has just handed over to his friend a pluralistic world.

And how is it a "blessing" that Adams will understand his all-faithful James? He will understand, James is saying, because the issue was for him enough of what William would call a "live option" to result in his reacting. Which is only to say that Adams, too, is still performing; it is still for him an act of life.

And what is the upshot with respect to the past as such? If, as William tells it, each tiny single ideal realized can be seen to be a moment in the world's salvation, can we not also say that each realization of the past by Adams and by James together constitutes another moment of the past? This can be a very creative way of thinking, and is clearly the presupposition that governs the novelist's autobiographical volumes, his "sense of the past."

But probably the most Jamesian of all of this is not even that he considers Adams's letter charming, but his expression that *he does not know what keeps him from* doing so. For something does, in a sense, prevent it: the possible other case that what Adams implies may in the end be one hundred percent right. One cannot separate pragmatism's hope, or its good humor, from its lack of certitude.

In attempting to convey the special mentality of James's expression to Adams, it will be best now to step away from him altogether and bring this long discussion of the "Jourdain" relationship to its end with another piece which might well be appropriated for this context—Robert Frost's poem "Neither Out Far Nor In Deep."

> The people along the sand
> All turn and look one way.
> They turn their back on the land.
> They look at the sea all day.
>
> As long as it takes to pass
> A ship keeps raising its hull;
> The wetter ground like glass
> Reflects a standing gull.
>
> The land may vary more;
> But wherever the truth may be—

> The water comes ashore,
> And the people look at the sea.
>
> They cannot look out far.
> They cannot look in deep.
> But when was that ever a bar
> To any watch they keep?[28]

We are of course involved in this lovely poem with the familiar, the everyday, the typical. The "people along the sand" are caught up by Frost in a practice we all recognize and have probably participated in. But if his typical world represents initially a "one way" look, we can observe it proceeding to mean the unfixing and unstiffening of any single point of view: our familiar world becomes such that all perception is limited perception, all knowledge partial knowledge, and that is precisely what is interesting and worthwhile. Hence there is no fixed world "behind" the familiar scene Frost depicts. It is a world of process: there is no saying "how long" it takes for the ship to pass, or where it came from, or where it is going—it *is* what it *does*, which is its proceeding, the "raising" of its hull; the same is true of the "gull"; it stands, to be sure, but it stands in reflection from the "wetter ground"—which is itself in constant change with the tide.

What, then, of a perspective which is wider than the "one way" look of the people? Surely their limitation will serve to point up a more comprehensive understanding of reality which the poet will then share with us. But Frost says instead that the land "may" vary more, and that truth is quite literally a "wherever" truth. And for that very reason, we arrive at the end of the poet's third stanza not to the "pronouncement" we might expect, but to a kind of anti-pronouncement. For he repeats the donnée:

> But wherever the truth may be—
> The water comes ashore
> And the people look at the sea.

Now we have been on much this same circular path in these pages, in connection with Henry James. One keeps coming back to where one was before, except that the "back" appears somehow to mean more than it did before. That, too, is William's "steering-function" of ideas, his notion of re-direction, his "same return[ing] not, save to bring the different." It is to be back once more, let us say, at the number twenty-seven, as the product of three and nine, having been there before as one hundred minus seventy-three. But if we would think radically empirically, let us then say that twenty-seven is but a point on the vector of our continuously felt life as we proceed to conceive of it. This last dimension is what Henry's later manner has preeminently, but Frost too has something of it: for now that "one way" look of the opening lines of his poem has by the end of stanza three become linked with the unending process of the water coming ashore. A "look" has therefore become look*ing*.

Yet again, the final stanza begins as though surely we *are* to get our pronouncement after all; to get, that is, the promise that the merely empirical realm of human experience will be subsumed by the poet into some higher understanding:

> They cannot look out far.
> They cannot look in deep.

But this suggestion of our consulting, so to speak, the profounder climes of insight and knowledge is then beautifully "redirected" back into the donnée again by a positive assertion as if rebuking the mentality of these two lines above, while at the same time confronting the issue which they raise:

> But when was that ever a bar
> To any watch they keep?

There are, indeed, many ways to be profound, and this is the pragmatistic way—by accepting the limited, the intellectually "local," and then persisting in finding one's meaning and one's truth in the dead center of that "lesser." Frost has brought us right "back" to where we began, the fact that they *do watch.* This is what William means by pragmatism's "friendly" conclusions: it is to find one's meaning and one's values in the consequences or "practices" of the matter in question. Frost has addressed the philosophical implications of the "one way" look by proceeding to bring out *its* meaning, not by making it a set of particulars for a higher transcendent meaning. "Any watch," he says, and, with his pluralistic sense in this poem, at least, that is just what he means. But also—what is so characteristic of the pragmatic mind—the conclusion is somehow the question of the matter, not the answer to it: "Dupery for dupery, what proof is there that dupery through hope is so much worse than dupery through fear"?[29]

William's pragmatistic thought is its tentativeness, is its apparency, is its question of the matter; as long as there is a possible other case, there is just that much reason to hope, and just that much to work with.

. . . and I don't know what keeps me from calling your letter a charming one!

> But when was that ever a bar
> To any watch they keep?

Part Three

Pragmatistic Thought

and the Art of Fiction

Ambulation into Polarity

VI. Psychology –
The Real and the Ethical
"*The Real Thing*" *and* The Spoils of Poynton

Prologue: Why Polarity?

With the exception of some relatively brief remarks in my first
chapter, pertaining to Henry James's ultimate ties with the assumptions of artistic creation voiced by the aesthetic tradition of
Coleridge, I have been endeavoring to present .the novelist's
most singular relationship with the pragmatistic thought expounded by his philosopher-brother. The last four chapters
have, I can only hope, brought to light rather fully the texture
and implications of the "Jourdain" relationship. At the very
least, I trust that these chapters have clarified what it was Henry
himself had in mind by his repeated claims of identity; and if I
can hope from the reader a little more than "the very least"—that
the novelist grasped William's thought most perceptively and
legitimately, grasped it indeed in just those ways that it deserves
and is perhaps only intermittently grasped: by Dewey and
Whitehead, say, on the philosophical side, and by Frost, Stevens, and Robinson on the poetic side.

It may or may not have also begun to surface, however,
that if William's thought does answer to just those qualities we
call "Jamesian" in his brother's work, there is at least one distinguishing facet that remains—or at least insinuates itself—
when we step back and think of their respective work. Henry,
we know, was a creative artist; and yet, William's own thought,
as we have seen, is itself most creative, dramatic, and even proto-
fictive, like his view of truth—"an event, a process." Nor does
the distinguishing facet lie where we might first imagine, in the

novelist's social world of manners and "super-subtle fry," because William's thought, as we have also seen, is precisely what legitimizes the world of Henry's "nuances" no less than his psychological orientation. To say that Henry's fictional arena, that of the novel of manners, is where he really parts company with William's thought, begs the question almost with a vengeance— or so it seems to me. It is something like saying that Coleridge's ancient mariner "differs" from the distinct view of the supernatural which justifies his spiritual voyaging, or that Keats's distinct choice of an autumn landscape "differs" from his grasp of "negative capability," which justifies his poetic treatment of that landscape.

The distinguishing facet between William and Henry actually comes into its own when we turn our attention back to the "Jourdain" relationship itself. William's pragmatistic thought has as the root and condition of its viewpoint the assumption that reality is both circular in mode and totally open-ended in its farthest projections. Not altogether unlike my own appropriation and use of the 1914 letter to Henry Adams in the last two chapters, William's thought, affirming an ambulatory reality of next-to-next, always "in the making," conceives what we call beginnings and ends as constructs and impositions: when viewed against the larger given world of "pure experience" and indeterminable flux, they assume an artificial and arbitrary status. Henry's own open-ended quality in his late work, both his in-process beginnings and distinctively open-ended "endings," arise naturally from and bespeak this "Jourdain" relationship. We see it again in his instinctive conception of his work as round or circular, by which I do not mean simply his titular image, say, of turning a screw, but his remark that *The Ambassadors* was the best "all round" of his productions. If we imagine that this is just a colloquialism, his pointing to its "superior roundness" when designating *The Portrait of a Lady* his second best should dispel our doubts.[1] William's theory of "transitional" ideas, their "re-directing" and "steering" function, is what parallels this general sense of "roundness," as it also names Henry's method.

The distinguishing facet between the two lies in the condition of Henry's best work as somehow genuinely and *positively* unified in a way that, as I read him at least, William's thought does not quite account for. In his best work Henry's beginnings and ends make a whole, a "seminal identity," which William's pluralism cannot adequately explain. As a devoted pluralist William necessarily "slighted" the unifying principle. Not that he denied one, or did not have one to espouse: for he insisted that unity occurred in experience itself—conjoined, concatenated, confluent. He did not, however, choose to explore the actual working relationship, the activity itself, of this unifying process. And why should he have? His task was, after all, to celebrate particularity, individual differences, and to teach us not to go immediately to some transcendent principle (like the prevailing German School with its Absolute) to solve the age-old problem at the expense of the living particular nuances of things. Let me say that even here Henry would have affirmed immediately William's own view of unity—he literally did, in fact, when he declared that *The Portrait of a Lady* "has that unity—it groups together."[2] Nothing could be more congruous with William's pluralistic unity of "relatedness." That too is the "Jourdain" relationship.

Thus, I am not even contending that this distinguishing facet—as I keep calling it—is something the novelist himself would have been particularly conscious of. All I am really saying is that the "grouping together" he refers to in *Portrait* achieves a very positive dimension that we in literary studies would instinctively recognize as "structural," "organic," or "selective." One could even say—and should, I think, where Henry's art is concerned—that the whole issue amounts to our walking up to and "peering inside" William's unifying network of connectedness and concatenation. What we would see in there, at least in relation to Henry's work, is the unifying relationship referred to in my opening chapter: we would see polarity, the interpenetration (not the juxtaposition) of opposites. But, as I also said at the beginning of this book, polarity *as such* does not make the novelist "Jamesian." The "Jourdain" relationship is what does that. Polarity is what he shares with other great creative artists. To put it another way, it is of greater interest that James thoroughly empiricized his creative imagination (which is what polarity is) than that he had it. It got expressed *as* the deeper psychology (which is why we have to "peer inside" William's unity of confluence and connectedness to see it). That is why I suggested, also in my opening chapter, that William's pragmatistic thought is, in effect, Henry's Coleridgean "fancy."

Ambulation diversifies, polarity unifies. Ambulation's great insight is that you ought not distinguish where you cannot divide, for fear of not doing justice to the actual "each" of next-to-next. Polarity's great insight is that you sometimes must distinguish where you cannot divide, for fear of never grasping the unifying principle. If we look at Henry James apart from the "Jourdain" relationship, we are liable not to address just those qualities that distinguish his idiom from Melville, Thoreau, or Twain; or even what relates that idiom to Hawthorne, Frost, or Robinson—much less to William's thought itself, and why he espoused it. If we look at him apart from polarity, we are liable not to address the fact, which we instinctively recognize as literary critics, that William's everyday human consciousness, no matter how creative, does not unify in positive fashion the blocks or segments taken from "pure experience" in quite the way Henry's fiction does. If I appear to belabor this issue, it is because the matter is of considerable importance. It is by now comparatively easy to discuss James's art of fiction apart from the "Jourdain" relationship, primarily because there is already such a fine articulate scholarship of Jacobite and even anti-Jacobite criticism to work with. It is far more difficult to address and elaborate the "Jourdain" relationship, because that amounts to penetrating and catching hold of James's own "way of thinking." But it is especially difficult to then *reattach* in a positive way the "Jourdain" relationship back to the fundamental aesthetic assumptions presupposed by the critical academy. For it amounts really to reattaching the "fancy" back to the "imagination," which shows itself through the fancy to begin with. For that reason most of us, I dare say, would prefer to point out, via Coleridge, how the "two" faculties differ, not how they positively relate. If we recall once again René Wellek's conclusion, that "James alone in his time and place in the English-speaking world holds fast to the insights of organistic aesthetics and thus constitutes a bridge from the early nineteenth century to modern criticism,"[3] we could say that the novelist's "Jourdain" relationship is the bridge *itself*, whereas polarity is the same bridge viewed as the "unity" of the two shores. And recall that William's whole point about ambulation, his "bridge of intermediaries," was that the walk across the bridge was real territory, and that we ought not to pretend the bridge was "not there" once we made it across and thought to ourselves: how nicely the two shores are "put together."

"Ambulation into polarity" is therefore my title for this final section of three chapters, in order that I may continue the focus of this study on the "Jourdain" relationship itself, while simultaneously allowing that unifying principle of polarity within Henry's fiction a little greater visibility than before. Polarity, it might be said, is what permits even a study of the "Jourdain" relationship to come to an end, so that a Henry James novel is not made to "yield itself" indeterminately (and interminably) like a letter to Henry Adams![4] All we need to do to really understand this general point is to recollect William's, "the same returns not, save to bring the different," or else his contention, while arguing for ambulatory relations, that his adversaries indulge in "hocus-pocus" to relate their "end-terms." In both cases we have reached the threshold of where, in Henry, polarity occurs. How *is* "the same" at once "the different"? How *do* we relate the "end-terms," except through polarity? Henry's fiction, like William's thought, insists on relating the same and the different in felt experience itself, and that is what is "Jamesian" about the novelist. But Henry's very capacity to achieve that same-different relationship, so that the dramatic issues exist simultaneously at each other's expense and for each other's sake, is the facet which distinguishes him from William. It is his third dimension, so to speak, occurring within William's own "felt" conjunction and concatenation of experience.

I should also mention that the following division of chapter headings into "pyschology," "pragmatism," and "radical empiricism" are not meant to imply that these three facets of William's thought are totally or even importantly separable. They point to emphases rather than divisions proper, and may perhaps be likened to "fields" in William's own view of consciousness. The analogue in Henry's fiction might be that of "manner," as in early, middle, and late: it is always impossible to say just exactly where one stops and the next starts, just as it is also clear that they do exist and refer to genuinely distinct "phases," or again "fields." This same analogy does not mean to suggest either that my following discussions are to be drawn from all three of the novelist's periods; as I have repeatedly indicated, the "Jourdain" relationship is realized primarily in the later James, which is also in part, I suspect, why the late James was able to perceive it. My reference just now to his three "manners" is therefore merely by analogy with my own chapter divisions—though I do wish to indicate that within Henry's later period there is at least one rather significant progression in his work after *The Ambassadors* which corresponds to William's own progression from his pragmatism and pluralism proper to his final and most far-reaching suggestions embedded in his doctrine of radical empiricism. In that sense, at least, I suppose one can think of these three divisions as "ascending" pragmatistic thought. But the more important point about such phases—and what distinguishes it from my previous remarks in this prologue—is that they do relate "confluently" only, and have nothing whatsoever to do with polarity.

"The Real Thing"

In a fairly recent essay on Henry James's much admired tale, "The Real Thing" (1892), David Toor challenges its traditional reading by reexamining the story "in terms of one of James's favorite devices, the unreliable narrator." Recalling the novelist's demands for "attentive" readers, and citing the painter-narrator's hint that he wished to be "a great painter of portraits," Toor argues that this same narrator is inadequate to his ambition and remains little more than "a hack," continually pronouncing Major and Mrs. Monarch "impossible" and ultimately blaming them, all too conveniently, for the "permanent harm" attributed to his work at the end. We thus discover in a tale that may have seemed ironic enough by virtue of an actual, even "model," lady and gentleman being pathetically unsuitable models for the imaginative rendering of ladies and gentlemen (while two lower class models are "natural" at it), that there is "deeper irony" still to James's piece—the narrator's incapacity as an artist in the first place, and even his destructive need to bring the Monarchs "down a few pegs," reduce them to menials, to find, in short, a scapegoat (since *he* is not "the real thing") for his limitations.[5]

Toor's reading points to a familiar pattern in the criticism of Henry James: the reverse reading, the "turn of the screw" on previous commentary, the opposite insight awaiting the "attentive" reader. It was Wayne C. Booth who in *The Rhetoric of*

Fiction christened James's practice "the unreliable narrator," but in doing so he was naming a critical perspective already current in James criticism. For Booth, "genuinely" unreliable narrators in James, if clearly and consistently presented as such, were quite acceptable to his rhetorical approach. On the other hand, James's penchant for something more like unreliable narration, in which *fundamentally* opposing readings can be entertained and appear to hold up under analysis, was not acceptable. Booth maintained that too many occurrences of the second in James had resulted in deleterious effects upon modern fiction and the critical academy: scholars trained and "attentive" to a post-Jamesian gestalt of "aesthetic distance" could no longer, as he put it, "accept a straight and simple statement when we read one."[6]

It may appear that I intend to dismiss David Toor's interpretation of "The Real Thing" and perhaps reaffirm something like Boothian common sense. But this is not the case. In many respects I am as sympathetic to the way he wants to read the tale as I am to the conventional reading found, say, in Matthiessen and Murdock, or in Harold McCarthy.[7] I would argue, however, that Toor's justification for that reading, James's "favorite device, the unreliable narrator," is not at one with the spirit of Booth in *The Rhetoric of Fiction*—surely the source for his parallel remarks about James's story "The Liar."[8]

Were we to put aside momentarily Toor's contention and think instead along more traditional lines, "The Real Thing" interests us primarily for its parallels with "The Art of Fiction." The story is usually seen as a kind of companion piece to the famous literary essay, in which James had affirmed the strongest of ties between the art of fiction and the art of painting: "the analogy," he writes there, "between the art of the painter and the art of the novelist is, so far as I am able to see, complete. Their inspiration is the same, their process . . . is the same, their success is the same. They may learn from each other, they may explain and sustain each other. Their cause is the same, and the honor of one is the honor of another."[9]

Apart from such ties with "The Art of Fiction," however, "The Real Thing" stands on its own and impresses its readers as "a little gem of bright, quick, vivid form"—to quote James's hopes for it in his *Notebooks*. "Little" is in fact his insistent recurring word in these notebook deliberations, because he is worried again and again by the need to "fix" the subject—"if I could only achieve this more as a habit!" The same need demands that he "keep down the lateral development."[10] These worrisome tendencies he acknowledges to himself are the very ones we shall find to be as basic to his art as is his successful ability in the finished tale itself to harness and achieve control over them.

Such modest aims perhaps suggest how unlikely "The Real Thing" at first appears to embody William James's (or anyone's) philosophy. Such unlikelihood expands the more factors we consider. There are no Americans in the story, no "international theme," no occasion for James's portrayal of the New England consciousness. Furthermore, the story belongs to that cluster of tales about art, a satellite group which may be said to isolate the aesthetic concerns we otherwise find merging with larger ethical and social explorations in the novels, or in tales like "The Pupil," "The Birthplace," or *The Aspern Papers*. In short, "The Real Thing," while it remains a fine piece from the late-middle period, and while it has a particular interest for us with "The Art of Fiction," and while it need not be antagonistic to William's thought, may strike us at first as simply indifferent to the issue. And yet, this very unlikelihood can perhaps address the "Jourdain" relationship as well as a work with more obviously potential ties, like *The Ambassadors*. For the relationship always involves, as we have seen repeatedly, James's own mentality, his way of apprehending and responding to *any* issue he engages creatively.

Of the "germ" itself (an incident related to him by George du Maurier), James says he was struck immediately with "the pathos, the oddity and typicalness of the situation." This reminds us that for James realism in fiction (growing in turn from his own sense of the real) relies as much on oddity (the unlikely) and pathos (sympathetic engagement) as on typicalness. This is so true of his work and so fundamental to his mind that in "The Real Thing" it shows up strongest in just those areas the notebook conception does not promise. Thus, he tells us he intends that the Monarchs "only *show* themselves, clumsily, for the fine, clean, well-groomed animals they [are]," by "just simply *being*"[11]—and assuredly he is most successful at this in the tale. And yet, how is it that by the end of the story these "well-groomed animals" have accrued such interest and humanity?

How is it that, especially when we watch Mrs. Monarch walk to Miss Churm and adjust her hair, we are moved and sense this to be perhaps the most satisfying touch in the tale?

There is no question of James's *initial* intent in the *Notebooks*. He wishes a crisp and Maupassant-like "juxtapos[ing]" of the "blank" Monarchs with the "pictorial sense" of the lower class models, and the bafflement of each at the others' claims.[12] And, again, no reader of the story can seriously question James's success at rendering this juxtaposition. Yet there is David Toor's reading of the destructive and unreliable narrator. And even without his argument, we can find now a tendency to put the primary emphasis on the narrator's plight, which James only hints at in the *Notebooks*. Thus, Virgil Scott argues that the story "is concerned essentially with the artistic conscience in conflict with the social conscience." According to this reading the narrator is forced to reject the Monarchs in order to preserve his artistic integrity, though he puts it off out of a sense of humanity, and ultimately suffers "permanent harm" at the end. But Scott concludes that "there may be some compensation . . . ; he may no longer be an artist, but he has become a human being."[13]

What such readings coupled with James's own acknowledged "habits" tell us is that he was never the best person for keeping his ideas "fixed." The evolution from notebook to tale in "The Real Thing" is similar to other such cases in his work, a number of which were cited by Booth in *The Rhetoric of Fiction*.[14] But whereas Booth's point was that they bespoke an ultimate deficiency in James's rhetoric, mine is that they can help us to grasp the "Jourdain" relationship. When James becomes "engaged" with his subject, the subject itself begins to "unstiffen," as alternative possibilities begin to show themselves. The only problem with such unstiffening in James, however, is that it does not always result in "cordial" readings by his critics. Booth aside, many Jamesians do not find the Master deficient, but they often find one another deficient in getting the "real" point or the "real" irony. Jamesians—to other Jamesians—are too often said to be "taken in." It is difficult for me to believe that the "Art of Fiction" parallel is misguided, or that Toor's insight is not "there," or that Virgil Scott is totally "wrong." The question is, how do we put them *all* together and make them positively cordial?

We can begin with the traditional reading and perspective. The Monarchs are the real thing—a real lady and gentleman—yet because they are so complete, finished, "always the same thing" (unlike William's reality, "in the making"), they stint the artist's imaginative faculty. This is what links the story with "The Art of Fiction," and not only via James's remarks there about the kindred arts, already quoted. The link is even stronger with James's central point that "the illusion" or "direct impression" of life, as he thinks of fiction, must always allow for the artist's own transforming process, activated by and acting upon the object from life which is its "donnée" or "germ." For example, when confronted with the axiom that the artist should write from his own experience, James accepts this dictum gladly and then proceeds to amplify it in a most unlikely way:

. . . the faculty which when you give it an inch takes an ell, . . . [t]he power to guess the unseen from the seen, to trace the implication of things, to judge the whole piece by the pattern, the condition of feeling life in general so completely that you are well on your way to knowing any particular corner of it—this cluster of gifts may almost be said to constitute experience. . . . If experience consists of impressions, it may be said that impressions *are* experience, just as (have we not seen it?) they are the very air we breathe.[15]

We saw earlier the astonishing parallel of these remarks (especially the entire passage they belong to) with William's view of experience and human consciousness. But it is also a passage intimately related to the theme of "The Real Thing." Yet what is perhaps most interesting is its unlikely amplification of the axiom that generated it—that one should write from experience. Notice that such unlikeliness is inseparable, however, from its dramatically illustrating what is being said: *he* is proceeding to transform the axiom, to make an "ell" out of *its* "inch," to use it as a germ. Let us see if there is not the selfsame process at work in "The Real Thing," both in connection with its germ and even in its connection with "The Art of Fiction"!

Since William has defined "the real" as "[a]nything . . . of which we find ourselves obliged to take account,"[16] we are obliged to take account of the fact that the Monarchs just will not "do" as models, despite the narrator's repeated attempts with them, a judgment shared by his friend Hawley, the publishing house for the "deluxe edition," and even some other unnamed painters. And the reason they will not do is given explicitly in passages like these: " 'Now the drawings you make from *us*, they look exactly like us,' [Mrs. Monarch] reminded me, smiling in triumph; and I recognised that this was indeed just their defect."[17] Or this one: "She was always a lady certainly, and into the bargain was always the same lady. She was the real thing, but always the same thing. . . . I found myself trying to invent types that approached her own, instead of making her own transform itself—in the clever way that was not impossible for instance to poor Miss Churm" [326-27].

Miss Churm (as the *Notebooks* promised) is just the opposite. Her name sounds of course like "germ," and indeed that association is in keeping with her mysterious gift: "After I had drawn Mrs. Monarch a dozen times I felt surer even than before that the value of such a model as Miss Churm resided precisely in the fact that she had no positive stamp. . . . Her usual appearance was like a curtain which she could draw up at request for a capital performance. This performance was simply suggestive; but it was a word to the wise—it was vivid and pretty" [327-28].

These passages point up the juxtaposition James sought in the *Notebooks*; and if we are to keep a William Jamesian spirit in approaching the story, that juxtaposition must really "count," for it is present in the tale. At the same time, if we are to be cordial to alternatives and unstiffen our understanding of his theme, we can be guided by William's other formulation about the novelty of reality: "the same returns not, save to bring the different."[18]

In this spirit we can observe a number of things about James's fine tale, not the least of which is that while the Monarchs will never do as models, what is conspicuous about the tale is how well they do—for James; or, if we prefer, how well James does with them. Neither Miss Churm nor Oronte is as living and rendered, nor as "germinated." Indeed that crisp juxtaposition of the *Notebooks* may be said to occur "only" thematically, for the equivalent proportions are not present in the ongoing reading experience, which favors the Monarchs. We may hold, of course, that James's demands at rendering his "little idea" became such that he had to do more with them. The narrator is a professional with a "ruling passion" against "the amateur," and the Monarchs are amateurs. But since James is no amateur, he could not do justice to his "little idea" without getting across their amateurishness, and to do that well meant they would eventually have to dominate a story the main point of which is that they lack interest.

But suppose we were to take William's proposition about the "transitional" function of ideas and apply it here; that is, take our own recognized "theme" and "re-direct" it back into the fluid reading experience. If we do that we will find, I believe, Henry's "possible other case." Even a William Jamesian reading needs a germ, however, and we have one at the beginning when the artist informs us of his situation. He says that his friend Claude Rivet must have told his two visitors, "how I worked in black-and-white, for magazines, for storybooks, for sketches of contemporary life, and consequently had copious employment for models" [309-10]. But he immediately disclaims this as his ultimate goal: "These things were true," he says, "but it was not less true—I may confess it now; whether because the aspiration was to lead to everything or to nothing I leave the reader to guess —that I couldn't get the honours, to say nothing of the emoluments, of a great painter of portraits out of my head. My 'illustrations' were my pot-boilers; I looked to a different branch of art—far and away the most interesting it had always seemed to me—to perpetuate my fame" [310].

We are surely "obliged to take account" of this aspiration for portraiture, especially since it is the only time we are to be addressed as readers. But this need not "fix" us into "unreliability," but rather open up the tale's resonating plurality from its opening language: "When the porter's wife . . . announced 'A gentleman and a lady, sir,' I had, as I often had in those days— the wish being father to the thought—an immediate vision of sitters. Sitters my visitors in this case proved to be; but not in the sense I should have preferred. There was nothing at first however to indicate that they mightn't have come for a portrait" [307]. The Monarchs, that is, have indeed come for a portrait, for that is what the narrator—the wish being father to the thought—immediately begins to present to us. His "vision" has already particularized them during the comic interchange when he and they speak at cross purposes—they for employment fee, he for portrait fee—so that when he does finally realize they wish to model for his sketches, he comments: "I was disappointed;

for in the pictorial sense I had immediately *seen* them. I had seized their type—I had already settled what I would do with it. Something that wouldn't absolutely have pleased them, I afterwards reflected" [310].

I think we must agree that someone makes good on this claim, or else we are not speaking of "The Real Thing." But he means, of course, painting them "within" the story, whereas I mean perhaps the story itself as a product of James's narrative consciousness. An important distinction, to be sure; but also one which relies on our remembering the difference between James's art of fiction and the plastic art the story treats—the very thing we usually want to bring together in this tale! At all events his statement does, clearly, reveal the narrator's aspiration for portraiture. The "pictorial sense," he speaks of is even James's very own phrase in the *Notebooks* for what the professional models will have and the Monarchs will lack!

What I am obviously suggesting is that James's story is cordial to such alternatives and plurality of meaning through a "conjunctive" relationship between them (in turn grounded within, I believe, on the principle of polarity). Thus we can now actually watch our narrator give us a living illustration of that same faculty from "The Art of Fiction"—of getting an "ell" from an "inch," of guessing "the unseen from the seen"—when he thinks about the past history of the Monarchs:

It was odd how quickly I was sure of everything that concerned them. . . . Their good looks had been their capital, and they had good-humouredly made the most of the career that this resource marked out for them. . . . I could *see* the sunny drawing-rooms, sprinkled with periodicals she didn't read, in which Mrs. Monarch had continuously sat; I could *see* the wet shrubberies in which she had walked. . . . I could *see* the rich covers the Major had helped to shoot and the wonderful garments in which, late at night, he repaired to the smoking-room to talk about them. I could *imagine* their leggings and water-proofs, their knowing tweeds and rugs . . . and I could *evoke* the exact appearance of their servants and the compact variety of their luggage on the platforms of country stations [316, my emphasis].

This can hardly be said to result from the Monarchs' lack of plasticity, their inability to activate the imagination. Of course it may be argued that this picture looks more like a Du Maurier illustration than a Rembrandt portrait. But what of this:

They gave small tips, but they were liked; they didn't do anything themselves, but they were welcome. They looked so well everywhere; they gratified the general relish for stature, complexion and "form." They knew it without fatuity or vulgarity, and they respected them-selves in consequence. They weren't superficial; they were thorough and kept themselves up—it had been their line. . . . I could feel how even in a dull house they could have been counted on for the joy of life. . . . Their friends could like them, I made out, without liking to sup-port them" [316-17].

These "impressions constituting experience" are all quite re-liable. The distortion is never in the narrator's vision of the Monarchs as such. It lies in his persistent refusal to see that their very inappropriateness for his illustrations is at once bound up with his own aspirations for portraiture, character, individual-ity. The terms of the one are the terms of the other: that is, James *con*joins the issue on the identical terms by which they are *dis*-joined by his narrator (polarity). The artist thinks, for example, that the couple have missed their vocation in advertising, for he can imagine " 'We always use it' pinned on their bosoms with the greatest effect" [313]. But he divines that the reason they have come to him instead of to an advertising agency is that "the re-production of the face would betray them" [317] to friends—an insight which can only come from his response to them as indi-viduals, as human beings, and as subjects for his creative impulse for portraiture. On their side, the Monarchs, who know nothing of art, assume that, since they have "been photographed—*im-mensely*" [314] in society, they will naturally be ideal models. This is, of course, no more viable than, say, the Major's proud announcement that his wife was once known as "the Beautiful Statue" [314]. But how anemic for us to say that what all this comes to is James's parable of the difference between art and photography, or, conversely, that our narrator is unreliable. What is "Jamesian" about such interchanges is that the Mon-archs' poor misguided view of their qualifications based on pho-tography is precisely what is rendering them individuals, the most unlikely thing for them to be. As for the remark *about* the "Beautiful Statue"—it is at the heart of what simply will not allow them to remain statues, not for the painter, not for us; they are "unstiffening" as they speak.

And so it happens that all the narrator's attempts to use

them for his edition are failures, while at the same time his relationship with them, the cognate of his impulse for portraiture, grows complicated. His drawings of Mrs. Monarch "always came out, in my pictures, too tall—landing me in the dilemma of having represented a fascinating woman as seven feet high, which (out of respect perhaps to my own very much scantier inches) was far from my idea of such a personage" [327]. He is projecting into her picture his own loftier aspirations. His "very much scantier inches"?—possibly a permanent limitation of his ability; but, just as possibly, an expression of his limited awareness at the time of what was going on within himself. In either case, whenever our narrator utters one of those "thematic" statements about art, the very application (i.e., "re-direction," "practical consequence") of that statement back into the ongoing context is James's "possible other case." Another such case occurs with his oversized drawings of the Major: "nothing I could do would keep *him* down, so that he became useful only for the representation of brawny giants" [327]. This complaint gives rise in turn to the following "apologia."

I adored variety and range, I cherished human accidents, the illustrative note; I wanted to characterise closely, and the thing in the world I most hated was the danger of being ridden by a type. I had quarrelled with some of my friends about it; I had parted company with them for maintaining that one *had* to be, and that if the type was beautiful—witness Raphael and Leonardo—the servitude was only a gain. I was neither Leonardo nor Raphael—I might only be a presumptuous young modern searcher; but I held that everything was to be sacrificed sooner than character. When they claimed that the obsessional form could easily *be* character I retorted, perhaps superficially, "Whose?" It couldn't be everybody's—it might end in being nobody's [327].

Like the great majority of ideological passages in James's mature work, the value here is not to provide us a thematic "touchstone" to get above the context, but to enrich the context and make plural James's meaning meaning*fully*. It functions, in short, to amplify the concrete fluid experience, psychological and dramatic, which come to the same thing in James. Thus, our narrator here upholds against his friends the priority of character over type; yet it is clear that he cannot get away from the Monarchs' character ("do what I would with it my drawing looked like a photograph or a copy of a photograph" [326]). He simply cannot help engaging the Major in his individuality and particularity; the distortion in the drawings reflects the human relationship; that relationship in turn the narrator's compelling need for portraiture; even the quarrel itself with his friends and his insistence to them that all is to be sacrificed before character, reflects the aspiration. He believes, of course, that he is ridden by a "type" when he draws them; indeed he is pyschologically "ridden" to individualize them, as he does naturally and genuinely when he projects their past history. It is rather the "friends," who cite Leonardo and Raphael, and claim "the obsessional form could easily *be* character"—it is these people who unwittingly speak to the narrator's situation with the Monarchs; in fact, he even spoke *their* doctrine to us earlier—"I had seized their type—I had already settled what I would do with it"— before, however, learning that the couple had not come to him for a portrait.

Of course, with so many "possible other cases" in the tale, we should remember that James did realize his crisp "juxtaposition" from the *Notebooks*. It is done beautifully in section 2, for example, when Miss Churm enters the studio while the narrator is still interviewing the couple. James counterpoints her facility ("she asked me what she was to get into this time") with their pathetic incapacity (" 'It's awfully hard—we've tried everything' "); her lower class station ("She couldn't spell and she loved beer") with their breeding and fastidiousness ("my visitors saw . . . that her umbrella was wet, and in their spotless perfection they visibly winced at it") [320-21]. A lovely "plain old" dramatic irony occurs when the Monarchs first begin to gain some confidence after seeing how obviously not the real thing is Miss Churm.

Yet even here, where James is closest to his *Notebooks*, he is still cordial to his alternative possibilities. When the Major hears that Miss Churm is to be that day a "Russian princess," he is startled and points to his wife as the real lady; whereupon she responds: " 'Oh I'm not a Russian princess,' Mrs. Monarch protested a little coldly. I could see she had known some and didn't like them. There at once was a complication of a kind I never had to fear with Miss Churm" [322]. The "complication" can be seen, I trust, as broader and multiple in its meaning, for just such remarks "unstiffen" her. It is one more instance in which type is *proceeding* to become character.

In the last analysis, then, "The Real Thing" is a story which refuses to "sacrifice character"—and not merely despite its recognized theme of plasticity, but because of it, in additive, unlikely respects. The Monarchs *become* increasingly the real thing in the tale, and for that reason more and more of a burden to the artist in his "crisis." "As I look back at this phase," he says, "they seem to me to have pervaded my life not a little. . . . and resembling the while a pair of patient courtiers in a royal antechamber" [339]. Indeed this is so. Jack Hawley, his friend, returns from abroad and pronounces categorically on the deterioration of our painter's work, calling the Monarchs a "ridiculous pair" [340]. Hawley "painted badly himself, but there was no one like him for putting his finger on the place" [336]. Hawley's criticism is well meant and quite legitimate as far as the illustrations themselves are concerned. But there is no reason to expect him to grasp the full "complication," unless of course he were a deep and perceptive man in James's sense, which he is not: "[Hawley] had been absent from England for a year; he had been somewhere—I don't remember where—to get a fresh eye. . . . He came back with a fresh eye. . . . He had done no work himself, he had only got the eye" [336-37].

Hawley's quality of mind is of a piece with this statement. He tells the narrator that the illustrations show "a screw loose somewhere" (which is not entirely wrong, but also not very penetrating—and based on the opposite reason for its really being "loose"), that his new models are "stupid" and should be shown the door. Hawley's "aesthetic" is also revealing: "There was a certain sort of thing you used to try for—and a very good thing it was. But this twaddle isn't *in* it" [339]. Once again James's verbal structures are at work in his operative irony: the "fresh eye" is anything but fresh, the "sort of thing you used to try for" the opposite of what the entire situation bespeaks, the painter's psychological trying-for-more. But Hawley's judgment is echoed now by the publishing house, which deems the "illustrations were not what had been looked for" [342]. Faced with the prospect of continuing a relationship which interferes with his assignment—i.e., what is "looked for"—and increasingly tense with the Monarchs, who interrupt his accelerated schedule with the regular models, the narrator finally blurts out: "Oh my dear Major—I can't be ruined for *you!*" [342].

This statement constitutes dramatically his repudiation of

the couple; but James, significantly, brings the tale to its final climax with an incident several days later, the effect of which is to round out the piece and leave us with not merely its theme of plasticity but also the full reading experience of it—which involves our seeing an opposing rationale added to the one which usually gives us that theme (conjunction through polarity). We may note, however, that the narrator's outburst is followed by his admission to us that it was a "horrid speech," but necessitated because the Major had not "read with me the moral of our fruitless collaboration, the lesson that in the deceptive atmosphere of art even the highest respectability may fail of being plastic" [343]. We have in this the most explicit statement of what most readers agree is the theme of the story. But I hope we have already seen how anemic is that "idea" when we treat it apart from its "life elsewhere," its "practical consequences" in the fluid experience of the story.

The ending of the tale in particular will make this clear. The Monarchs return three days after the "horrid speech," while the narrator is busy and finally making real progress at his assignment. It is a touching and beautifully rendered scene. The couple stands around awkwardly and silently while the work proceeds (everybody "fixed" and in place except them!), trying to discover some way to participate in the small community. Presently Mrs. Monarch asks to go over and adjust Miss Churm's hair, to dispose it better for the pose: "she was staring with a strange fixedness at Miss Churm, whose back was turned to her. 'Do you mind my just touching it?' she went on—a question which made me spring up for an instant as with the instinctive fear that she might do the young lady a harm. But she quieted me with a glance I shall never forget—I confess I should like to have been able to paint *that*" [344].

Indeed he would—as we have seen again and again. The Major's last act is equally touching, individual, and even heroic. " 'I say, can't I be useful *here*?' " he calls out, and begins cleaning the dishes. Our painter cannot continue, for his realization of what these actions bespeak—a realization that cannot be separated from his own projections into their past history—causes his drawing to be "blurred for a moment—the picture swam" [345]. Such eloquence is their character, the last step in their transformation from type to character, the final touch to their portrait: the illustration is thus most appropriately "blurred." The Major's final pathetic plea to the narrator—" 'I say, you know—just let *us* do for you, can't you?' "—begins to resonate like an emblematic utterance, although (like James's "symbols") it functions to reinforce the dramatic and psychological matrix, and means literally to allow them to be his servants. But he sends them away, reluctantly, and the story closes with his informing us that he "obtained the remaining books, but my friend Hawley repeats that Major and Mrs. Monarch did me a permanent harm, got me into false ways. If it be true I'm content to have paid the price—for the memory" [346].

James never tells us what the "permanent harm" or "false ways" consist of, but since our narrator calls it a "price" paid "for the memory"—a *dis*junctive line of thought—we can perhaps do worse than see it as simultaneously a *con*junctive affair for James. Thus, the "permanent harm" is itself equivalent to the memory, if by memory is meant the total experience of the painter's relationship with the Monarchs and its fundamental implication from the mind of Henry James: that there is always character and meaning to be found in even the most unlikely circumstances, individuality and depth in even what appears the quintessential case of surface. In short, it implies just about everything James stood for as a Realist. Such "memory" signifies that mode of apprehension which responds to all experience in its concrete particularity, its fluidity, its novelty—William's reality. We cannot know whether our narrator will actually become "a great painter of portraits." What is important is that his "memory" has provided us "The Real Thing," and if James means it also to suggest the narrator's imaginative and plastic faculty in "time present," then the aspiration may, perhaps has, come to pass—"I leave the reader to guess." But the point of this reading has been neither to take a fixed position on that question nor, more obviously, to merely legitimize "unreliability," nor to rest in the "conflict" of the artistic conscience versus the social conscience. Rather, the more central matter made present by Jamesian conjunction (and within it, polarity) is always the genuine possibility for a more valid art which itself expresses the humane sensibility—and that *is* what "The Art of Fiction" says. The Monarchs have provided the occasion, if not the impulse, for our narrator to develop this sensibility. Had James himself not had it, the tale would never have amplified from the neat juxtaposition of the *Notebooks*: like William's philosophical opponents he would have kept his idea "fixed," and he would not have been "M. Jourdain." Perhaps the entire matter can be summarized by our recalling again the narrator's "thematic" complaint about Mrs. Monarch: "Meanwhile I found myself trying to invent types that approached her own, instead of making her own transform itself." If at that time he had possessed the faculty of "making her own transform itself," the result would not have been an illustration but a living portrait which managed somehow to capture the history of its subjects, from the earlier days, to the first meeting with the narrator, to the abortive attempts at modeling, to the act of cleaning the slops. This is what James has done. Whether our narrator will do its equivalent in his later work is another matter, and another story—unless it is also this one.

The Spoils of Poynton

In turning from "The Real Thing" to *The Spoils of Poynton* (1897), we turn from a virtually flawless tale which can engender opposing interpretation to a novel whose problematic nature has elicited disagreement only less notable than that of *The Turn of the Screw*. Neither our alpha nor omega critical reader of "The Real Thing" would ever consider that James was there "uncertain of his intention." But these are R. P. Blackmur's words about *The Spoils of Poynton*,[19] and many readers would agree, I suspect, if only because it is clearly established that the novel marks an important transition in James's career: it is his attempt to salvage the debacle of the playwriting period by appropriating the scenic art into his longer fiction. According to Leon Edel the novel was literally "a turning point in the fiction of Henry James."[20]

At the same time, this book has been the recipient of at least one small tributary line of consistent argument, though it is well overshadowed by its general problems of interpretation. It has been regularly cited—if not really examined—as the demonstrable source for Henry's ethical repudiation of William's pragmatism. The repudiation lies, according to this argument, in the contrast between the moral sensibility of the heroine Fleda Vetch and that of Mrs. Gereth, the widow and mistress of Poynton Park, whose antique home and unsurpassing collection of art objects and furnishings are subject by English law to possession by her son Owen upon his marrying. Mrs. Gereth, the argument continues, is someone with whom we initially sympathize in her plight and (like Fleda herself) we admire for her aesthetic capacities embodied in Poynton, but who ultimately shows up morally as expedient, materialistic, utilitarian—"pragmatic"; Fleda, on the other hand, is ultimately shown to be the spokesman for Henry's own opposing ethic—absolute, idealistic, categorically imperative.[21] The repudiation of William's pragmatism as such is said to occur late in the story when the two ladies have their celebrated quarrel and each gives her respective view of life. When entertaining this argument, we must remember, obviously, that it rests in turn on an entirely sympathetic (or completely "reliable") reading of the heroine and "register," Fleda Vetch, and not on the possibility that she is a classic study in hysteria or neurotic behavior, tending toward that of the famous governess. That is what the larger critical argument centers on.

If my examination of William's thought in relation to Henry in this study has pointed to anything, it points to the fact that this last possibility, that Fleda is an unreliable neurotic, is too easy and inappropriate a line to take in responding to the ethical issue just mentioned. The governess, after all, is left at the end of the tale with her arms around a child she may have frightened to death, whereas Fleda's only tangible harm, assuming she is neurotic, is to herself in the form of renunciation of all her best chances—something endemic to Jamesian protagonists even when we do not think them neurotic. Besides, this is the same lady James was to praise as a "free spirit" and the embodiment of "appreciation" in his later "Preface" to the novel.[22] More to the point generally might be Henry's own unawareness that he "unconsciously anti-pragmatised," but even there we could perhaps say that he was several years away from knowing what he was to believe about William's thought. And meanwhile we do have William by 1897 becoming increasingly critical of Henry's later manner—except that he certainly failed to see any repudiation of his own ethic in *The Spoils of Poynton*, which is a piece he happened to single out for praise.[23]

The real issue, on William's side at least, is of course whether his thought really is mere expediency and materialism; and if I have not answered that already in these pages, I do not see how I possibly can. That he is a utilitarian is another matter, and one that perhaps can use some further amplification. The issue grows more engaging in its complexity when we turn back to Henry's side of it. For it is perfectly possible to assume, as Yvor Winters does, for example, that Fleda Vetch represents James's own "absolute" moral viewpoint,[24] while not necessarily having William's pragmatism in mind as the opposite and repudiated ethic of the novel. In my remaining remarks I should like to address this last point along with the question of a repudiation of pragmatism. If I seem therefore to slight some of the other thematic content—the novel's implicit Ruskin- or Arnold-like critique of Victorian society, for example—it is the result of this particular ethical focus.[25]

Mrs. Gereth, we must remember, is designated by James in his "Preface" as one of the "fools" or "figures" along with the more obvious cases of Mona and Mrs. Brigstock and Owen. They are all of them "fixed constituents," he says, and *on that basis* different from Fleda Vetch, the "free spirit."[26] It is most significant that James would proffer such a distinction—and most appropriate, given the "Jourdain" relationship. A "fixed constituent" means a character who cannot change, cannot grow, a static instead of a dynamic character, as we would say. But this very distinction is for James's art fundamentally grounded in turn on his engagement with reality in its flux and process. A "fixed constituency" can no more comprise James's sense of human freedom than it can his view of fictional rules, like those of Walter Besant; and it likewise cannot comprise William's view of reality or human choice, both of which must allow for the genuine "novelty" in human affairs and which thus disallows "moral holidays" implied by fixed systems, ethically as well as epistemologically. And so to call Mrs. Gereth a "fixed constituent" is practically to have prima-facie evidence that, whatever she represents, it is mostly unlikely to be William's thought.

In the story itself she is not motivated in her conduct or in her views just by her passion for the lovely objects themselves at Poynton: she is "fixed" by her all-consuming idea in respect to them and in connection with which she has spent most of her life in assembling and, like a monarch, surveying them. The objects are the particulars she finds meaning in, in the same sense that William's intellectualist opponents make particulars serve their notion of the real:

It was not the crude love of possession; it was the need to be faithful to a trust and loyal to an idea. The idea was surely noble; it was that of the beauty Mrs. Gereth had so patiently and consummately wrought. Pale but radiant, her back to the wall, she planted herself there as a heroine guarding a treasure. To give up the ship was to flinch from her duty; there was something in her eyes that declared she would die at her post. . . . Her fanaticism gave her a new distinction. . . . She trod the place like a reigning queen or a proud usurper; full as it was of splendid pieces it could show in these days no ornament so effective as its menaced mistress.[27]

These observations come to us via our "register" Fleda Vetch, and we may, of course, choose to distrust them. But there is certainly nothing in their import that is out of joint with the conduct and stance of Mrs. Gereth throughout the novel. Perhaps the more discriminating point is that Fleda here chooses a viewpoint and expression which also reveals her own idealism and absolutism. Then again, the passage as a product of James's narrative consciousness seems to participate in irony, even while presenting the sentiments which have caused Fleda to side initially with Mrs. Gereth in the dispute. Already, then, we find ourselves, in evaluating such passages, having to keep quite a number of matters distinguished: James's view of Mrs. Gereth, his attitude toward Fleda, the modifying context of this relatively early point in the story, and even his viewpoint on the issue of beauty. In order to clarify my own general position about so many intersecting matters, I am first going to engage in a "Jacobite" evaluation and reading of the passage above. I believe it would read something like this: James, as he so often does, is employing here a "double consciousness"; we are early in the story; Fleda has yet to discover that her fine moral sensitivity cannot be superseded even by her equally fine artistic one; nevertheless, James has managed here to convey masterfully not only the erroneous view which she holds, at this point, of Mrs. Gereth's position in the dispute, but also her own warmth and generosity: qualities which may take her for a while into a wrong turning, but will, in the long run, take her far beyond the merely "artistic" norm she imputes to Mrs. Gereth and on to the truly artistic one where, with her author, moral values and "patiently wrought beauty" are one; James accomplishes all this, and at the same time stands "behind" his heroine and, with comic discipline and rhetoric ("heroine guarding a treasure," "menaced mistress"), points delicately and satirically at the limitations of Mrs. Gereth, all of which is the more remarkable for his not detracting from Fleda's own superior qualities.

I cannot conceive of a Jamesian enthusiast disapproving of that reading, unless he happens to believe that Fleda Vetch is the Master's brilliant portrait of a neurotic and not his ethical spokesman. I myself do not disapprove of it—or I would not have made it as elaborate as I have. I subscribe to it almost, wholeheartedly, if perhaps a little less rhapsodically, one octave lower on the keyboard (as also, doubtless, my hypothetical enthusiast). Nevertheless, it is that octave lower which makes me ask: what does it mean to say that Fleda's view of Mrs. Gereth is at this point erroneous? Is she not rather perfectly correct about Mrs. Gereth, her error lying in her very accuracy rather than the expression of a temporary mistake "despite" her good parts? In other words, is the issue fundamentally a conjunctive or a disjunctive one? Her error resides in her accuracy at assuming, as she does here with Mrs. Gereth, that someone's behavior ("practice") can be justified primarily by recourse to a noble idea alone—even the idea of beauty. For as she becomes more and more involved in this dispute, and more and more "unfixed" in her own loyalties, she will discover that this present lovely idea itself has consequences which get her enmeshed with people and people's feelings, including her own. Then comes the difficult question of how one best "uses" all concerned. The attempt to *use* people well is not shoddy because it is utilitarian: it is in fact the heart of any ethical question, even though one sometimes hesitates before employing the word "use" in this way, so little currency does it seem to have now.

At the same time, Fleda's notion, insofar as it pertains to Mrs. Gereth, is quite correct. Mrs. Gereth has the classic intellectualist mentality: concepts for her are not things to come back into experience with; they stand stately and removed from "mere" occurrences and consequential process. Let us see:

The great wrong Owen had done her was not his "taking up" with Mona—that was disgusting, but it was a detail, an accidental form; it was his failure from the first to understand what it was to have a mother at all, to appreciate the beauty and the sanctity of the character. . . . One's mother, gracious goodness, if one were the kind of fine young man one ought to be, the only kind Mrs. Gereth cared for, was a subject for poetry, for idolatry [49].

This passage is not, like the previous one, complicated by the "registering" viewpoint of Fleda. It belongs entirely to Mrs. Gereth, even though not a direct quotation, and can remind us that James has as many "in-between" areas in his panoramic-scenic method as in his view of reality itself. In any case, this passage is supposed to represent William's thought? If it has to represent anything along these lines, I would rather call it a caricature of William's opposition. But of course it represents nothing along these lines, and is Henry's very solid characterization of Mrs. Gereth. It is just that, James's mind being what it is, such a flawed viewpoint probably will appear intellectualist in William's sense. Mrs. Gereth's captivation by an idea is correlative to her prescriptiveness and "infallibility." The absolutist, not especially bothered by particulars, is secure in his knowledge of what is central and what is peripheral. Thus Fleda to Mrs. Gereth: "'I gave [Owen] my opinion that you're very logical, very obstinate and very proud.'" And Mrs. Gereth replies: " 'Quite right, my dear: I'm a rank bigot—about that sort of thing!' Mrs. Gereth jerked her head at the contents of the house. 'I've never denied it. I'd kidnap—to save them, to convert them—the children of heretics. When I know I'm right I go to the stake. Oh he may burn me alive!' she cried with a happy face" [114].

We shall want to remember this extravagant remark about a possible "burning" and the context in which it is uttered, when we later come to address the novel's conclusion. Meanwhile we see once again the quality of Mrs. Gereth's presumption, which remains intact throughout the greater part of the novel. She is one of James's many Walter Besants, those who think a priori, who know in advance what is what, and are therefore not embued with the possible other case. Mrs. Gereth has presumed, practically from the start, that Fleda, unlike Mona Brigstock, would be just the person for Owen—i.e., just the sort of daughter-in-law who would continue to cherish and properly administer the lovely Poynton objects. And it is precisely because James's own mentality differs from hers that this presumption is quite accurate—Fleda really *is* just the person for Owen. She has fallen in love with him, and because she really does love him honorably, she therefore cannot *be* "just the person" for Owen in Mrs. Gereth's scheme. The same is true of the elder lady's presumption that Fleda, like herself, has the true artistic empathy for the spoils. Again, she could not be more wrong for being right. Fleda's difficulty here is that, not unlike the poor pragmatist, she cannot take any moral holidays: her empathy for the objects is "true," all right; so true that she is eventually compelled to respond to them *contextually*, in all their relations and ramifications ("consequences"), which is what gets her embroiled with them as the occasion for people's conduct. If I may be forgiven such a "utilitarian" perspective—it is exactly her having the artistic sensibility ascribed to her by Mrs. Gereth that impels her to deal with the spoils in terms of what they are "proceeding-to-do," how they are "known-as," and hence she cannot play the game according to Mrs. Gereth's prescribed injunctions. But Henry James *can*, because he knows artistically that the value of such injunctions, like those of Walter Besant, lies wholly in the meaning one attaches to them. That is the mentality of his operative irony because it is thoroughly conjunctive (and within, polar) in its dramatic manifestation.

In the blurb of the Penguin edition of this novel we find the following quite typical sort of comment and paraphrase: "[Fleda] is in love with Owen Gereth and genuinely appreciates the contents of Poynton for themselves. But she scrupulously stands aside when he gets engaged to the coarse and insensitive Mona. . . ."[28] The whole import of my previous remarks is that, except for the very beginning—and then again at the very end, as we shall presently see—Fleda cannot and does not appreciate the objects "for themselves"; her refusal to find inherent properties or essences in them throughout the conflict is only less than James's own throughout the entire novel from cover to cover. As for such expressions as "but she scrupulously stands aside"—we must try to remember that James's art is not primarily a "but" art; it is a "because" and a "for-that-very-reason" art. It is the art of—"the same returns not, save to bring the different."

Mrs. Gereth's many presumptions culminate in what is one of the more satisfying structural "re-directions" in James's fiction. Fleda, having confronted Owen's own eventual declaration of love and marriage proposal to her at her sister Maggie's house, has after considerable excruciation refused him unless the affianced Mona herself releases him from his pledge. She sends Owen back in the hope that he will be released, since Mona has become so adamant and furious over not getting the objects

(Mrs. Gereth having carted them off to the dower house at Ricks), that she appears ready to break things off. Fleda then returns several days later to London in answer to a summons from Mrs. Gereth, only to learn that the elder lady has, in her latest— and last—melodramatic move, packed up and sent every last "spoil" back to Poynton itself:

> Mrs. Gereth stood there in all the glory of a great stroke. "I've settled you." She filled the room, to Fleda's scared vision, with the glare of her magnificence. "I've sent everything back."
> "Everything?" Fleda wailed.
> "To the smallest snuff-box. The last load went yesterday. The same people did it. Poor little Ricks is empty." Then as if, for a crowning splendour, to check all deprecation, "They're yours, you goose!" the wonderful woman concluded, holding up her handsome head and rubbing her white hands. But there were tears none the less in her deep eyes [211].

Thus we see the tenacity of Mrs. Gereth's "fixed" idea, the logical extension of her fanaticism. She has properly fixed Fleda's wagon by virtue of that presumption of hers. Not duped for a moment, when she heard that her son had gone searching for her young protégée, she saw (naturally) the embodiment of her own plan. Her great act is her "sign," her "token" of knowledge. The only trouble with such knowing what you are about intellectualist-fashion is that the consequences may not always allow the curtain to drop amid the applause. She has done the one thing that can lose Owen back to Mona, as Fleda, in sending him away, has done the one thing Mrs. Gereth could never entertain in her anticipation. It is at this point—and not before—that we turn the page and have the well-known quarrel between the two ladies wherein Henry is supposed to have repudiated William's "pragmatism." But let us look back at Fleda's character and ethic more closely.

I would be the last to say that Fleda Vetch is not idealistic. William's ethical pragmatism, if we can grasp it without supplying present-day connotations of the word, is itself most idealistic. The point is here that we must see Fleda's particular quality of idealism, not just call her idealistic and then quasi-mechanically equate that with absolutism. That she speaks ethically for Henry James (whatever her "ism") is not cut and dried, for his later fiction remains a "more-and-less" affair in this as in other matters. That she is his "viewpoint" is not definitive, for so are the narrators of "The Liar," *The Aspern Papers*, *The Sacred Fount*, and *The Turn of the Screw*; as well as John Marcher and Herbert Dodd in *The Beast in the Jungle* and *The Bench of Desolation*—to name several narrative "deputies" not, to my mind, at least, his ethical spokesmen. Nor should we overlook the possibility that a central James character with whom he is on the whole sympathetic may proceed from one ethical orientation to another, and then back again—though always remaining, to a greater extent than with almost any other writer, "in character." Nevertheless, I do think that James's comments about Fleda Vetch in his "Preface," stressing her "appreciation," her "character," and her "free spirit" are genuine and adhere correctly to the reading experience of the novel. I would even say that her "appreciative" qualities as James defines them—her capacity to "both see and feel" as well as her not being "able," like the stronger-willed Mrs. Gereth and "triumphantly" willed Mona— do constitute ethical qualities James admires; [29] furthermore, they are the very ones implicated in William's claim, earlier quoted, that anyone who thinks his law lax ought to try keeping it one day.

I have several times pointed out that in William's pragmatistic thought the ethical view just cannot be divorced from the epistemological view. The character of Fleda Vetch is a particularly apt illustration and parallel. When she accidentally meets up with Owen Gereth on a shopping trip, and he seems to want to lengthen their meeting, Fleda reflects: "He unduly prolonged their business together, giving Fleda a sense of his putting off something particular that he had to face. If she had ever dreamed of Owen Gereth as finely fluttered she would have seen him with some such manner as this" [63].

This is most "Jamesian," a quality not, we see, necessarily dependent upon sentences a page long, although to accomplish what he just has above usually demands longer sentences. The quality lies in Fleda's previous impressions of Owen as terminating and tumbling into the present one. She does not think of her present perception as something to be explained or modified through attachment to some preconceived reality. She thinks in just the reverse fashion: i.e., Owen seems to be putting something off; I have never seen him act like this; and with respect to my previous knowledge of him, were I now to imagine that person as nervous, his behavior would resemble the phenomenon I presently perceive. Of course it would be easier for James to have Fleda thinking: "Good heavens, he's acting differently: he must really be fluttered." And such a statement would be far easier for a conceptualist or "saltatory" reader (or critic) to accommodate. But it would also take us out of James's world, implying as it does a disjunction between the present, nervous Owen and the former un-nervous Owen. And, viewed in this light, the *former* Owen would be the *real* Owen; the present nervousness only a new "attribute" intruding on the scene. Instead, Fleda's thinking makes Owen's most recent behavior in effect the continual and ongoing basis for "Owenness." It captures the very heart of William's whole point about pluralistic "novelty."

But the real issue now is the ethical correlative to such epistemological considerations. Fleda's "use" of others morally is the cognate to the sort of thinking above. What the epistemology insists upon is the undermining of the subject-object separation. Fleda's "appreciation" is her constantly imputing to others her own best and most recent motives—always making them morally "present." Let us go to her celebrated scene with Owen, when she sends him back to Mona, the scene that has irritated quite a number of critical readers as much as it will upset Mrs. Gereth herself when, after sending the spoils back to Poynton, she later learns from Fleda that this scene had taken place:

"Then in God's name [Owen pleads] what must I do?"

"You must settle that with Mona. You mustn't break faith. Anything's better than that. You must at any rate be utterly sure. She must love you—how can she help it? *I* wouldn't give you up! . . . The great thing is to keep faith. Where's a man if he doesn't? If he doesn't he may be so cruel. So cruel, so cruel, so cruel!" Fleda repeated. "I couldn't have a hand in that, you know: that's my position—that's mine. You offered her marriage. It's a tremendous thing for her." Then looking at him another moment, "*I* wouldn't give you up!" she said again [196-97].

This entire scene has perplexed many a reader, and I do not wish to diminish some of its problems—for example, Fleda's characteristically retreating "upstairs" (like a Victorian heroine) for fear of breaking down before Owen's passion. My concern is that of the ethical content of Fleda's character. For the Jacobite critic she is either James's surrogate moral absolutist or else the

Master's brilliantly done neurotic, and for the anti-Jacobite she is the second without the Master's knowledge. It seems to me that, even if we are to find her excessive, the quality of her ethic remains utilitarian; and if it seems awfully "fine" for being utilitarian, then so much the worse for our understanding of utilitarian. It is utilitarian because she refuses to prescribe ("'You must settle that with Mona'"); utilitarian because she does not base her position on anything transcendent, but rather on the human contracts and pledges made by fallible people. The "faith" she speaks of is that everybody, including even the Monas of the world, must get the fairest shake possible, because we do not have the final word that their position is less ordained than ours. It is utilitarian because its eye is to consequences: no matter how deserving we are convinced that we are, our actions can cause cruelty. Utilitarian, finally, because the matter remains provisional: if Mona will agree to call off the engagement, then Fleda and Owen can marry.

Her ethic here is furthermore pragmatistically oriented— that is, parallel to William's own broadening or "radical" aspects of utilitarianism—in that Fleda characteristically *creates* a possible other case about Mona, projects a version of the other girl as someone for whom Owen's earlier proposal is "a tremendous thing," someone who "must" love him because Fleda herself does. The saltatory mind can immediately say that Fleda is merely creating Mona in her own image; and that is so to the extent that she does project, in Henry's language, the "possible other case" for what "*might*, blessedly be," and makes Mona's feelings coalesce with her own. To the same saltatory mind that sounds simply like making others into yourself. In fact it is just the reverse: it is conceiving of each person as so distinctively individual that you are willing continually to subsume your own views into them rather than classify them as Other, which would then take the spark of human life and dignity out of them—one which you know is there because you have it yourself. That is the sort of "use" Fleda makes of Mona, and it is characteristic of her throughout the novel.[30] The fact that neither Mona nor Owen deserves such good usage cannot alter Fleda's fundamental response in this regard. It is an extreme position and an extreme ethic, and one which is rather easy to confuse with its conceptualist opposite—making others conform in an extreme way to your own idea. The reason the two are easily confused is that they *are* both extreme and opposite and therefore seem to resemble one another; and the reason Fleda's is likely to be thought the other is that we rarely see *her* ethic in people, but we do see the other one. James himself is most capable and adept at presenting the other one: John Marcher, the narrator of *The Aspern Papers*, and the governess are good examples of it in his fiction. Fleda is instead an extreme case of William's ethic.

Late in the novel, in the aftermath of Owen's marriage to Mona, Mrs. Gereth expresses her bewilderment to Fleda, this time about Owen himself; that is, if Fleda had been "idiotic" in pursuing her "scruples" beyond all reason, there was still Owen's discovery in the whole dispute of the ugliness of Mona's character—and yet he now seemed content. Fleda, however, observes: "'[Mona's] a person who's upset by failure and who blooms and expands with success. There was something she had set her heart upon, set her teeth about—the house exactly as she had seen it.'" And Mrs. Gereth cries: "'She never saw it at all, she never looked at it!'" But Fleda counters:

"She doesn't look with her eyes; she looks with her ears. In her own way she had taken it in; she knew, she felt when it had been touched. That probably made her take an attitude that was extremely disagreeable. But the attitude lasted only while the reason for it lasted. . . . When the pressure was removed she came up again. . . . her natural charm reasserted itself."

"Her natural charm!"—Mrs. Gereth could barely articulate.

"It's very great; everybody thinks so; there must be something in it" [254-55].

The novel never allows us to test this evaluation of the couple by Fleda. But one thing, I hope, is clear: this evaluation could never come from someone who is supposed to embody Henry's repudiation of William's thought. And note that it continues Fleda's characteristic "use" of others. Moreover, it is one time we could hardly confuse such usage as its opposite of making Mona into Fleda's idea and self, for Fleda is certainly not someone who blooms and expands with success.

In the celebrated quarrel scene between Fleda and Mrs. Gereth (occurring, we must remember, only after the elder lady's comic "apotheosis" in sending the objects back to Poynton as well as Fleda's sending Owen back to Mona) the two women do not so much reveal their opposing ethics, or ideologies, as they reinforce and enrich the full meaning of the dramatic context— much like those "thematic" statements earlier discussed in "The Real Thing." Shortly after Mrs. Gereth condemns Fleda's "wonderful exactions" and "sweet little scruples," and wonders why her son had not "snapped his fingers at your refinements" [219, 220], Fleda cries out her defense that many readers consider— along with the statements to Owen about keeping faith—the touchstone of her ethical consciousness and that of Henry James:

"You simplify far too much. You always did and you always will. The tangle of life is much more intricate than you've ever, I think, felt it to be. You slash into it," cried Fleda finely, "with a great pair of shears; you nip at it as if you were one of the Fates!" [224].

If this is a touchstone of Jamesian morality, we should at least include the finishing line to it: " 'If Owen's at Waterbath he's there to wind everything up.' " Not only does this take away some of the bloom of profundity, it shows that Fleda could not be more wrong for being right: Owen, we later learn, is indeed winding things up, but not as Fleda bravely imagines.[31] What James is again doing is making his ideological pronouncements arise out of a context only to be "re-directed" right back into it, and making the very relationship itself totally "empirical" in William's sense. Fleda, in short, has become increasingly apprehensive that Mrs. Gereth's unforeseen act may have lost her Owen, and that her own earlier insistence to Owen that he keep his pledge may have the dire consequences she was willing to risk. The quality of James's art lies just in such unstiffening and mediating. It is really beginning to come home to Fleda that she *is* going to lose Owen, just as earlier she so nobly said that she might. Such is James's actual "tangle of life" and "intricacy" of the human comedy. Like William's unseverable stream of reality it cannot be cut with a shears, because it is thoroughly conjoined.

Mrs. Gereth, for one, perceives what is involved in Fleda's fine rhetoric about "the tangle of life": " 'You don't believe a word you're saying,' " she responds: " 'I've frightened you, as you've frightened me: you're whistling in the dark to keep up our courage' " [224-25]. But the recognition here is not gratuitous either. It does involve Mrs. Gereth's inability to comprehend Fleda. In fact Fleda's present fright, which the elder lady perceives, drives it home to *her* that all expectations are lost. She immediately continues: " 'I do simplify, doubtless, if to simplify is to fail to comprehend the inanity of a passion that bewilders a young blockhead with bugaboo barriers, with hideous and monstrous sacrifices. I can only repeat that you're beyond me. Your perversity's a thing to howl over' " [225].

Mrs. Gereth begins this speech with a "slow austere" shake of the head, and becomes increasingly furious until she is almost ready to howl. And, once again, she too could not be more wrong for being right: her simplifying *is* her incomprehension; and she creates for herself a Fleda in the image of her incomprehension—blockheaded and perverse; her imputation to Fleda of monstrous sacrifices comes from the same source: Mrs. Gereth *will* have a sacrifice, after her own "crowning splendour" of having sent back the spoils! But what is almost of equal importance is that Mrs. Gereth's anger, culminating in these remarks above, also expends itself with them. Not only does she calm down, and the two ladies exhaust themselves with their argument, but their relationship reestablishes itself for the remainder of the novel, if anything on the closest and most legitimate footing since they first met. Thus, not only does a reading of Fleda's repudiation of Mrs. Gereth's "pragmatism" do violence to the context leading up to the quarrel but even to what follows afterward. It also, as we have seen, thoroughly misconstrues the ethical bases for both Mrs. Gereth and for Fleda. Henry James's "tangle of life" proceeds and is in the making.

The difficult and controversial dénouement, the burning down of Poynton Park, is for the most part outside of the ethical focus I have been addressing. But I would like to comment on its possible place or appropriateness, if only to stress what are often the implications for James's art of the "Jourdain" relationship. The critical problem with the potentially melodramatic conflagration that closes the novel has been one, first, of deciding whether James knew his full intention in the story and, second, assuming he did, what the fire was then meant to symbolize. More recently Leon Edel has said that it stands for James's own theatre period and vocation going up in smoke,[32] and that seems plausible; but it neither supports nor rejects the critical question of its symbolic content or artistic appropriateness for the novel as a whole. The general tendency has been to see it as some kind of symbolic underscoring of Fleda's necessary renunciation of earthly or material gain—poetic justice which deprives her of tainting her pristine fineness and absolute morality; or else the parallel aesthetic point of tainting her hard won recognition that true art exists beyond its mere physical embodiment. [33]

If we were instead to shift our basic orientation away from such symbolic realms proper and "re-direct" our focus back into the context in which it occurs, I believe we can see another quite different rationale for it, and one at least as satisfying as those proposed above. It should be remembered that Fleda only begins to think of the lovely objects once again as "too proud, unlike base animals and humans, to be reducible" to anyone's mere ownership—Mona's or her own—after the conflict has been resolved against her and she faces the prospect of a future alone with only lost alternatives [235]. In other words, just as we have seen that she initially joined up with Mrs. Gereth on the basis of a lovely "idea," then had to discover through the conflict that such ideas cannot be divorced from their consequences, she now as a lonely and rejected girl becomes vulnerable to responding— or re-responding—to the same lovely "idea" of the spoils detached from time, place, or human conflict.

The advantage of our keeping this perspective is that it adheres so well to the text during those chapters following the quarrel with Mrs. Gereth and culminating in Fleda's trip to Poynton and discovering the fire. First there is the pathetic search for Owen, the telegram, the full reconciliation with Mrs. Gereth, the response to Ricks and the modest furnishings of the "maiden-aunt," and the growing acquisition of her "serene" and "lucid" stoicism. Owen's surprising letter, requesting that she go to Poynton and take the "gem of the collection," is a Jamesian tour de force of mystery and ambiguity, but its effect on Fleda, coming when it does in her situation, triggers a response from her that is unmistakable and unambiguous. We can literally watch her becoming increasingly enamored of an "idea." Starting with natural bafflement, she proceeds "little by little" to endow it with significance and idealism. She "would go down to Poynton as a pilgrim might go to a shrine"; she "would act with secret rapture"; she would have a gift more splendid and joyful "than the greatest she had believed to be left her"; the time was "to dream of and watch for; to be patient was to draw out the sweetness"; it was "an hour of triumph, the triumph of everything in her recent life that had not held up its head." And still her response builds and expands:

She moved there in thought—in the great rooms she knew; she should be able to say to herself that, for once at least, her possession was as complete as that of either of the others whom it had filled only with bitterness. And a thousand times yes—her choice should know no scruple: the thing she should go down to take would be up to the height of her privilege. The whole place was in her eyes, and she spent for weeks her private hours in a luxury of comparison and debate. . . . [S]he would on the spot so handle and ponder that there shouldn't be the shade of a mistake [259-61].

In one conjunctive, seamless, sequence (a single two-page paragraph in the text) Henry James has modulated his heroine's response from one of initial bafflement at Owen's request to the heady imaginings seen here. This very progression equates perfectly with the description by William, given in an earlier chapter, of how the human mind can mistakenly arrive at a "sublime" saltatory explanation or Idea.[34] But we need not revisit William's epistemology to see that Fleda's initial perplexity has turned into "triumph," her sense of the possible other case which characterized her conduct has evaporated into "completeness," her commitment to human fallibility becomes now no "shade of a mistake." Henry's own doctrine for all of this is his well-known distinction between the real and the romantic, contained in his "Preface" to *The American*. Fleda has cut the "rope" which keeps the "balloon of experience" tied to the earth.[35] And that means, vis-à-vis William, that she is out in the great conceptualist Beyond.

The Poynton fire, then, is what brings her back. For what all "symbolic" readings of the fire inadvertently distort is that the fire qua fire is never given in the text; that is, the final scene takes place at the train station, and is rendered through high comedy— Fleda's impassioned remarks to a most bewildered porter followed by her conversation with the stationmaster, who tells her what has happened. This does not mean, however, that the scene exists and is written satirically at Fleda's expense. There is great sympathy for her when, after finally grasping that Poynton is gone, she feels herself "give everything up" and, standing in the smoke from the fire a mile away, covers her face and speaks the final lines of the novel: " 'I'll go back' " [266].

It is the appropriately written scene, then, for what has happened to Fleda since she lost Owen. Her "go[ing] back" symbolizes, if you will, her reattachment to actuality, and even conveys that circular quality we have seen again and again in connection with the letter to Henry Adams—one seems to be back again at the beginning, except that being "back" means more than it did. Similarly, Fleda's built up reveries and imaginings have been "redirected" back into their ongoing consequences, and the result is a rude awakening. Thus, in contradiction to the many "symbolic" readings of the Poynton fire, I am suggesting the purpose and effect of the denouement is almost one of setting up and then rejecting such symbolic realms—or at least the transcendent correspondences such readings imply. Judged this way, the scene would function basically like the concluding stanzas of the Frost poem earlier examined in this book.

It cannot be too greatly stressed, however, that the deflation of Fleda's "idea" in no way undermines what is basically James's compassionate and sympathetic view of her. For that very reason the scene is a delicate "compromise" between its comic and tragic elements. And if we do not respond to them both simultaneously, we are again rejecting that positive middle territory demanded by a mediating view. If I may appropriate the ethical language and criteria of my discussion of Fleda herself, James is here "using" his character well. Had he not subjected her to this rude awakening, he would not have fully respected her as a created "center"—in effect a real person, a someone who, like Isabel Archer, is not a "fixed constituent." And not to have allowed her to fall prey to her lovely "idea" at the particular *time* and *context* she did, would have disallowed her fallibility as a human being, also making her a "fixed constituent." The pragmatistic mind cannot give favors in those ways.

At the same time, my reading of the novel's ending does come round to making the point that commentators have sensed about the conclusion, that it somehow recapitulates the central conflict. It does indeed, as Fleda once again engenders her aesthetic ideal disembodied from time and place and people, and then must give it up. James has seen his character through in the "Jourdain" way; his consistency in this respect is fully intact.

If, then, *The Spoils of Poynton* remains, as I suspect it will, an important "problem" novel in James's canon, perhaps the reason must be sought elsewhere than in the character of Fleda as such: if the problem is not at the level of fancy, perhaps it is at the level of imagination; if not at the "Jourdain" level, perhaps at the level of polarity. Walter Isle observes that the free spirit is necessarily "fixed" by the conditions of life in which it finds itself, and that the novel reveals the "gap between perception and act," the "irreconcilable split between the self and life."[36] Such seem the effects of Fleda's successive defeats and Mona's triumphs. At the same time Laurence Holland maintains that the novel "turns on the paradox that the renunciation and the hope, the sacrifice and the vision, virtually create each other; the act of renunciation and the vision of possession are the source and image of each other."[37] To the extent that readers sense these various contraries to be reconciled through the work, to that extent the novel becomes less of a problem. These relationships—between freedom and conditions, perception and act, self and life, renunciation and possession—*are* cases of genuine polarity. That they are made to relate *as* polar—relate, that is, in the positive way Holland speaks of—would be altogether clear were the novel under discussion *The Portrait of a Lady*, in which these very same cases of polarity sustain it throughout. To the extent, however, that a reader senses what Isle calls a "gap" or "irreconcilable split" between them (not as a thematic issue, but in the full matrix of the work itself), to that extent one can speak of James's "uncertainty" in intention—or ambiguity. The issue, once again, is between dichotomy and polarity, between juxtaposition and interpenetration. In my judgment *The Spoils of Poynton* is ultimately unified organically through polarity, but not nearly so clearly and obviously as in much of James's comparable best fiction—such as the two works to be discussed in the next chapter.

VII. Pragmatism—
"Remoulding" Experience and Violating Ideas
The Ambassadors
and The Beast in the Jungle

> *Experience is remoulding us every moment, and
> our mental reaction on every given thing is really a resultant of
> our experience of the whole world up to that date.*
> **WILLIAM JAMES**, *The Principles of Psychology*

It is most appropriate to the "Jourdain" relationship that Henry
James should have chosen *The Ambassadors* (1903) his best
work, and equally appropriate that the novel has sustained such
penetrating literary criticism validating his judgment. Beyond all
others it is the textbook illustration of the relationship, the embodiment's embodiment, so to speak. The reason is that we have
in *The Ambassadors* the rare instance of a "register," Lambert
Strether, who himself happens to exemplify William's thought
and thus participates in the same "way of thinking" as his creator. Just as the statement and formulation above from *The Principles of Psychology* (1890)[1] is one which captures what is
innovative in William's psychology, thus pointing directly ahead
across his career to the later philosophy; so it is also the perfect
motto and key signature for Henry's Lambert Strether, the one
protagonist in his canon who, despite his many fine female creations, seems to capture the essence of James's career, both synthe-
sizing and summarizing his international work up to that date
and reincarnating in particular the young decent Western American financeer Christopher Newman (of *The American*) as the
older decent New England writer and editor Strether. Indeed *The*

Ambassadors is such a focal illustration of the argument of this study that in coming to it now I am almost compelled to say, anti-climactically, that the argument for it has already been made in the third, fourth, and fifth chapters above dealing with the "Jour-dain" relationship and with ambulation. For that reason, as well as the superb critical exegesis of the novel, I shall try wherever possible to explore and emphasize some less examined byways and, perhaps more than before, shall allude to the central ma-terial with the assumption of the reader's familiarity with the main lines and dominant patterns of the critical literature as well as the novel itself.

One such byway is James's own recognition that from the very beginning of his work on this book he was literally amazed by the way he progressed without a hitch, quite as if the book wrote itself out. In no other work of comparable scope and am-bition was this the case. If we reflect that his entire artistic career, with its three or perhaps even four "phases" (if we include the *Finer Grain* tales), expresses quintessentially his growth and the stretching of his aims and powers, always confronting the "beautiful difficulty" spoken of in connection with *The Portrait of a Lady*, then it begins to dawn on us how astonishing it is that his masterpiece should have been *the* case of something the re-verse of his reach exceeding his grasp. Yet that is apparently so true of *The Ambassadors* that James all but makes it his motif in the "Preface," in a series of statements we will necessarily over-look—or at least de-emphasize—when we focus instead on the critical gems there dealing with his single "point of view," Strether's "process of vision," the "ficelle," and so forth. "Noth-ing is more easy than to state the subject of 'The Ambassadors,' " his "Preface" begins, because such surprising ease is also his subject in these remarks. "Nothing can exceed the closeness with which the whole fits again into its germ,"[2] he says shortly after, not because he thinks his other works lack the organic relation-ship between germ and completed work (as the other "Prefaces" will amply attest) but because he is delighted and amazed at the effortless expansion of this particular germ—which is why we get the image in reverse, as if to say the whole work could shrivel right back into its germ and then expand back out again without friction or abrasion. Remarking again on the "suggested wealth" of this germ, he generalizes about "degrees of merit in subjects," and about the possibility, even among already "supremely good" ones, of "an ideal *beauty* of goodness," which can then raise "the artistic faith to its maximum." And he states:

Then truly, I hold, one's theme may be said to shine, and that of "The Ambassadors," I confess, wore this glow for me from beginning to end. Fortunately thus I am able to estimate this as, frankly, quite the best, "all round," of my productions; any failure of that justification would have made such an extreme of complacency publicly fatuous.[3]

In other words he would never venture to speak in such nothing-to-it fashion were it not for the fact ("Fortunately") that the book will hold up against the most discriminating examination. All of which is only to say that James is himself as amazed as anyone else at such a development. He continues:

I recall then in this connexion no moment of subjective intermittence, never one of those alarms as for a suspected hollow beneath one's feet, a felt ingratitude in the scheme adopted, under which confidence fails and opportunity seems but to mock. If the motive of "The Wings of the Dove" . . . was to worry me at moments by a sealing-up of its face . . . so in this other business I had absolute conviction and constant clearness to deal with; it had been a frank proposition, the whole bunch of data, installed on my premises like a monotony of fine weather.[4]

Some remarkable comparison this, the process of composing *The Ambassadors* with the "monotony of fine weather"! But James insists that, even with such potential difficulties as his older hero and the different ages of Chad Newsome and Madame de Vionnet, "I could still feel it serene. Nothing resisted, nothing betrayed . . . ; it shed from any side I could turn it to the same golden glow."[5] This "turning" image here is that same instinctive sense of the book's "superior roundness," the circularity that characterizes the ambulatory view of reality that I have had occasion already to discuss. The point is here that the novel seems to have had this desired quality all along the way. And James, too, it might be said, keeps circling back to this issue in his "Preface." Thus he remarks presently how so often "the Story is just the spoiled child of art," that is, in the resistance it puts up against the artist's executing faculty of bringing to light its meaning. But in this case the child practically exhausted the artist, not by resisting him, but, so to speak, by sprinting ahead of him:

the *steps*, for my fable, placed themselves with a prompt and, as it were, functional assurance—an air quite as of readiness to have dispensed with logic had I been in fact too stupid for my clue. Never, positively, none the less, as the links multiplied, had I felt less stupid than for the determination of poor Strether's errand and for the apprehension of his issue. These things continued to fall together, as by the neat action of their own weight and form, even while their commentator scratched his head about them; he easily sees now that they were always well in advance of him. As the case completed itself he had in fact, from a good way behind, to catch up with them, breathless and a little flurried, as he best could.[6]

Such reiterated claims of extraordinary ease and confidence suffuse the tone and spirit of this "Preface" and are really what cause him to remark, in conclusion, on the novel in general as "the most independent, most elastic, most prodigious of literary forms."[7] My reason for drawing out and emphasizing this issue is that it seems to me to speak to the "Jourdain" relationship in a particular way. The reason, in other words, for such quasi-automatic progress is that this book has a pragmatist for its "center" which, combined with a "Jourdain" for its author, puts James thoroughly at home and in "familiar territory" from start to finish. And when we think in turn of pragmatism's own cultural ties with "The Rise of Realism," we can see an expanding appropriateness to James's ease and familiarity: the fact that it was William Dean Howells who actually spoke the novel's germ is something we usually want to divorce—and properly—from the fictive creation of Strether; but the reverse is true when considering James's singular ease in composition. The very "organicism" of his germ to the written work implicates the whole cultural gestalt of Howells, of New England, of William's world—the "way of thinking" which is itself the inner mentality of late-nineteenth-century America, and which thus comes full circle and implicates "Jourdain" himself too: for there is, as many critics have recognized for various reasons, just an uncommon degree of James himself in Strether.[8] And how appropriate this same condition even in its aesthetic implications, in which his reach did not need to exceed his grasp: for it is preeminently the Realist aesthetic associated with Howells and his school that emphasizes the lesser or ordinary subject done well, whereas it is the Romantic school that stresses, like Ruskin's concept of the gothic, the attempt to convey more or to stretch beyond one's normal or mundane capacities. James's career, and most certainly including *The Ambassadors*, is always a unique combination of the two schools, as we have already seen. I am speaking now only of his particular situation in composing the book and its relationship with the rare case of a pragmatist for its center and "deputy."

To speak of Strether as a pragmatist is only to say what we already know about him, that his entire mission to Europe to return Chad is a case, continually, to use his own language for Madame de Vionnet, of matters having "taken all his categories by surprise."[9] It is to say, again as we all know, that the novel presents as its central subject Strether's abandonment of the preconceived moral absolutism of Mrs. Newsome and Woollett in favor of his new and ongoing experience of Europe, his changing allegiance from what has been presumed and imposed from afar to what he yields from the immediate "sea of sense" in the milieu of Chad and Mme. de Vionnet and of Paris; yet this action develops without Strether's ever abandoning in the least his moral seriousness by virtue of relocating it contextually instead of a priori.[10] Strether himself explains the nature of pragmatic openness negatively in his description, late in the novel, of Mrs. Newsome's limitations:

"That's just her difficulty—that she doesn't admit surprises. It's a fact that, I think, describes and represents her; and it falls in with what I tell you—that she's all, as I've called it, fine cold thought. She had, to her own mind, worked the whole thing out in advance, and worked it out for me as well as for herself. Whenever she has done that, you see, there's no room left; no margin, as it were, for any alteration" [II, 239].

But understanding Strether as a pragmatist, while it seems, significantly and appropriately, to take us at once to the heart of *The Ambassador's* Aristotelian action, while it illuminates James's striking ease of composition, and while it speaks directly to the unusual degree of identity between protagonist and author, cannot by itself adequately do justice to the novel as the work of "Jourdain," as the realization, that is, of pragmatistic thought. Or rather, it can do justice to this only if we enlarge Strether's pragmatism to the point where it meets and intersects with James's full "roundness" in seeing his hero through the labyrinth of his "gropings," the "rich rigour" of which, James tells us in his "Preface," gave him "a large unity."[11] Just as James himself, in other words, is not the pragmatist (William is that) but the pragmatism itself, so Strether's being a pragma*tist* is not sufficient to the novel's embodiment of William's thought, although obviously there are closer ties here in this regard than elsewhere in James, especially in view of Strether's extraordinarily full role as the dramatic center—the trait which more than any other has made this book famous and the perennial touchstone of Jamesian "point of view."

By virtue of James's method as well as Strether's unique character, then, we find throughout that Strether's "experience is remoulding [him] every moment, and [his] mental reaction on every given thing is really a resultant of [his] experience of the whole world up to that date." Strether's "whole world," which he brings with him across the Atlantic at the outset of his ambassadorial mission, is comprised of a New England conscience and consciousness second to none, a mediocre career as Woollett's decorous intellectual-in-residence, an all but assured betrothal (provided he succeeds in his mission) to the reigning queen of industrial power and *"moral* swell," Mrs Newsome [I, 67]; beyond and behind this, however, his "whole world" is also his early marriage, the loss of his young wife, and then his son, and the promises long ago made to "the higher culture" and "the temple of taste" upon first coming over to Europe and to Paris newly married, which he then failed to keep [I, 85, 87]. The fact that all these matters and more—"his blest imagination,"[12] his "dog-tired" state when he sailed, even his belief in "the illusion of freedom" [I, 29, 218]—seem to resonate with new meaning and simultaneously yield to reconstruction and redefinition with each successive event or next experience in the novel, is what makes *The Ambassadors* the preeminent realization of the statement by William which heads this chapter. The quality noted before in Fleda Vetch, in the passage where her previous impressions of Owen Gereth are made to project forward and terminate in the present perception, is literally the function of Strether's cognition throughout: his "experience of the whole world up to that date" is thus his Fleda-like *way* of thinking: "[Waymarsh's] head was bigger, the eyes finer, than they need have been for the career; but that only meant, after all, that the career was itself expressive. What it expressed at midnight in the gas-glaring bed-

room at Chester" is the "rigour" of Waymarsh's immediate awkward "posture" on "the edge of his bed," and by extension "the
angle at which poor Waymarsh was to sit through the ordeal of
Europe" [I, 26]. The only discrimination one might want to make
between Fleda's passage and this one is the almost doctrinal
quality here to William's epistemology ("but that only meant,
after all, that the career was itself expressive . . . "), as though
we practically have Moliere's "Philosophy Master" with us along
with "Jourdain." Because we *do* have "Jourdain," however, the
same passage is characteristically cordial and additive in its operative irony: Strether himself is on the threshold of a European
"ordeal," he, too, will be in a "posture of prolonged impermanence," he, too, will eventually be "in a railway-coach with a
forward inclination" (when he rides back with Chad and Mme.
de Vionnet from the Cheval Blanc). Here as before the same returns to us as the different: "poor Waymarsh" is also poor
Strether. Strether's "whole world," then, in all its elements is
constantly defined and rendered by each new facet of the present,
no matter how deceptively trivial.

In such a novelistic hymn to ambulatory rather than saltatory relations, in which the "intervening parts of experience"—
i.e., the "demonstration of [Strether's] process of vision"[13]—
supersede every other consideration, we are forced to attend in
particular to those occasional moments when we are given a
quasi-ideological expression from James's pen which in effect
"names" the very ambulatory process of the book itself. Thus
Paris, for Strether, sitting in the Luxembourg Gardens shortly
after his arrival, "hung before him this morning, the vast bright
Babylon, like some huge iridescent object, a jewel brilliant and
hard, in which parts were not to be discriminated nor differences
comfortably marked. It twinkled and trembled and melted together, and what seemed all surface one moment seemed all
depth the next" [I, 89]. Most appropriate, therefore, is Strether's
analogous response to the woman who eventually comes to represent for him the embodiment of Parisian culture and history—
Marie de Vionnet: "She fell in at moments with the theory about
her he most cherished, and she seemed at others to blow it into
air. She spoke now as if her art were all an innocence, and then
again as if her innocence were all an art" [II, 115-16].

Both passages are noteworthy in explicitly articulating the

same returning *as* the different, which is to say they tell to a greater degree than usual what is also the basic felt reality and mode of presentation of the novel as a whole. They are of course at the center of Strether's "gropings" and of James's "large unity." For these very reasons, then, they can be said to take us at once to the process of the book as a "Jourdain" work, just as before Strether's role as pragmat*ist* was able to take us immediately to his rejection of preconceived absolutism. The felt reality and process bespoken by these passages is fundamentally William's "apparent" in its affective flux. Strether's whole exploration and initiation is, in contradiction to Woollett, a matter of learning to respond to and respect the "mere" apparent. This motif is announced from the beginning, with Strether's first "note" of Europe, that of giving himself "to the immediate and the sensible," followed shortly by his sense before the dressing-glass of "a sharper survey of the elements of Appearance than he had for a long time been moved to make" [I, 4, 9]. It is reiterated in his meeting and dinner with Maria Gostrey in "the rose-coloured shades and the small table and the soft fragrance of the lady," as well as the "cut down" dress and the charming "red velvet band"—all in such marked contrast with evenings out back home with Mrs. Newsome [I, 50]; yet those contrasting evenings are made *present* by Strether's "fresh backward, fresh forward, fresh lateral flights" [I, 51], so that "Jourdain's" conjoining method is never more intact and William's "whole world up to that date" never more demonstrable than when Strether is differentiating what is present from what is distant in time and space. Indeed Miss Gostrey's—"how intensely you make me see [Mrs. Newsome]!"—spoken to Strether, is itself implied by the "Jourdain" method and points to the realization of William's "whole world," for it is the much noted effect on the reader of the novel; and it also becomes, finally, the achieved recognition and conversion of Strether himself when, at the end, he will say back to Miss Gostrey that *he* can now "*see* [Mrs. Newsome]" as never before after his extended absence and "the whole affair" that makes up the novel [I, 63; II, 323]. Thus, the response to the integrity of the pragmatistically apparent yields new meaning not only close up, but brings the "whole world up to that date" into the present with increased vividness. Strether's inability to have "seen" Mrs. Newsome properly back home when, presumably, *she* was "immediate and sensible" is of course an issue that takes us outside of the novel proper; but, by inference, at least, it can be understood as the result and index of Strether's prior participation in Woollett's and Mrs. Newsome's own a priori mentality. Nevertheless, it must be remembered that he clearly brings his pragmatic predisposition with him across the Atlantic fully as much as he "finds" a new viewpoint on foreign soil. That, too, is "Jourdain's" same and different, and perhaps the most central one, as we shall presently see, that can be reconciled *ultimately* only by the principle of polarity.[14] But before our walking up to and "peering inside" William's confluent and concatenated world, "all surface . . . all depth," to discover within Henry's empiricized polarity in this novel, we need to keep to the pragmatistic focus and do *it* justice.

Strether's growing openness to pragmatistic novelty, which is the correlative of James's ambulatory medium of his hero's rendered consciousness, culminates first in the discovery—or rediscovery—of Chad himself as "a case of transformation unsurpassed" [I, 137]. Chad, having purposefully stayed out of Strether's way and sight for a week or so, thereby adroitly allowing for Strether's series of concatenating impressions—the young man's tasteful rooms in the Boulevard Malesherbes, Strether's acquaintance with his young friends, particularly the amiable Little Bilham, whose "mention of [Chad] was of a kind to do him honour," and above all (as Miss Gostrey perceives) simply "Europe" and "dear old Paris" itself [I, 117, 134]— finally makes his calculated appearance by walking into a box at the *Théâtre de Comédie Française* at 10 P.M., thus creating for Strether an enforced period to observe him without the two being able to speak because of the performance. This high point of James's almost inexhaustible use of playacting and performance to reinforce, extend, and complicate the novel's inner drama[15] has the effect of totally reversing Strether's preconceptions while, simultaneously, providing the copestone for his expanding response to "the elements of Appearance" operative since his arrival at Liverpool:

The phenomenon that had suddenly sat down there with him was a phenomenon of change so complete that his imagination, which had worked so beforehand, felt itself, in the connexion, without margin or allowance. It had faced every contingency but that Chad should not *be*

Chad. . . . [W]hat could be more remarkable than this sharp rupture of an identity? You could deal with a man as himself—you couldn't deal with him as somebody else [I, 136-37].

James's cordiality and "unstiffening" here is of course the fact that it is also Strether himself who more than anyone else, is undergoing transformation, the very thing counted on and abetted by Chad himself when making his calculated entrance and displaying his new "refinement" and "streaks of grey" hair [I, 140]. Strether's "gropings" are never more present than in this portion of the book, for his developing response to the "elements of Appearance" culminating in Chad in no way diminishes his ethical sense. Like William's ethic there can be no "moral holidays" for Strether; in fact, again like William's doctrine, the moral sense increases in its activity at the same ratio as the response to the new "phenomena." Thus, Chad's transformation, inasmuch as it includes a disjunction of previous resemblance to his mother, "produced in Strether . . . one of those frequent phenomena of mental reference with which all judgement in him was actually beset" [I, 140]. This involves, clearly, Strether's own "besetting" alienation from Chad's mother, his gradual process of "seeing" her as never before. Strether's intensified moral activity in apposition with his response to immediate "phenomena" is here underscored by James himself: Strether's sense of duty impels him to communicate "quickly with Woollett" his new discovery; but the very same "burden of conscience" makes "his heart always [sink] when the clouds of explanation gathered." And James continues:

Whether or no [Strether] had a grand idea of the lucid, he held that nothing ever was in fact—for any one else—explained. One went through the vain motions, but it was mostly a waste of life. A personal relation was a relation only so long as people perfectly understood or, better still, didn't care if they didn't. From the moment they cared . . . it was living by the sweat of one's brow [I, 141].

If he cannot telegraph to Woollett an adequate "explanation" of what he has seen, his very puritan ethic of "living by the sweat of one's brow" does issue forth in his collaring Chad immediately after the play and at the height of his own astonishment and discomposure blurting out: " 'I've come, you know, to make you break with everything, neither more nor less, and take you straight home; so you'll be so good as immediately and favorably to consider it!' "[I, 147]. But such a rapid-fire expression of a viewpoint and a mission actually held and undertaken is itself the present index of Strether's "remoulding" process by his experience, the reconstructing of his "whole world up to that date." For he finds Chad "an absolutely *new* quantity," a man "made over," a possible "specialty of Paris"; the old Chad was "rough," the new Chad "actually smooth"; and in the smoothness somehow "marked out by women" and an "irreducible young Pagan" [I, 150, 152, 153, 156]. But then this "Pagan" (like the "Jewel" of Paris) most iridescently expresses himself like the "gentleman" he looks, simply by asking, with mixed amusement and disgust, if Woollett thinks " 'one's kept only by women?' " and adding, to Strether's discomfiture: " 'I must say then you show a low mind!' " Hence, for poor Strether:

It was a dig that, administered by himself [i.e., as he might have, having seen Chad's tasteful rooms and amiable friends]—and administered even to poor Mrs. Newsome—was no more than salutary; but administered by Chad—and quite logically—it came nearer drawing blood. They *hadn't* a low mind—nor any approach to one; yet incontestably they had worked, and with a certain smugness, on a basis that might be turned against them. . . . There was no doubt Woollett *had* insisted on his coarseness; and what he at present stood there for in the sleeping street was, by his manner of striking the other note, to make of such insistence a preoccupation compromising to the insisters. It was exactly as if they had imputed to him a vulgarity that he had by a mere gesture caused to fall from him. The devil of the case was that Strether felt it, by the same stroke, as falling straight upon himself. He had been wondering a minute ago if the boy weren't a Pagan, and he found himself wondering now if he weren't by chance a gentleman. . . . What it accordingly amounted to for [Strether] was that he had to take full in the face a fresh attribution of ignorance [I, 159, 160-61].

It is ultimately this willingness to take things "full in the face" that defines Strether's pragmatism and ethical sensibility. And it is James as "Jourdain" that provides both the comedy and operative irony of Strether's affair. That Strether can be duped bespeaks his pragmatic openness and his idealism, but the particular terms of his dupery bespeak James's as "Jourdain." Strether, responding to the new Chad, "was at this period again and again thrown back on a felt need to remodel somehow his plan" [I, 165]. And James, requiring one more element to make his hero's *volte-face* with respect to Chad full in its artistic "roundness" provides it with Little Bilham's assertion that Chad's involvement with his Parisian lady is a "virtuous attachment" [I, 180]. This gives Strether the link and clue his sensibility requires, for it is the only way he can reconcile the new Chad, on the one hand, with the young man's own insistence that he is free to stay or leave for home, or, on the other, with Miss Gostrey's and Little Bilham's contradictory assertions that Chad is *not* free in his involvement. If the "attachment" in other words is "virtuous" (i.e., not sexual in nature), then Chad's declaration of freedom combined with his transformation, and combined also with Gostrey's and Bilham's countercontention—all come together for Strether. For it is a composition of elements that bespeaks Strether's own character: his own sense of freedom felt both positively and negatively by his commitment to duty and to virtue, and his aesthetic and cultural propensities nourished and defined by such moral criteria. Strether, like Fleda Vetch before him, has "used" Chad generously by subsuming his own best and present values into him.[16]

What makes *The Ambassadors* correspond in its "roundness" to the jewel metaphor, "all surface . . . all depth," is that Strether will proceed to take this reconstructed and "remodeled" view of Chad into the successive phases of his European adventure: he will have it during the famous scene in Gloriani's garden when he utters the famous germ passage, " 'Live all you can' " [I, 217]; he will find what he feels is the very foundation for it when he meets and repeats the same "transforming" process respecting the person of Mme. de Vionnet; he will insist upon it to Sarah Pocock when Mrs. Newsome sends over her next wave of ambassadors to recoup the vagrancy of her first. And it will come full circle in its "superior roundness" when Strether ultimately discovers in the famous recognition scene that Chad and Mme. de Vionnet are sexually intimate, and that Chad's initial claim of freedom to leave was in all likelihood the initial "germ" of his willingness to disassociate himself from the lady responsible for the "transformation"!

The recognition of the couple's sexual intimacy at the Cheval Blanc, which Strether, as always, is compelled to take "full in the face," engenders in regard to Chad Strether's reconstructing of his own reconstruction—again, significantly, on the basis of what is empirically presented. Once again a high point of James's use of playacting and performance, Strether perceives, among other things, that Chad simply sits by and contributes next to nothing while Mme. de Vionnet fabricates a story of the two coming out for the day, as if they were not spending the night together at a quiet retreat. What this in turn communicates to Strether is that Chad "could let her know he left it to her. He habitually left things to others, as Strether was so well aware, and it in fact came over our friend . . . that there had been as yet no such vivid illustration of his famous knowing how to live" [II, 264]. That is, Strether perceives a parallel between Chad's diffidence and lack of participation in the make-believe story to his increased willingness, especially since the arrival of Sarah Pocock, to leave the whole dispute to Strether's own handling. Hence it shows as a "vivid illustration" of the young man's "knowing how to live," because it demonstrates anew that his entire transformation with its great quantity of expertness and sophistication has always required for its real implementation, so to speak, the active response and embroidery of Strether's own imagination. My point is that, although it is obviously true that Strether's famous epiphany means, as one critic has recently said, "his vision of Chad darkens,"[17] it is important both for our grasp of his character and for our understanding of James as "Jourdain" to remember that even at the cutting edge of Strether's surprise and/or "disillusionment" his "way of thinking" remains intact. This re-reconstruction of Chad continues when, responding to Madame de Vionnet's summons, and surmising her imminent despair at Chad's emergent disaffiliation, Strether reflects:

[S]he had but made Chad what he was—so why could she think she had made him infinite? She had made him better, she had made him best, she had made him anything one would; but it came to our friend with supreme queerness that he was none the less only Chad. Strether had the sense that *he*, a little, had made him too; his high appreciation had, as it were, consecrated her work. The work, however admirable, was nevertheless of the strict human order, and in short it was marvelous that . . . [Chad] should be so transcendently prized [II, 284-85].

That this is no more than just, and not merely Strether's sour grapes or tragic disillusionment, is fully verified by James's last element in the fabric of Strether's re-reconstruction of Chad, the young man's decision to embrace the "great new force" of "advertisement." The two men are standing under a street lamp, thereby reenacting that first night after the play at the *Comédie de Française*:

"[Advertising] really does the thing, you know."

. . . "Affects, you mean, [says Strether most disconcertingly] the sale of the object advertised?"

"Yes—but affects it extraordinarily; really beyond what one had supposed. I mean of course when it's done as one makes out that, in our roaring age, it *can* be done. . . . It's an art like another, and infinite like all the arts. . . . In the hands, naturally, of a master. The right man must take hold. With the right man to work it *c'est un monde*" [II, 315-16].

"*C'est un monde*"—indeed poor Strether's "whole world" is "remoulded" again as James brings his hero full circle in the novel's "superior roundness." Chad has completely fulfilled the metaphor of the "iridescent object," the "jewel brilliant and hard," but only with Strether's help. Chad's transformation now appears a quintessential case of masterful proto-advertising, accomplished with Strether's own active participation, his tribute to the "virtuous attachment." Chad has proved his mettle at the new art he espouses by selling Strether so completely that he has just now been pressing the young man, " 'You'll be a brute, you know—you'll be guilty of the last infamy—if you ever forsake [Mme. de Vionnet]' "; and again: " 'You'd not only be, as I say, a brute, you'd be . . . a criminal of the deepest dye' " [II, 308, 311]! This is the strongest language he has yet employed with him, rivaled only by his earlier and opposite, " 'I've come, you know, to make you break with everything.' " As we have seen, Chad's response earlier was to accuse Woollett and Strether of low-mindedness; his response now is the above encomium to advertising. Strether's earlier perception that Chad's transformation might be "a specialty of Paris" can now have for the reader the most unlikely and resonating implications. "Jourdain" has thus made "transitional" the terms of the whole issue, thoroughly "unstiffened" the meaning of Chad's transformation, the same literally returning as the different. Strether as pragmat*ist* has genuinely rejected Woollett's a priori injunctions in his conversion; but James himself, once again, has been able to show that the value of Woollett's injunctions, like those of Walter Besant, lies wholly in the meaning one attaches to them.

Woollett has been wrong for the right reasons, Strether right for the wrong reasons—and James supremely cordial and conjunctive at rendering the terms of the one as the terms of the other.

But if Chad's change has been a Paris "specialty," the primary source of that change, and Strether's imputed embodiment of Parisian civilization and history, comes to be Mme. de Vionnet. His response to her is a recapitulation of his response to Chad. It differs of course in that there has been no prior relationship, but there is the a priori assumption of a "base, venal" woman which serves equally well [I, 55]. There is also the distinction that, once he is surprised and captivated by her, as well as by her lovely and innocent daughter, it serves for him as the pragmatic ongoing extension of his previously accomplished reconstruction of Chad himself culminating in the "virtuous attachment." Mme. de Vionnet, in other words, provides for Strether the incarnation of the phrase and the "proof" for him that his interpretation of it must be the correct one.

The very process of Strether's next and ultimately strongest of his new allegiances shows again how inexhaustible is "Jourdain's" reality of the same returning as the different in "superior roundness." For in this case his initial response to the lady contrasts with the immediate astonishment we have seen at the new Chad by being more restrained and unobtrusive, an indication that it will be ultimately more substantive. He feels Mme. de Vionnet's "common humanity. She did come out, and certainly to his relief, but she came out as the usual thing."

There might be motives behind, but so could there often be even at Woollett. The only thing was that if she showed him she wished to like him—as the motives behind might conceivably prompt—it would possibly have been more thrilling for him that she should have shown as more vividly alien. Ah she was neither Turk nor Pole!—which would be indeed flat once more for Mrs. Newsome and Mrs. Pocock [I, 213-14].

It is instead Chad who has shown as "vividly alien" to Strether's expectations. At the same time, as this passage hints, there is to Strether's series of responses to Mme. de Vionnet a constant recurring to Woollett, and to Mrs. Newsome in particular, for comparison and evaluation. It shows for his ubiquitous "burden of conscience," his "living by the sweat of one's brow," James's serene command of his hero's "gropings." Thus, he decides that the lady, "oh incontestably, yes—*differed* less; differed, that is, scarcely at all—well, superficially speaking, from Mrs. Newsome or even from Mrs. Pocock. She was ever so much younger than the one and not so young as the other; but what *was* there in her, if anything, that would have made it impossible he should meet her at Woollett?" [I, 212-13].

What, indeed! The final answer to that question is, like so many others asked in the text, the entire European experience of Strether and the novel's own "roundness," a pattern intact from "Strether's first question"—the opening words of the book. The more immediate answer is above all else Mme. de Vionnet's organic extension of an entire complex of cultural values "vividly alien" from those of Mrs. Newsome and Woollett. Strether's educative process in this direction will make up the subsequent phases of the novel. But what adds to the already rich complications of his "gropings" at this point is his sharp perception, when first introduced to her in the midst of the free, sensuous, and expert crowd surrounding the sculptor Gloriani, that *she* at least precludes "with the others, any freedom used about her. It was upon him at a touch that she was no subject for that" [I, 210]. Hence his train of associations presumably linking her with Mrs. Newsome and Mrs. Pocock, as though on his puritan side he has discovered in her a temporary relief from the hint of moral wilderness present in the ambivalently attractive "assault of images," where there seems to him " 'so much visual sense that you've somehow all "run" to it' " [I, 196, 206]! Thus James's proceeding and accretive irony—not because Mme. de Vionnet is actually immoral, but because the terms of her virtuousness no less than the respect treated her are of course totally other than the train of associations she here evokes for him. Such irony is unending and circular, like the book itself, inasmuch as the specific context for these evaluations is that she fulfills in a pleasant way for Strether the *"femme du monde."*

But Strether's increased association with the lady is marked by his quick realization that any comparison of her with his Woollett ladies is false indeed. In looking back at his re-appraisal of Chad, followed by his introduction to Mme. de Vionnet, then, we can see how James has had them begin from opposing directions only to make them function, as I have said, on a single linear plane to extend and verify for Strether the interpretation given by him to the "virtuous attachment." If Chad bespoke a new refinement, Marie de Vionnet evokes the cultural roots of the transformation. Even her unfortunate marital situation, her husband a "polished impertinent reprobate," is for Strether first and foremost a matter of "history" [I, 229]. Most compelling of all in this regard are her quarters in the Fauberg St. Germain, which tell him of "possessions not vulgarly numerous, but hereditary cherished charming," of "old accumulations" the reverse of "any contemporary method of acquisition," of "the spell of transmission," and "the air of supreme respectability" [I, 244, 245]. These rich associations, the complement of her personal charm and manner, give her an attractiveness for him well beyond that of Miss Gostrey, his European confidante and up to now the first woman to have put Mrs. Newsome in a less attractive light. In contrast to Miss Gostrey's "museum of bargains" in her rooms, Mme. de Vionnet's possessions are "objects she or her predecessors might even conceivably have parted with under need, but Strether couldn't suspect them of having sold old pieces to get 'better' ones" [I, 244-45]. In short:

At the back of his head, behind everything, was the sense that she was —there, before him, close to him, in vivid imperative form—one of the rare women he had so often heard of, read of, thought of, but never met, whose very presence, look, voice, the mere contemporaneous *fact* of whom, from the moment it was at all presented, made a relation of mere recognition [I, 252].

Some measure of Mme. de Vionnet's greater attractiveness for Strether than Maria Gostrey (in addition to his own comparisons frequently given during this period) can be seen if we merely recollect Strether's " 'You're the very deuce' " to the American lady shortly after encountering her and responding to her sophisticated knowledge of things [I, 67]. One could never imagine him responding to Mme. de Vionnet in such language. Strether's enormously warm view of Chad's friend determines his conclusion that " 'She keeps *him* up—she keeps the whole thing up. . . . She has simply given [Chad] an immense moral lift' " [I, 283-84]. Such language of morality, while it is appropriate to Strether's puritan sensibility, and while in James's proceeding irony it bespeaks his inability to entertain the possibility of a sexual relationship, is, as always, at one in Strether's mind with his aesthetic response. For Marie de Vionnet as no one else embodies for him his own earlier promises and response to the "higher culture." In a scene that clearly anticipates the famous recognition scene late in the book, Strether accidentally encounters her at Notre Dame, the effect of which is to solidify his view and interpretation of her virtue, the scene thereby relating to the later more famous one through "Jourdain's" reality of the same as different. Just before recognizing her, he perceives a lady in prayer as "one of the familiar, the intimate . . . for whom these dealings had a method and a meaning," language unmistakably adumbrating that of the couple in the boat, just prior to recognition, as "expert, familiar, frequent" [II, 6, 256]. Such yoking of the sacred and profane is of course basic to Strether's European initiation, but in Notre Dame the encounter serves, again empirically, to convince him that someone who frequents her church in this fashion is hardly going to be anything but "unassailably innocent." The much-discussed luncheon on the quay with her shortly after this chance encounter at the cathedral exists itself in a sacred-profane relationship with the previous scene, and is one of the high points of Strether's conversion to the "agreeable and the sensible" which is Europe. The warm, human, and sensual quality of this luncheon has been much noted, and Strether himself reflects that he has "travelled far since that evening in London, before the theatre, when his dinner with Maria Gostrey . . . had struck him as requiring so many explanations."

He had at that time gathered them in, the explanations . . . but it was at present as if he had either soared above or sunk below them—he couldn't tell which; he could somehow think of none that didn't seem to leave the appearance of collapse and cynicism easier for him than lucidity. How could he wish it to be lucid for others, for any one, that he, for the hour, saw reasons enough in the mere way the bright clean ordered waterside life came in at the open window?—the mere way Madame de Vionnet, opposite him over their intensely white table-linen, their *omelette aux tomates*, their bottle of straw-coloured Chablis, thanked him for everything almost with the smile of a child, while her grey eyes moved in and out of their talk, back to the quarter of the warm spring air, in which early summer had already begun to throb, and then back again to his face and their human questions [II, 13-14].

That this moment represents in a sense the high point of Strether's conversion, and exists (to recall Emily Dickinson's words) "Between the Heaves of Storm," is suggested among other things by the fact that in the very next chapter Chad will announce to Strether his willingness to leave, thereby introducing a series of re-complications which will in turn carry into Sarah Pocock's arrival, and eventually take Strether away (he thinks) from the embroilment to rural France—and to the boat scene. But what makes this moment itself so "confluent" in the ambulatory process of "Jourdain's" book with all that precedes and succeeds it is that even—or particularly—here Strether, we note, is again finding "explanations" impossible. His wonder at having either "soared above" or "sunk below" them reinforces our sense of his still living by the sweat of his brow, while it likewise epitomizes an episode which structurally "hinges" together the halves of the book. Similarly, Strether's very reason for being here with her simply cannot be separated from the "moral" impression just given him at the cathedral. Again, his thinking now of the earlier dinner with Maria Gostrey functions—as that dinner at its time did—to reaffirm Strether's inescapable need to re-evaluate morally as well as aesthetically. If he *is* "Between the Heaves of Storm," in other words, that "between" territory like William's "bridge of intermediaries" is connected and conjoined with the storm, not disjoined from it. Thus Strether's unforgettable luncheon, his appreciation of the simple sensuous joy of a Parisian meal with a woman whose thankful "smile of a child" communicates to the reader and to James's hero her sensual vitality, is no "moral holiday" for poor Strether—as the language and syntax of the passage above clearly demonstrates.

What this means is that Strether's important allegiance to Mme. de Vionnet in the novel, his promise to her to "save you if I can" [I, 255], her "publicly [drawing] him into her boat" at Sarah's arrival [II, 94], and his final affirmation of her is the recapitulation and extension of his active response to Chad's transformation. For that reason it, too, has the same "all surface . . . all depth" complication and unstiffening—the "all an innocence . . . all an art" parallel which was noted earlier. Hence, when he does eventually have his famous Cheval Blanc epiphany, his re-reconstruction of *her* occurs no less than with Chad, with the added factor that, just as he has understood her to be the source of Chad's transformation, her transforming agency itself must then be pragmatically evaluated on a continuing basis—and that must include Chad's ultimate "advertising" superficiality. This is not to say, however, that Strether's re-reconstruction of her makes her for him identical to Chad. To assume that would be, precisely, saltatory and monistic thinking. She is the one, as we have seen, who must fabricate to Strether in their chance encounter, for she is the one who has always done all the giving.[18] While it is true, then, that "the quantity of make-believe involved and so vividly exemplified" is what "most disagreed with his spiritual stomach" [II, 265], the burden of such "disagreement" is, for Strether, on Lambert Strether himself, and not on the couple as such. What makes Strether remain a pragmatist to the very end, in other words, and the novel complete in its "superior roundness," is that Strether is compelled to account as empirically real both the make-up of his own re-introduction to his "spiritual stomach" while simultaneously affirming, as in his final interview with Mme. de Vionnet, that "once more and yet once more, he could trust her. That is he could trust her to make deception right. As she presented things the ugliness—goodness knew why—went out of them" [II, 277]. The conjunction of this with Strether's "spiritual stomach" bespeaks again a mediated view to which the reader must positively respond in its plurality, or, put epistemologically, in its "in-between" territory.

Similarly, Strether is not prevented from recognizing that "their eminent 'lie,' Chad's and hers, was simply after all such an inevitable tribute to good taste as he couldn't have wished them not to render" [II, 277].[19] This pragmatic cordiality to multiple meaning and awareness does not prevent his perception that within the couple's corporate good taste "Chad had, as usual, let her have her way [i.e., in sending for Strether]. Chad was always letting people have their way when he felt that it would somehow turn his wheel for him" [II, 278]. The justice of this we have already seen. Strether's pragmatism even rises to a "Jourdain"-like level in his humorous sense, given all his previous assumptions, that it shows for "the general spectacle of his art and his innocence, almost an added link and certainly a common priceless ground for [himself and Mme. de Vionnet] to meet upon" [II, 278].

So in speaking of Strether's last re-reconstruction of Mme. de Vionnet at the end, it hardly means his repudiation of her and the values and associations she has come to represent for him. It *does* mean his inevitable re-definition of those very values and associations in the light of his most recent empirical knowledge: her sexual tie to Chad, Chad's rapid disinterest in her, his own "spiritual stomach," and the exploitative possibilities attending Chad's new vocation. The positive plural expression of such diverse elements is precisely what we get in Strether's last associations of her historical embodiment of Paris as now the troubled "days and nights of revolution. . . . the smell of the public temper—or perhaps simply the smell of blood" [II, 274]. Such intimations are borne out by the sight of her pain:

She was older for him to-night, visibly less exempt from the touch of time; but she was as much as ever the finest and subtlest creature, the happiest apparition, it had been given him, in all his years, to meet; and yet he could see her there as vulgarly troubled, in very truth, as a maidservant crying for her young man. The only thing was that she judged herself as the maidservant wouldn't; the weakness of which wisdom too, the dishonour of which judgement, seemed but to sink her lower [II, 286].

The strong language he will use with Chad in their final interview we have already seen. Strether genuinely affirms Mme. de Vionnet in the fullness of his experience in a way that, given the pragmatic evidence, he cannot affirm Chad. At the same time, inasmuch as her transforming powers have only made Chad what he is, Strether's previous evaluation of her powers is to that extent modified.[20] Put positively, her own powers in conjunction with the cultural viewpoint they represent have had a lasting effect on Strether himself, have produced in him an unforgettable response to a whole way of life previously unappreciated or else interrupted after its beginnings many years ago with his first trip to Europe—whichever way we prefer to put it. As he tells Maria Gostrey at the end, like the pragmatist he is, " 'I shall see what I can make of it' " [II, 325].

The fact that the book begins, "Strether's first question," and ends, " 'Then there we are,' " points by itself to the extent to which James has kept to William's world of the ongoing given and apparent. Strether's unusual parallel with his author's "way of thinking" even results in frequent passages that literally amount to William's doctrine as such. For example, when determining in his mind the quality of Chad's " 'high fine friendship' " with Mme. de Vionnet, he remarks, " 'as to *how* it has so wonderfully worked—isn't a thing I pretend to understand. I've to take it as I find it' " [I, 280, 281]. As always James's operative irony is intact here: Strether must indeed eventually "take it as he finds it," including the sexual intimacy. But his very viewpoint here is what will always enable him to readjust. The most striking of all of his "doctrinal" statements of William's viewpoint is the rejoinder he makes to the angry accusations about his conduct by Sarah Pocock:

"I don't think there's anything I've done in any such calculated way as you describe. Everything has come as a sort of indistinguishable part of everything else. Your coming out belonged closely to my having come before you, and my having come was a result of our general state of mind. Our general state of mind has proceeded, on its side, from our queer ignorance, our queer misconceptions and confusions—from which, since then, an inexorable tide of light seems to have floated us into our perhaps still queerer knowledge" [II, 200-201].

This passage literally brings us to the nexus of William's pluralistic universe, the ambulatory relationship of next-to-next, the confluently related elements of experience, in which one simply must not distinguish where one cannot empirically divide. The passage is also pragmatic of course in the attitude taken toward a priori preconceptions, but that is comparatively minor, in this instance, at least, to its positive expression of William's coalescing process-reality; the "queer ignorance," for example, literally conjoined and coordinated syntactically with the "perhaps still queerer knowledge," and expressed through the inevitable water imagery. But this is only to say that Strether's statement here recapitulates the process and the rendered felt world of "Jourdain's" book.

Strether's statement, inasmuch as it does take us to the heart of William James's ambulatory relations and principle of unity through felt confluence, can likewise serve to bring us to the threshold of Henry's polarity—that point at which we "peer inside" William's unity to discover Henry's Coleridgean imagination. To the reader who has followed the argument of this study it must be clear that my foregoing discussion of *The Ambassadors* implies (and I expect also reveals) two things: first, that a *full* pragmatistic approach to the novel would be literally endless in its circularity and "roundness," revolving without halting, like the world of process it explicates, or like the "old clock at Berne" that Strether images at the end [II, 322]; second, that the very terms of "Jourdain's" continuing irony, his relationship of same and different, his conjunction of Strether's aesthetic and moral sensibility, his rendering of surface and depth, innocence and art, and any number of such "contraries" permeating the novel—ultimately bespeak the inner presence of polarity as its ultimate unifying principle. For *The Ambassadors* is clearly a novel in which James's empiricized polarity is commandingly at work, ultimately the source for its perfection of form and the organic relationship of that form to its vision. It is in short a work of artistic genius and the creative imagination. For this reason perhaps a discussion of *The Ambassadors* is the place at which some further remarks pertaining to James's polarity are in order, if only to add some light both to the fine critical attention the book has received as well as to one problem it seems to have raised in this same critical literature.

Polarity, let me say once again, differs from dichotomy by virtue of involving interpenetration rather than juxtaposition. It is a life-endowing relationship through opposition and, according to Coleridge anyway, the fundamental source and principle of life itself. However we may view Coleridge's conclusion about the latter, his view of its aesthetic domain needs no defense. The important point, rather, is our grasp of the polar relationship itself in its positive—or again life-endowing—quality even if we prefer to call it "tension" or "paradox" rather than polarity. One of the implications of genuine polarity is that, even when one pole, or its opposite, is predominating at a particular time and place (for perfect equilibrium is not the constant state of things), it is at such a time fully dependent on its opposite pole to *be* predominating—which is precisely the time when most of us are likely not to fully appreciate that we have an interpenetrating relationship in the first place, and are thereby tempted toward one "side" or the other—to think more along the lines of dichotomy.

In *The Ambassadors*, then, genuine polarity occurs in the first place in the relationship between what Strether brings with him across the ocean and what he discovers during his adventure in Europe. This is why, for instance, his given aesthetic requirements, his feelings of guilt and responsibility over his lost son, his sense of a lost youth, and his imaginativeness are all matters that get themselves defined and affirmed only by response to everything about Paris, Chad, and Mme. de Vionnet which is "new," unexpected, or "different." His natural affiliation with Little Bilham, who is really a young Strether who did not return in his youth to America, and who becomes Strether's teacher in the new definition of "virtue," has its source, too, in polarity; just as it is also Little Bilham who is the recipient of Strether's impassioned "Live!" speech and, conversely again, the young man who tells Strether *he* really preferred the "old Chad"—i.e., the Chad who first arrived in Paris before being transformed. James the empiricist does not, as I have pointed out before, tend to express himself *ideologically* in terms of polarity; but there are occasions where he comes close to doing so. One instance in particular is an early hint to the reader of the fundamental quality of Strether's character and therefore the complications that await him:

That he was prepared to be vague to Waymarsh about the hour of the ship's touching, and that he both wanted extremely to see him and enjoyed extremely the duration of delay—these things, it is to be conceived, were early signs in him that his relation to his actual errand might prove none of the simplest. He was burdened, poor Strether—it had better be confessed at the outset—with the oddity of a double consciousness. There was detachment in his zeal and curiosity in his indifference [I, 5].

It is the last sentence here that expresses the polar relationship as such. But, as such, it simply comes closer than usual to naming the relationship that is fundamental to the novel's aesthetic unity, as before the "jewel" image and similar expressions come closer than usual to naming the novel's rendered and felt reality. With respect to the "jewel" image itself, it, too, referred now to its ultimate unifying principle, derives from the polarity between Henry's same and different. Similarly, Strether's astonished appraisal of Chad in the theatre box as a "sharp rupture of an identity," when understood, simultaneously, as the copestone of his concatening responses since landing to "the elements of Appearance," relates through polarity. Likewise the opposing directions of his initial evaluations of Chad and Mme. de Vionnet that yet simultaneously affirm, reinforce, and extend his view of their relationship. In short, everything we have already seen that is "Jamesian" in its ambulation ultimately refers itself to and unifies within through a vast network of polarity.

This vast network expands exponentially to a number of larger issues naturally raised by the book and accounts for their aesthetic integrity in treatment and vision. The relationship between innocence and experience is grasped and rendered as polar in this book, as well as its cognate, that between the moral and aesthetic. The international subject of America and Europe, which is correlative to them both, relates through polarity: they all exist simultaneously by virtue of each other as well as at each other's expense. Because of this they can literally transform into each other, back and forth, which they do within and through the unifying medium of Strether. At the same time, the representatives of James's polarity at its international level considered momentarily apart from Strether himself—Mrs. Newsome and Sarah Pocock on the one hand, Mme. de Vionnet on the other— do not relate in polarity; that is, as characters in and of themselves they really *do* juxtapose in clashing dichotomy (or are "polarities" in the way the word is usually meant!). But as representatives within James's encompassing international vision in *The Ambassadors*, these same ladies participate in its international polarity. My only reason for stressing this is that it is obvious to any and all readers that Mme. de Vionnet emerges as far more preferable to Strether and to the reader than Mrs. Newsome or Sarah. And what this bespeaks in the larger polarity in which they participate is that *The Ambassadors* in its international theme is a case in James of the European pole "predominating" over its new world opposite, more so than in either of the successive novels of the major phase, *The Wings of the Dove* and *The Golden Bowl*. But this is precisely when we must keep hold of the nature of polarity itself, as I have just indicated before, when we do have a particular case of predominance. The international theme in this book is the initiation and positive response to Europe. But this very predominance of the European pole never ceases to require its new world opposite to sustain it. That is why the particular New England quality of Strether's response to Europe is indispensable to the book's comedy and irony, and ultimately its artistic integrity of form and vision. And it is also why Strether's decision to return home at the end is both appropriate and inevitable.

Another major polarity in *The Ambassadors* is that of freedom and determinism. Strether's celebrated "illusion of freedom" speech in Gloriani's garden was discussed in an earlier chapter with William's doctrine; and the same equation between the brothers can be quickly recalled in the echo of Strether's encompassing image of the "tin mould" with William's "remoulding experience" passage much quoted in this chapter. But with regard to this same issue, if we move downward from its pragmatistic expression at the level of felt life and refer it to the domain of James's aesthetic unity, the "Jamesian" mediation between freedom and determinism too has its source in polarity. Strether's new "consciousness of personal freedom as he hadn't known for years" [I, 4] at his arrival in Europe depends for its existence and meaning on his character as irrevocably "set" in a certain way. Similarly "the illusion of freedom" operative in the novel's unity is a condition shown to be both positive and negative in character, and related through polarity. Strether himself almost feels it in this sense in his speech to Little Bilham, but he expresses the relationship between these poles as coordinate and mediating, which is most appropriate for a "Jourdain" character who is also a pragmatist. But polarity is what is ultimately *doing* the mediating, *doing* the coordinating. The illusion of freedom is most positive in its capacity to entertain alternatives, respond to new impressions, and choose new allegiances—all of which Strether does. It is negative in that the very quality of such alternative-taking, such responsiveness, and such choice reaffirms what is predetermined in Strether's make-up.

There are also, of course, "outside" determinations, which range from Chad's early strategy of appearance, to Mrs. Newsome's second group of ambassadors, to the "chance" discoveries of Mme. de Vionnet at Notre Dame and then, most dramatically, of Chad and Mme. de Vionnet at the Cheval Blanc. Such "outside" determinations also exist in a reciprocal relationship with Strether's character and ultimately have their source in James's network of polarity. The arrival of the Pococks, for example, serves among other things to redirect Strether's energies so to speak in favor of his conversion, for the news he now receives from Mme. de Vionnet that she and Chad have arranged for the marriage of her daughter Jeanne has disturbing intimations for him of exploitation and insensitivity at variance with his own elevated view and interpretation of their relationship. Sarah's antagonism and evocation of her mother serve to check such disturbing intimations on the other side, while at the same time these same intimations clearly intensify Strether's apprehension that the Pococks see only " 'the same old Chad they've been for the last three years glowering at across the sea' " [II, 111]. In the case of the two chance meetings at Notre Dame and Cheval Blanc, we have already seen how they parallel while giving off opposite meaning for Strether. Still another polarity involved in them is that both trips are made with the expectation of a temporary respite from "the obsession of his problem" [II, 3] and of course take him in both cases to the heart of it. *The Ambassadors*'s network of polarity involving innocence and experience, moral and aesthetic values, America and Europe, and freedom and determinism is also correlative to the polarity of nature and art. The Cheval Blanc episode recapitulates this entire network by virtue of presenting itself as an extraordinary case of the nature-art polarity. James's commentators have pointed with admiration to his handling of Strether's walk through the French rural countryside as a trek "inside" a Lambinet painting he had wished to buy years ago in Boston and could not afford, and of the artistic landscape of the quiet river into which the boat of Chad and Mme. de Vionnet floats. James's creative imagination, his commanding expression of polarity, is most striking here in that everything about the episode articulated and rendered as "art" serves to conspire in the discovery of Chad and Mme. de Vionnet's sexual relationship, the fundamental requirement and expression of nature. Strether's warm aesthetic response to the scenery reaches its apotheosis in his sight of the boat—"What he saw was exactly the right thing" [II, 256]—which then throws into light his puritan morality. Strether's appreciation of the old world artist Lambinet, itself first engendered in the new world, and then given incarnate life back in the old world (the same polarity coming from the other direction), finally culminates in his sharp rediscovery of his new world ethical presuppositions. Strether's last major initiation from prior innocence to experience is the condition of his rediscovery of present innocence, itself the terminus of the whole experience-acquiring process which has led him to this appointed time and place. Strether's unforgetting memory of the high cost of art in Tremont Street has generated his appreciation for its now being "free" in his walk, the Lambinet "frame . . . drawn itself out for him, as much as you please" [II, 252]—all in the very process of defining once again the high cost for him of a "Lambinet."

Such an extraordinary case of James's aesthetic unity through polarity is nevertheless "only a supreme illustration of the general plan"—to quote James on Isabel Archer's recognition scene in *The Portrait of a Lady*.[21] What is most important, again, is our grasp of what polarity actually is and means. There is now increasingly strong and persuasive critical opinion that expands on F. O. Matthiessen's observation years ago that Strether essentially fails to fulfill his own advice to "live," as well as Philip Rahv's opinion, also of years ago, that James's work reveals both an "ardent search for 'experience,' " and simultaneously a withdrawal or "dread of approaching it in its natural state."[22] Certainly it is true that Strether's two memorable declarations " 'Live all you can; it's a mistake not to," or "Do what you like so long as you don't make *my* mistake. . . . Live!' "; and then: " 'That, you see, is my only logic. Not, out of the whole affair, to have got anything for myself' " [I, 217-18; II, 326]—seem by themselves in dichotomy.[23] Of course Strether's many remarks framing his exhortation to "live" (along the lines of "don't make *my* mistake") suggest that his renunciation at the end is not at such variance with his outbreak in Gloriani's garden. The real issue is not so much Strether here as James himself. The very ties between Strether and his author which make *The Ambassadors*, as Christof Wegelin has said, the story "of the making of an American cosmopolitan" and perhaps a "spiritual autobiography,"[24] could be brought to bear on the possible limitations embedded in and signified by Strether's final retreat from sexuality in the example of Mme. de Vionnet and Chad followed by his renunciation of the proffered love of Maria Gostrey.

In my judgment this issue, if pursued, could take us to the primal and universal level of all polarity—that of activity or energy as such in its relation to thought or form. In James's best work the relationship between "experience" and "imagination," between "living" and "seeing," is a case of genuine polarity in which the latter pole is predominating. Unquestionably in *The Ambassadors* it does predominate, which is perhaps only appropriate in a book whose international theme favors Europe and whose formal excellence is striking even for James. Nevertheless, I would be the first to say that in James generally form or thought is predominating over activity or energy—or is the centripetal force to which his work is to be referred in any universal perspective. My only reply, again, is that we understand what polarity actually is. If James's characteristic predominance in this area leads us to conclude that his work is narrow or thin in its "retreat" from life, we inadvertently repeat the same error, though to a lesser extent, of early readers who denied him any "content." James's predominance in this regard is precisely the occasion when we must recognize the sustaining presence of life or experience for seeing or imagination to *be* predominating—that is, these nonpredominating poles are themselves concentrated at *their* opposites *as* seeing and imagination: for that is what all predominance itself ultimately is, the energy of the nonpredominating pole concentrated at its own opposite. We must appreciate this predominance in James just as much as the generally reverse condition of concentration in, say, Walt Whitman. And we should not lose sight of the fact that all great imaginative literature, including now literature whose characteristic concentration may be quite the reverse of James's, as well as cases of less *degree* of concentration either way, is itself a universal case of energy in polarity with meaning in which meaning predominates. Viewed in this perspective James is simply a case of literature's own natural and universal predominance predominating below on the exponential scale and network—thus our habitual sense of him as the artist's artist, or at least novelist's novelist. Strether's—and James's—"renunciation" is about as life-denying as Whitman's assimilation of the phallic universe into "himself" is thereby a denial of consciousness.

These last remarks come admittedly from my momentarily projecting outward Coleridge's aesthetic view proper toward his larger theory of life; and I recognize that this theory of life will not have the general assent given his aesthetic, despite the fact that the aesthetic itself depends on it.[25] To bring matters back closer to home, to the "Jourdain" relationship, let us recall that Henry's "problem" between living and seeing closely resembles the perennial problem in interpreting William's doctrine. The reader will remember that in *The Meaning of Truth* William reminded his critics that, in construing his pragmatism "an appeal to action" rather than a way of making ideas themselves living and experiential, they "ignore our primary step and its motive, and make the relation to action, which is our secondary achievement, primary."[26] Henry, it would now appear, elicits the same sort of problem in reverse with the "living versus seeing" issue. The very clarification William gives his critics is something Henry's can find too strong and insistent in his work. All of which can serve to remind us of two things: first, the nature of the "Jourdain" relationship between the brothers; second, our necessity in the last analysis to grasp positively how it is possible for fundamental contraries actually *to* reconcile themselves.

We have just seen that *The Ambassadors* is a rare case in James of a novel whose hero shares his author's "way of thinking." But we have likewise seen that this never prevents James his fulfillment of the "Jourdain" relationship over and above his hero's pragmatic mentality, and even at Strether's expense with respect to the novel's proceeding irony and comedy; at the same time, Strether's pragmatic openness makes him a most attractive character, whose "cordiality" gets communicated to the reader as well as to his European associates. It may be of interest, therefore, to consider briefly the situation of John Marcher, hero of James's most famous nouvelle *The Beast in the Jungle* (1903), with Strether still in mind. It can serve in a particular way to remind us that all the exceptionalness surrounding *The Ambassadors* still does not make it *the* William Jamesian piece in his canon by virtue of Strether; that the "Jourdain" relationship this study has endeavored to define and present is always prior even to the creation of a pragmatist like Strether.

To begin with, any inclination we might have to link the two works by their common "theme" of "too late" is precisely our own share in saltatory instead of ambulatory thinking, the inevitable result of which is to overlook—literally "jump over"—what is "Jamesian" in both stories. This is especially true if we think of Strether and Marcher as similar characters. Strether's cordiality, whether we associate it with pragmatism or not, makes him among other things a visibly public man whose interaction with his community is preeminently social and healthy. John Marcher's intense privacy and alienation from his social community is a striking contrast. Yet Strether's social affability in no way prevents him from private and imaginative reflection —who could be more privately reflective and imaginative than

Strether? The social complement is notably absent in Marcher, however, whose "theory, as always," is "that he was lost in the crowd."[27] Marcher, as we come to know him, "wore a mask painted with the social simper, out of the eye-holes of which there looked eyes of an expression not in the least matching the other features. This the stupid world, even after years, had never more than half discovered" [82]. Marcher's entire "community" is of course May Bartram, and, as all readers of the tale know so well, he only discovers this fact accidentally at the beginning, when she astounds him by declaring to him she knows his obsession. More importantly, as all readers also know so well, Marcher then embarks on his career of killing her by inches, so that, for example, at her funeral he is as completely unknown by and alienated from her family and relatives as from the rest of the "stupid world." Among our many ways of viewing James's famous tale could be that of its showing how a man totally cut off from the rest of the world proceeds carefully to eliminate the only person who strays into his private universe, thereby reestablishing its pristine emptiness once again.

But I certainly do not mean to imply that the great majority of James's commentators would deny the significant difference between Marcher and Strether. Even a negative view of Strether's renunciation would never have the appalling implications of Marcher's "sacrifice" of May Bartram. In fact my interest here for the brief point I wish to make is perhaps less with Marcher himself, whose condition has engendered outstanding commentary befitting the tale's perennially haunting quality, than with establishing again the presence of "Jourdain" dealing with a set of fictional requirements altogether different from those that govern *The Ambassadors*.

Considered philosophically, Marcher is the perfect dichotomy (yes, dichotomy) to Strether's pragmatic openness of mind. Marcher is a supreme illustration in James, to recall again T. S. Eliot's famous remark, of a mind "violated" by an "Idea." He is therefore an epitome of William's philosophical opponents: a priori, monistic, intellectualist—someone for whom immediate experience or novelty does not "count" except expressly to reattach and define itself to his preconception, his pristine "Idea." The Idea is his celebrated conviction that he has been marked out and "kept for something rare and strange, possibly prodigious and terrible," that is "sooner or later to happen" to him [71]. What makes him the supreme case of the intellectualist is the sheer extent of his monistic *"the* thing"—the phrase and the tenacity of conviction it signifies reappearing throughout the tale. Such a mentality and viewpoint—again, simply viewed philosophically—by definition repudiates the "mere" apparent, the actual, the self-sufficient experience of next-to-next, process itself. Considered as an anti-pragmatist, Marcher appropriately rejects out of hand what might be called the "Rise of Realism," mundane or ordinary, commonplace reality and all its associations; whereas Strether, by contrast, is the sort who invests it with elaborate possibilities of meaning and "remoulds" it again and again as it keeps coming at him. Marcher's typical anti-"Rise of Realism" propensity is his wish, for instance, that he had done something extraordinary for May in the past, "saved her from a capsized boat," or "recovered her dressing-bag, filched from her cab in the streets of Naples by a lazzarone with a stiletto" [66]. Such reflections, though they sound harmless enough in themselves, proceed in his case from the most fundamental disregard for and disinterest in the "usual" thing, including even the "common doom" of human love and death. Marcher's obsession in its prescriptive absolutism and monism can have no truck with the Realist's "lesser" or "local" world as in itself of value and appreciation.

But here again, Marcher's violation by an Idea is just the condition and occasion of his author's characteristic refusal to be so violated and determines "Jourdain's" mode of presentation. *The Beast in the Jungle* is finally pragmatistic not on account of Marcher's anti-pragmatism anymore than *The Ambassadors* on account of Strether's pragmatism, although I do think James's moral evaluation of these two men can be inferred from this. James's *own* task, however, is to take Marcher's Idea and proceed throughout the tale to "unstiffen" it by making it conjoin with every felt moment of next-to-next, make it occur, vis-à-vis William's "steering-function" and "re-direction," in the ongoing experiential process: if William's famous "Truth *happens* to an idea" could be said to refer to any one person's life story, that person would be John Marcher. All of Henry's operative irony *proceeds* on this basis (and grounded within, again, in polarity), that Marcher's own prescribed conviction that he is specially marked for experience becomes the basis by which he can be shown to be having none. "Jourdain" provides the pluralism lacking in his character. It is not that Marcher turns out to be wrong about himself, but right—his special mark does come "round" to his being "the man of his time, *the* man, to whom nothing on earth was to have happened" [125]. What must be stressed here, though, is not just the ironic "upshot" that my last sentence points to, but the operative irony of each and every passage in the tale which is that irony "in the making," as William says of his reality, and Henry's "possible other case."

At one point, for example, Marcher reflects that a personal relationship as close as his and May's should take "the form of their marrying"; but, he opines, since "the basis" of their relationship comes from "her first penetrating question in the autumn light there at Weatherend," consequently "the very basis itself put marrying out of the question" [79]. This is pure "Jourdain" in its circularity and contextual irony. Their personal relationship is what requires marriage, and we naturally condemn Marcher's failure to respond to the love relationship offered him; but then, as he says, "the basis" of their relationship does put marriage out of the question, because the relationship has come about in the first place and defined itself only through his obsession; which obsession, in turn, *is* his incapacity for love or human warmth; the continually dramatic expression of which incapacity is just such typically "careful assessment" as this here. Such assessment itself, we might go on to say, then feeds back into the relationship and nourishes Marcher's self-fulfilling prophecy. All of which is only to say more generally that, if Marcher himself is convinced of a "mysterious fate" in wait for him " 'in the lap of the gods' "[85]—or *dis*joined from himself and without—it is "Jourdain's" task to *con*join Marcher with his fate, to render his character as one and the same *as* his fate. In short, an idea or concept like fate must be "re-directed" in its "steering-function" back into the proceeding experience or felt life it "happens" to. Viewed this way the beast that springs in the tale is not so much any particular point in the story as it is a kind of slow motion spring*ing* that begins with the first line and completes itself with the last.

In a sense it is the ending of this tale that provides the greatest challenge to James as "Jourdain," his decision to give Marcher a true and shattering epiphany. In marked contrast to the ending of *The Ambassadors*, for example, with its empirically open-ended " 'there we are,' " so appropriate to its central character, *The Beast in the Jungle* ends with unusual finality—Marcher's realization of everything followed by his hurling himself on May's tomb. It is significant that, with all the "unreliable" readings of James's characters proliferating in the critical literature, it would never occur to us to question Marcher's epiphany. We might object to James's decision to give him the epiphany, object that the sight of the stranger's face at an adjoining grave is not convincing in its preparation for Marcher's illumination,[28] but not the epiphany itself. And how could we? The unreliability, as we say, has occurred in the story itself, not in Marcher's final discovery of it. It is certainly not my intention to argue that Marcher's illumination is "unreliable"; hopefully my earlier consideration of 'The Real Thing" in particular, as well as my entire argument generally, has expressed my own belief that that whole perspective is by no means the best way to read James. What *is* of interest here, however, is that James as "Jourdain" is required to provide the "roundness" in a situation where everything militates against it: we can hardly expect Marcher the anti-pragmatist to give us that "Jamesian" quality of the prospective and continuing process of things at the end; rather, his mentality and viewpoint call for an absolute or "final" end to things. And that is the kind of ending we do get in the tale, so to speak an anti-pragmatistic one.

Where, then, is "Jourdain" specifically at the tale's conclusion? He is where he always is, seeing his character through. But what that means in Marcher's case is that James makes the quality of Marcher's "reliable" epiphany identical in mode to his whole way and manner of responding to his obsession previously, and even caps it in language of avoidance and retreat:

He saw the Jungle of his life and saw the lurking Beast; then, while he looked, perceived it, as by a stir of the air, rise, huge and hideous, for the leap that was to settle him. His eyes darkened—it was close; and, instinctively turning, in his hallucination, to avoid it, he flung himself, face down, on the tomb [126-27].

A careful reading of Marcher's full realization, beginning with the stranger's "deeply stricken" face, rising in intensity, and culminating in these final sentences, reveals (at least to this reader) that we are in the process of watching Marcher create in the very discovery of his old beast a brand new one in exchange—the sacred memory of May Bartram and his missed opportunity. He lies there in ironic sexual posture on her tomb, which means that when he finally arises to go home, a sadder and wiser man, we can only hope he does not meet another sympathetic lady: for she will have no chance competing with May's memory. Although such speculation obviously goes beyond the tale, its import is only to stress again the tale's own portrayal of Marcher's paralysis and sterility of person, just as speaking of his epiphany as a "brand new" beast only means that he always requires his Idea. Rather, the "brand new" or "novel" part of all this belongs to "Jourdain." How could Marcher love May (or anyone) other than in the tomb? Or why do his travels following her death give him nothing except the sense that his whole "life" is back at her grave, thereby engendering the train of associations and intimations finally released in epiphany on occasion of seeing the stranger? Because John Marcher just *cannot* live in response to any immediate or present experience: May *must* be receding from the present sufficiently into the past for Marcher to begin to have any "throbbing" response to her. Put another way, the very height of Marcher's "thematic" realization that he is "the man of his time, *the* man, to whom nothing was to have happened," has that unmistakably monistic ring and meaning correlative to his paralysis and deep requirement to be someone apart from the world and a nonparticipant in its merely usual affairs. It is remarkable, as I have said, that, despite the innumerable "unreliable" readings of James's pieces, so dependent for the most part on assuming that his own critical remarks about the pieces in question merely "cover up" the real "irony" (or else flatly contradict what is "there"), it would never occur to us to question the reliability of Marcher's epiphany. James himself, on the other hand, goes out of his way in his "Preface" to acknowledge and alert us to the very point about Marcher's realization that I have just argued, and even "grants" that the tale's merit depends on it![29] What this shows, especially in view of this nouvelle's great popularity and the ubiquitous discussion of it, is our own predisposition for saltatory thinking.

When we reflect on Marcher's and Strether's stories and careers, then, we find them as characters epistemologically at odds. Strether is open in the pragmatic way, Marcher is the opposite. Viewed as such they clash in dichotomy. But viewed as participants in two works uniquely "Jamesian" and ultimately unified artistically, they assimilate themselves into "Jourdain's" characteristically rendered reality—his "great negative adventure," as he puts it in Marcher's case[30]—which reality is in turn unified within through polarity. In Strether's story we are struck by the way his full entertaining of alternative possibilities keeps coming back to the same locus. In Marcher's story his refusal to ever consider the "possible other case" is precisely what keeps describing it to us. Strether seems never so right as when wrong. Marcher seems never so wrong as when right.

VIII. Radical Empiricism—
"Beyond the Laboratory Brain":
The Quasi-Supernatural Drift
after The Ambassadors

The word "astonish" in its various inflections has more than once been used in this study to describe the nature of the "Jourdain" relationship. Without apologizing for using it as often as I have, I should like to use it one last time in coming now to a most extraordinary and far-reaching element in the relationship between the work of the two brothers: the fact that their respective life-long odysseys into the domain of human consciousness took them both to its same outer edge poised just short of "com[ing] out on the other side"—to use Henry's language for Strether's situation in his "Project of Novel."[1] The "other side" in this case, however, is one that significantly extends the limits of Strether's world, although it includes his world and can even be said to remain *primarily* within it. This is to say that William and Henry's view of conscious reality brought them gradually to a view of it in regard to its last questions concerning immortality and the soul which is all but identical, if only that the view itself is sufficiently unique as to be literally "Jamesian"—to use the term for once in reference to them both. But pointing out similarities in positions held, even regarding final questions like this one, has not been the principal aim of this study. What is always most important is the application it might have to their work, especially Henry's. To appreciate what this last convergence means and involves, therefore, it will be necessary to consider the particular context it has in their respective careers.

Whoever reflects very long on the quality and character of Henry James's major phase must, I believe, eventually recognize that *The Ambassadors*, his chosen favorite, is a work that can be viewed in relation to the novels and tales preceding and following it in two different ways at once. Perhaps a brief survey of critical attitudes and trends past and present is the best means of clarifying this point. For many years *The Ambassadors* has held the position of initiating the major phase itself, the first in a "trilogy" with *The Wings of the Dove* and *The Golden Bowl*, the three of them linked by their return to his international subject, by their "poetry" or quality as "poetic dramas of the inner life of the soul," and by the increased "spiritual" nature of his late vision.[2] Generally speaking, James's principal commentators during the twenty years or so following F. O. Matthiessen's pioneering study in 1944 emphasized the departure of the three major novels from his work of the "middle" period for the reasons above. The middle period thus understood would be said to include not only such novels as *The Princess Casamassima* and *The Tragic Muse* but also the "experimental" novels of the late 1890s—*The Spoils of Poynton*, *What Maisie Knew*, and *The Awkward Age*—as well as *The Sacred Fount*, written in 1900. Such a perspective unquestionably rests on some very solid and important ground, most especially James's return to the international subject as well as his putting together in the late method and later manner the alternating components of "picture" and "scene" for his dramatic rendering. Furthermore, the period or era of Jacobite scholarship to which I refer, deriving from Matthiessen and Blackmur primarily, has been responsible for giving James's late work the attention and perceptive analysis it merits, the very sort of sympathetic critical engagement James sought during his lifetime, largely without success.

With the inevitable diminishing emphasis on James's international subject (as well as the natural reaction against any prevailing school of critical opinion after a number of years) things have now begun to change: critically speaking, the "trilogy" appears to have broken up or been resolved back into three separate books; the "poetry" or "poetic dramas of the inner life of the soul" is in process of being discarded for features more earthy (or else rejected to the extent James fails to keep to his "own" better earthy features and tendencies); and, perhaps above all else, the "spiritual" in James, particularly if it occurs in conjunction with sacrificial "renunciation," seems en route to becoming the worst possible combination of elements in his work.[3]

All of which is perhaps a long way round, as James would say, to my remarking again that *The Ambassadors* can be viewed in two different ways. There has always been an argument to be made for *The Wings of the Dove* and *The Golden Bowl* constituting a departure from *The Ambassadors* as significant on its side as the three novels together from those, say, of the nineties. Sallie Sears, a critic who belongs to the more recent group of commentators just referred to, says of *The Ambassadors* in relation to its two successors:

> Though James typically is concerned with the *relation* of consciousness to the external human scene, finding in aspects of the latter analogues for the former (or items of special significance to it), the nature of that scene becomes progressively more abstract in each of the last three novels until, in *The Golden Bowl*, the external world has receded as an "interesting" tactile and visual field. . . .
>
> In *The Ambassadors* (completed before but published after *The Wings of the Dove*), . . . the "setting"—though as we have indicated it stands in analogic relation to conflicting aspects of Strether's consciousness—*is* projected in its three-dimensionality and detailed concreteness.[4]

Another recognition of something like a point of departure between *The Ambassadors* and its two successors, though on different grounds, has been noted by Oscar Cargill, whose ties are with the earlier group of Jacobite critics. Referring to *The Wings of the Dove*'s "Wagnerian" facet, Cargill observes:

> Conscious of making his novel match up to the [Tristan] legend, James speaks of himself as a poet and of his composition as a poem in both the book and its Preface—a thing he does nowhere else before this in his fiction or in his self-criticism. It is this consciousness which leads him into the extended metaphors of the book. The ever-present water imagery of the novel, so very differently used from that in *The Ambassadors*, is to put us in mind of Tristan's legend which has more seascapes and sea journeys than any other Arthurian legend.[5]

One very striking critical development which owes, I believe, to the breaking-up of the unified "trilogy" is the willingness now to consider both *The Wings of the Dove* and *The*

Golden Bowl something less than the crowning achievements earlier assumed—to be works less vital and cohesive than, say, *The Awkward Age* or *What Maisie Knew*, or even *The Bostonians*, a novel James did not even choose to include in his New York Edition. Critical disagreement about James's novels is hardly unusual, but there is considerable difference in this newer development from the controversy, for example, that has surrounded *The Turn of the Screw*, or the reliable-unreliable arguments attending individual tales. It involves, in a way these other disagreements do not, an evaluation of the major phase itself, which in turn involves James's own view of the determination and direction of his career. It even involves, in a sense, the New York Edition of his works, insofar as it can be said to express, both in his extensive revisions and the *Prefaces* on which he labored so long and hard, the justification of the late work.

This is admittedly putting it more strongly than the case actually admits of, and there is no question in any event that James himself thought he had succeeded better in *The Ambassadors* and *The Portrait of a Lady* than in either *The Wings of the Dove* or *The Golden Bowl*. Nevertheless, he did believe these last two novels to be among his most important and central contributions, his "advanced course" (as he told the young man from Texas), and the very locus of attempted achievement by which to evaluate, therefore, the excellence of the two novels he did pick as his "all round" best. *The Wings of the Dove* in particular exemplifies this whole question, if only because it has in the past been assessed by James's most knowledgeable and sympathetic examiners as his masterpiece beyond even James's own two choices. How can the book which, according to F. O. Matthiessen, provides us "the essential design" in James's "carpet," constituting "his masterpiece" and thus being "that single work where his characteristic emotional vibration seems deepest and where we have the sense, therefore, that we have come to 'the very soul' "; the book, furthermore, that Oscar Cargill, after reviewing and assimilating all previous scholarship on all James's novels, major and minor, judges to be the greatest achievement in the group; the book, finally, "that many will account James's masterpiece," according to Dorothea Krook[6]—how can such a book be then as seriously flawed as Sallie Sears and now even Leon Edel maintain, or as fundamentally "confused" as Charles

T. Samuels recently declares? The poor *Wings* is even becoming clipped or folded to the extent that a brand new edition of it cannot draw a favorable verdict from its own introducer.[7]

The difficulties posed are precisely those that consort with the changing perspective on the major phase generally. Specifically the "problem" posed by *The Wings of the Dove* centers on two matters essential to James's purpose and theme: first, that Milly Theale, his young American heiress, stricken with illness and then brutally exploited, is nevertheless ultimately a redemptive force in her death and forgiveness; second—and implicated in the first—that Merton Densher, English journalist, lover of Kate Croy and participant with her in the exploitation of Milly, ultimately undergoes a conversion from Kate as if by the infusion via Milly of grace (her role as "dove" or proto-"Holy Spirit"). Densher himself reflects on the phenomenal gift he has received on the occasion of Milly's last interview with him before her death: "The essence was that something had happened to him too beautiful and too sacred to describe. He had been, to his re-covered sense, forgiven, dedicated, blessed; but this he couldn't coherently express. It would have required an explanation . . . of the nature of Milly's wrong." Even without a coherent explanation, however, Densher and Mrs. Lowder, to whom he is now trying to express what occurred—"had the sense of the presence within—they felt the charged stillness." Densher even finds in his remembrance of the unforgettable occasion with Milly that he cannot picture it as happening to himself:

He saw a young man far off and in a relation inconceivable, saw him hushed, passive, staying his breath, but half understanding, yet dimly conscious of something immense and holding himself painfully together not to lose it. The young man at these moments so seen was too distant and too strange for the right identity; and yet, outside, afterwards, it was his own face Densher had known. He had known then at the same time what the young man had been conscious of, and he was to measure after that, day by day, how little he had lost.[8]

It will be quickly seen that such ingredients could conspire to affirm and reinforce a generic view of James's major phase novels as a "trilogy" in distant analogy with Dante, with "poetic dramas" of the "inward life," and with an increasingly "spiritual" vision. It will be seen just as quickly how the very same ingredients will be at odds with a more "earthy" perspective accom-

panied by an anti- "religion of renunciation" stress; or how re-
pellent, say, such ingredients must be to Sallie Sears's general
view of the major-phase James as a brilliant tough-minded dark
determinist, "remorseless" as a "pathologist of human nature."[9]
It is remarkable—and pertinent to my general point—to reflect
for a moment that *The Wings of the Dove* results in two of its
three major characters embracing sacrifice and renunciation;
and the third who does not, Kate Croy, is the supreme creative
accomplishment in James's work of a magnificent character who
is "greatly damned—with Lady Macbeth and Becky Sharp"—in
her tenacious acquisitiveness.[10] Even *The Scarlet Letter*, it might
be said, does not "stack the deck" any more in favor of the moral
value of renunciation. In short, whereas *The Ambassadors*
seems to take place entirely on a humanistic and secular plane,
deriving its moral vision quite apart from any insinuating possibilities or "presence" of a supernatural—or a quasi-supernatural—agency, *The Wings of the Dove* appears to be admitting
into its rendered universe certain intimations of immortality as it
were. To express it another way, the measure of idealism always
present in the pragmatistic vision of *The Ambassadors* begins to
run the "risk" of its being given a spiritual basis in *The Wings of
the Dove*.

My reference just now to *The Scarlet Letter* was not entirely
gratuitous, for this same issue has its parallel in the question of
The Wings of the Dove's—and, in its own increasing tendency,
the late work's—basic allegiance to realism or romance. Is *The
Wings* still a work stemming essentially from the Realistic Movement, still a linear extension from James's earlier work, the
expression of that school deriving from Balzac and practiced by
James's literary ally and compatriot William Dean Howells? Or
does *The Wings of the Dove* in its very continued expansion of
James's realism, an expansion through "phases" or "manners,"
as we say, so notably absent in Howells, finally then come down
"on the other side" of romance after all, thereby revitalizing the
earlier genre of Hawthorne, whose work had provided him such
an important point of departure at the beginning of his career?
James himself denied lucidly in "The Art of Fiction" that there
was any real substantive difference between the novel and the
romance, calling such divisions "clumsy separations."[11] At the
same time he did argue, several years after the composition

of *The Wings of the Dove*, that *The American* had been an artistic failure because of his unwitting participation in "arch-romance."[12] James, I think it is clear, understood and made a lucid distinction between the undesirable quality of "arch-romance," or "the romantic," in the novelist's obligation to his "illusion of life," and the romance genre as such, which could at its best always fulfill the desired "illusion" properly. And this is very much the basis of his retrospective praise of Hawthorne late in his career on the occasion of the Hawthorne centenary.[13]

The real question here, as with the matter of his spiritual "intimations," and as with every issue involving the "Jourdain" relationship, is whether we can respond positively to the actual territory located in an "in-between" state or condition. Matthiessen, to recur again to *The Wings of the Dove*, believes it James's masterpiece because it expresses definitively in its conception of Milly Theale James's idealism of the American girl (nourished in turn by his lifelong regard for his cousin Minny Temple who died young); furthermore, because the important growth and conversion of Merton Densher traced in the last portions of the book is what artistically validates that conception. And Matthiessen reflects: "the more one scrutinizes the technique of this novel, the more one perceives that, despite James' past masterly command over the details of realistic presentation, he is evoking essentially the mood of a fairy tale."[14]

The opposite of Matthiessen's view is Charles T. Samuels, for whom the novel is fundamentally "confused," owing to its excessive idealism regarding Milly together with its unconvincing "offstage" conversion of Densher. "Not only is Milly's goodness meager," he writes, but "being meager it cannot fill up so cavernous a moral vacuum as Densher."[15] For Samuels as for Sallie Sears the novel is appropriately successful and convincing in its portrayal of the evil, individual and social, of *this* world—Kate Croy and the London group surrounding Mrs. Lowder. In general it can be said that the critic who wishes to evaluate *The Wings of the Dove* "realistically" now finds it defective, so long as he agrees that James's intent is to persuade us of Milly's supreme act of goodness and of Densher's conversion—that the novel really means the redemptive theme implicit in its title. Conversely, a reader or critic who is more inclined, like Matthiessen, to see the novel ultimately "transcending" its "realistic details," whether because of a renewed interest in Hawthorne or else, say, because of its affiliations with the "poetic" novel, is inclined to accept James's conception of Milly and also Densher's conversion.[16] In short, we find again that *The Ambassadors* is not only less "Wagnerian" in grandeur and less abstract and internalized in its rendering of consciousness, as Cargill and Sears pointed out, but that it also appears to have much closer ties with the realistic novel as such. And certainly the absence from *The Ambassadors* of Biblical language and analogy such as that found in *The Wings* reinforces our sense that its ethical content occurs entirely within the realm of social and individual conduct without taking account of any theological or religious proposals per se underlying the given social and individual ethic. *The Wings of the Dove*, while it, too, takes place on the very same ethical plane as its predecessor, nevertheless seems to invite some correspondence between the individual and social ethic which defines its rendered center and the religious and theological proposals attending the given society and community. Hence, we find not only Milly's remarkable act and Densher's response to it, but matters ranging from Dr. Luke Strett's name and his extraordinary function in the story, to the arrival of Milly's behest on Christmas day, to Densher's unusual attendance at the Oratory, to the Biblical analogies, to the allusions to Veronese's religious paintings—all elements which begin to insinuate, if they do not actually express, the more transcendent realms of the romance. Finally, of no little importance, there is the fact that *The Ambassadors* is among the most consistently humorous of James's novels, whereas *The Wings of the Dove* has next to none.

These various issues and questions surrounding James's work and vision after *The Ambassadors*, which I have been attempting to clarify by focusing on *The Wings of the Dove*, have their parallel in another facet of his work as a whole—his increasing preoccupation with the "ghostly" tale. In speaking of the "intimations of immortality" quality about Milly's redemptive power, I earlier used the phrase "quasi-supernatural," which is also, of course, a conventional phrase for James's tales in the ghostly genre. *The Beast in the Jungle* is among the finest of these, although my discussion of it in the last chapter does not really confront it on this plane. The distinct eeriness conveyed in the ghostly tales proper, several of which predate both *The Ambassadors* and *The Wings of the Dove*, is a quality with significant ties to the eventual surfacing of the spiritual insinuations of a nonghostly novel like *The Wings*. In other words the line of departure between *The Ambassadors* and *The Wings of the Dove* may well be emblematic of James's gradual application and transference of his quasi-supernatural explorations into the central domain of his work. Thus, once again, when Merton Densher attempts to recall or "evoke" the memory of that last interview with Milly, both he and Mrs. Lowder "had the sense of the presence within—they felt the charged stillness." This has, as Poe might say, "collateral" relations with James's ghostly presences proper, and perhaps more than collateral relations at that. The even greater internalizing of rendered consciousness in *The Golden Bowl*, which Sears has pointed to, suggests this possibility, despite the absence in that novel of death or redemption through immortality and its "intimations." Rather, we might think, for example, of Maggie Verver's famous walk outside her father's country place, her gazing in at Mr. Verver, Amerigo, Charlotte, and Mrs. Assingham at the card table. There is an apparitional—or proto-apparitional—quality to such sights, which is only to say there is a quality or atmosphere to much of the novel that has, again, "collateral" relations with the ghostly realm. Or, again, in Maggie's great epiphany, when she does not speak out what she knows, the language chosen by James for her conscious thought is unmistakably reminiscent of his eerie world of the quasi-supernatural: "the horror of finding evil seated all at its ease where she had dreamed only of good; the horror of the thing hideously *behind*, behind so much trusted, so much pretended, nobleness, cleverness, tenderness. . . . it had met her like some bad-faced stranger surprised in one of the thick-carpeted corridors of a house of quiet on a Sunday afternoon."[17]

Perhaps the most fully suffused and incorporated of all James's works that are nonghostly with the atmosphere and rendered reality peculiar to the ghostly realms are the tales of *The Finer Grain*, published in 1910, the last he wrote. Two of his finest pieces of writing, "A Round of Visits" and *The Bench of Desolation*, are from this collection. In the first of these the world of New York through which Mark Monteith passes is rendered in elaborate conceits of tropical jungle imagery, the decor and social atmosphere constantly exuding a phantasmagoric quality; similarly, Monteith's mysteriously fateful visit to Newton Winch, wherein "Providence . . . was breaking him to its will by constantly directing his attention to the claims of others,"[18] a visit which inadvertently causes Winch's suicide, is rendered like a confrontation with an apparition—Winch's transformation in looks and manner reminding us of Chad Newsome's, yet elevated into the terrifying wonder-realm of the quasi-supernatural. The same is true of the rendered atmosphere of Herbert Dodd's world in *The Bench of Desolation*, particularly in the evocation through Kate Cookham of "Meg Merrilies" and in the later apparitional quality, again, of *her* transformation into a "real lady," when she returns to her Herbert after all the years of separation to reendow him with the very money she has bled from him.[19] These two tales, as well as the other three which make up the collection, are bleak and acrid in their social vision; at the same time, James's explanation to the English publisher for the title of his collection is cast in the language characteristic of his realm of the quasi-supernatural—the "finer grain of accessibility to suspense or curiosity, to mystification or attraction—in other words, to moving experience."[20]

James never did complete a full-length novel in his ghostly genre proper, but he did leave unfinished *The Sense of the Past*, first begun in 1900. *The Turn of the Screw* is not by design a ghostly or quasi-supernatural work strictly speaking, although its celebrated controversy is indicative of its de facto ties with the quasi-supernatural, rather than with the ghost story or "fairytale pure and simple" he meant it to be. His own view of its slightness, its "amusette" quality, and "ingenuity pure and simple" derives from his own most articulate distinction between psychical ghostly reality as such and the traditional "elves" or "goblins" attending the fairy tale; and he insists that Peter Quint and Miss Jessel belong to these latter.[21] There is now, after all the years of controversy, increasing opinion that *The Turn of the Screw* has been irreducibly ambiguous all along and unworthy of its great critical preoccupation.[22] This is perhaps closer in spirit to James's own view in his belief that the story was "least apt to be baited by earnest criticism," and as "pure romance."[23] It must be remembered, however, that this "pure romance" he "cast [his] lot with" in the governess's story differs from the "arch-romance" plotted and performed in *The American*: the first was intended, the second unintended. What was *unintended* in *The Turn of the Screw*, rather, was precisely the overpowering effect of its psychological medium and register, the governess, the source of all future complications of interpretation. This came about however because of a basic decision he made regarding its execution: James decided that the quality most lacking in the fairy tale proper was, despite its fine degree of "improvisation," any given "roundness," any "returning upon itself," any "keeping on terms with itself" from beginning to end.[24] This is really tantamount, as we have seen in this study, to James's making his tale "Jamesian" in its rendered felt life: hence the inevitable "possible other case." The upshot is that the supernatural realm presumed by the tale becomes undermined by its psychological mode of presentation. The story seems to me artistically valid and successful only to the extent that the supernatural agency of evil deriving from the two deceased servants at Bly can be said to have found, as a supernatural agency good or evil always must, the appropriate medium or instrument here in this world to work itself through and *manifest* its evil—the psychologically disturbed governess. This is in effect what we do have in the tale, but I do not think James initially set out to present it with this relationship in mind. The real lesson about *The Turn of the Screw* respecting James's career is that, even when he meant otherwise, he was clearly headed in the direction of the *quasi*-supernatural.

The quasi-supernatural realm as such for Henry James— whether we are speaking specifically now of the ghostly pieces themselves or of the increasing atmosphere or "intimations" present in his nonghostly works, particularly after *The Ambassadors* (or even the existence of a strange book like *The Sacred Fount* just prior to *The Ambassadors*), is perhaps best defined as follows: it is a felt relationship with the supernatural in which human consciousness, by the sheer extent of its own cultivated activity, its own exploration of its expanding realms or receding limits, thereby comes right up to the edge of the supernatural realm per se and stops just short of entering it; but then of admitting (or, if we prefer, not being able *not* to admit, given the proximity) effects and activities that come from just "over the line" making their presence felt *here*, on this side. The key point for our understanding this precarious state in James—the last in our series of "in-between" ones—is that it owes its very existence *as* the unique state it is from his deeper and ever deeper penetration into human consciousness, which is no more than a description of the basic direction and tendency of his entire adult life. For the same reason the locus of reality, the central "field," if we will, obviously remains always that of human consciousness itself.

Let me say at this juncture, even at the risk of the bad habit of "second guessing" one's reader, that we must resist rather automatically responding to this matter differently from so many earlier ones not involving the supernatural; that is, in speaking, for example, throughout this study of the *actual* realm of alternative possibilities demanded by pragmatistic novelty, I have obviously not been speaking "metaphorically" but literally. The same obtains here. My own description above of James's quasi-supernatural is, of course, expressed metaphorically with respect to the "edge" and "over the line," but the *condition* it refers to in James's own mind is actual and literal. We have not come all the way with the "Jourdain" relationship only to speak now as if James in his quasi-supernatural facet were merely working with a "convention" or an "emblem." Rather, he was the one who created the new convention, the new psychological terror or ghost story, as we say. His "Jamesian" innovation here as before proceeds from his own fundamentally developing habit of mind.

Because James came increasingly to realize in the later part of his life that the quasi-supernatural realm was only "induced" —i.e., itself defined—by the increased intensity of human consciousness, he portrayed this realm characteristically in the ghostly tales as the condition of an obsession. We can trace the evolution of James's own gradual clarifying consciousness of consciousness itself in this regard, if we look again at his three best-known tales in this dominion, this time in relation to one another: *The Turn of the Screw*, *The Beast in the Jungle*, and "The Jolly Corner" (1907)—this last among the greatest of his writings and a substitute version of the unfinished *Sense of the Past*. The first, as I have already indicated, was not even intended initially as a quasi-supernatural exploration, but does in effect amount to one; or, suppose we do say that James, perhaps having access to hysteria literature, really did set out to discredit the governess: I have no final quarrel with this or any other allied views of intention, although I obviously have my own opinion and have expressed it. The real issue, rather, is how he then chose to deal with and present the subject in comparison with what was to become his more characteristic way. The primary value of *The Turn of the Screw*, to repeat, is not found in our solution to its particular problems of interpretation, but in its relationship to James's other work in this line—at once its oddity and correspondence. The story, then, does not begin with, is not grounded upon, the presumption of an obsession. Not only is it introduced by the framing episode of the storytelling party, but the governess herself, once we get into her account, does not say: I have this obsession. She may *eventually* come to refer to her prescribed "heroic" task of saving the children as her "obsession" (it is significant that she does!), but her point is, she has seen the spectres at Bly and become convinced they wish to possess Miles and Flora. The governess's de facto obsession, her idée fixe, is rather what *we* as readers may, after a full evaluation of her case, wish to declare; but the genesis of the narrative framework is not that of obsession.

The importance of this distinction is clear as soon as we turn to the other two tales. In *The Beast in the Jungle* the very terms of its haunting quality or ghostly element are grounded on Marcher's given obsession. His rendered world is thus genuinely quasi-supernatural in that he and he alone must be continually "inducing" his mysterious fate by the sheer cultivation of his Idea. The beast that springs in his "hallucination" at the end is genuinely ghost*ly*, in other words, because it caps his long "inducing" or bringing-it-forth process re-enacted by the tale itself. It is in fact a process begun many years before the tale's dramatic opening. The reason Marcher told May Bartram his secret ten years before their encounter at Weatherend, and then forgot he had told her, is that at the time he told her it was less intense and cultivated an obsession than presently: the deeper and more intense it became, the more inevitable he would forget he had ever spoken it. This is why he is ever so "careful" (the obsession's own incarnate manifestation) to make her "name" it back to him at Weatherend, even after it is quite clear from her preliminary remarks that she knows it. And when she does name it, her own description of it as "very simple" can remind us both that it is not an obsession for her and, by inference, how much less a one it had been for Marcher at the earlier time he told her of it. The only dimension to Marcher's problem that May herself does not eventually come to know after all the years of "watching" with him is precisely the quasi-supernatural dimension. This is why she predicts— and who would not in her situation?—that he will never "find out." Even here her prediction, as I tried to point out in the previous chapter, is right in the sense that Marcher cannot ever be a person capable of love and response to immediate experience, a condition reinforced even by his own "epiphany." But May is wrong in the sense that he will never come to see his own induced apparition, thereby glimpsing what amounts to a figuration of his "self" and the essential meaning of that self. Thus Marcher simultaneously discovers the meaning of the riddle of his life while the very process of discovery nourishes the meaning he discovers —a relationship that can be maintained only through polarity.

In "The Jolly Corner" James extends his conception of the quasi-supernatural to its most logical conclusion, the psychologically induced *alter ego* proper through obsession. In doing this he has come full circle in his now clear grasp of the nature of the ghostly itself from his earlier composition of *The Turn of the Screw*. Whereas, in the governess's story, the narrative events are not grounded on the issue of her obsession; and whereas, in *The Beast in the Jungle*, the narrative is grounded on the obsession rendering itself and culminating in the induced hallucination (so that what is slowly "earned" in *The Beast* is immediately "given" in *The Turn of the Screw*)—in 'The Jolly Corner" James now constructs a narrative framework on behalf of the obsession: this gives us a story comparable to the governess's, and even on good terms with the traditional ghost story, because the components of the ghostly relationship—the cause and effect or the cart and the horse of it—are now for him in their proper order. Furthermore, he now appropriately extends the given fact of an obsession, as in *The Beast*, by including in his narrative framework its own original act of creation, as though in his clarity of the whole issue of the quasi-supernatural he can take us from its very inception to its last terminal results; or he can re-enact and recapitulate its total pattern and process as he had come to grasp it.[25] Thus, when Spencer Brydon returns home to

America after thirty-three years living abroad and shows his old friend Alice Staverton the new apartment house he is building, she says that "he had clearly for too many years neglected a real gift."

If he had but stayed at home he would have anticipated the inventor of the sky-scraper. If he had but stayed at home he would have discovered his genius in time really to start some new variety of awful architectural hare and run it till it burrowed in a gold-mine. He was to remember these words, while the weeks elapsed, for the small silver ring they had sounded over the queerest and deepest of his own lately most disguised and most muffled vibrations.

It had begun to be present to him after the first fortnight, it had broken out with the oddest abruptness, this particular wanton wonderment: it met him there—and this was the image under which he himself judged the matter, or at least, not a little, thrilled and flushed with it— very much as he might have been met by some strange figure, some unexpected occupant, at a turn of one of the dim passages of an empty house. The quaint analogy quite hauntingly remained with him, when he didn't indeed rather improve it by a still intenser form.[26]

Thus we watch the creation of Brydon's obsession; and the incantatory repetition in the first two lines—"If he had but stayed at home"—as well as James's expression that Brydon's condition begins *first* as an "analogy" which eventually he is to "improve on" by "a still intenser form," makes clear at which end the process for reaching the quasi-supernatural must start from. This is not to say, however, that Brydon is not also already dramatically involved like John Marcher in his obsession from the opening line: " 'Everybody asks me what I "think" of everything' "— the tale begins, not without good reason.

"The Jolly Corner" has elicited much attention, primarily on account of its multileveled incorporation of just about every facet of James's work in a remarkably concentrated amount of space. One thinks, for example, of his recurrent problem, so vividly exemplified in the *Notebooks*, of wanting initially to do a short piece, only to see it then proliferate in size. In this sense, especially, though by no means confined to it, it is understandable that he described this tale to his agent as a "miraculous masterpiece."[27] "The Jolly Corner" and its own nonghostly *alter ego*, "A Round of Visits" (1910)—both dealing with American expatriates who return to the same phantasmagoric and rapacious New York society after living abroad their adult lives; both portraying individuals who are haunted by questions they mean to pursue until answered; and both just extraordinary in their indissoluble fusion of what seem at once personal, social, and well-nigh mythic statements—could be said to illustrate together the coalescence of the entire direction of James's work and mind in its post-*Ambassadors* extension, although the tendencies involved had started several years before *The Ambassadors*; and even as *The Ambassadors* itself was to cap in its "superior roundness" the pragmatistic vision on its secular and empirical plane apart from any "intimations." What makes the two very late tales together so expressive of this basic direction is the extent to which ghostly and nonghostly realms seem so interchangeable in them that the distinction itself no longer appears substantive.

Despite the critical attention paid to one of these two tales ("A Round of Visits," sadly, has been comparatively ignored), there are at least two facets to "The Jolly Corner" that should be examined in view of its culminating place in James's evolutionary process regarding the quasi-supernatural. The first is that James allows Alice Staverton, as he did not May Bartram, to share in the psychic experience with Brydon. Not only has she seen Brydon's *alter ego* "twice over" in a dream prior to the climactic night that makes up the center and heart of the tale, but has also seen "him" and been given a sign on the crucial night itself. Furthermore, she participates with Brydon in the act of creation, as I have called it, by her own "inducing" or incantatory remarks mentioned above, the very ones that "sounded over the queerest and deepest of [Brydon's] own lately most disguised and muffled vibrations." It is Alice, finally, who at the end of the tale insists that the *alter ego* is not the "horror" and the totally disjoined "other" that Brydon has found him to be.

The main reason for Alice's different function in this regard from May Bartram is primarily owing to the ultimate success of her power of love and the active part it plays in making Brydon undergo the psychic experience which, when confronted, can then release him from the obsession itself and permit him to love back—to get outside of the private universe that Marcher so conspicuously remains in. This is, admittedly, perhaps just another way of saying that the two tales have very different outcomes or "upshots," which I dare say is no great surprise to anyone familiar with them. Nevertheless, the implications here are rather important. Alice, in her active participation in "inducing" the obsession, indeed, in her very condition of being "ahead" of Brydon (with her two dreams, her early mention of a "ghost," and so on), is a striking contrast to May Bartram. May's character and circumstances, as James presents them, bespeak those of a lovely person who is nevertheless a most unusually passive and dependent individual. Her relationship with her own family, no less than—and superimposed by—her relationship with Marcher, is always that of someone with no life of her own independent of either. I am not speaking now of her being "at fault" in not more aggressively declaring her love to Marcher: she does, in fact, to the extent that she can, for the very condition of Marcher is such that, had she been more aggressive, she would have lost him instantly. And yet, her very capacity to "watch" with him, even though it is clear from the start that she hopes "watching" will not comprise the whole of their relation, reinforces our sense of her acquiescence in her own exploitation—an acquiescence we could never attach, for example, to someone like Milly Theale.

Alice Staverton is the reverse of May in this respect. She has lived in New York during the entire cultural transformation that so shocks Brydon. She has lived by herself, retaining in her tasteful house in Irving Place the continuity with the past that Brydon finds an attractive refuge; but she also "sallied forth and did battle when the challenge was really to 'spirit'. . . . She made use of the street-cars . . . affronted, inscrutably, under stress, all the public concussions and ordeals; and yet, with that slim mystifying grace of her appearance, which defied you to say if she were a fair young woman who looked older through trouble, or a fine smooth older one who looked young through successful indifference" [439-40].

These unmistakably plucky qualities have a great deal to do with her active participation with Brydon in the psychic experience and her own share with him in inducing it. Her "mystifying grace" of "appearance," often referred to in the tale, suggests her own proto-apparitional quality of presence, and it is not a quality that James wishes us to separate from her pluck. Once again we can see how he has come full circle since *The Turn of the*

Screw: the governess was plucky enough, destructively so in her de facto obsession, her de facto condition of being herself "spooky"; May Bartram does not share in the quasi-supernatural dimension of her story, as we saw, whereas James does work out there, via Marcher, the relationship of obsession itself *to* the quasi-supernatural; but now Alice Staverton in a sense brings us back the governess, except that Alice knows what she is about. Her sympathetic attitude toward the ghost both reinforces her character and contributes to the tale's thematic content. It is appropriate that, having lived in New York during the period of change, she would not be as horrified as Brydon by the condition of the *alter ego*: she has had, let us say, an "ambulatory" rather than, like Brydon himself, a "saltatory" relation with the enormous changes in America. On a personal level she is still ahead of him in realizing that Brydon is someone she could have loved either as *alter* or *ego*; that Brydon would not have been irrevocably destroyed even with the impaired vision and mutilated condition of life accruing from "downtown" work, for he could not ultimately be dispossessed of the very qualities that had in fact sent him abroad—anymore than Brydon has been irrevocably dehumanized by building his apartment house, the very occasion for his search into his own "organism." Alice, in other words, grasps the real meaning of an *alter ego* itself, the positive allegiances involved. Brydon has not yet grasped this at the end of the tale, although, now released from his obsession and capable of love, he will presumably do so rather soon. The sort of insight Alice has about the two "Brydons" has been implicit in his entire life, for he has lived abroad on the money coming from his "property"; and its increasing value has nourished his expatriate life. The social vision of America as such is not an optimistic one in the tale, but the personal vision is hopeful. What is perhaps most significant in terms of James's development and grasp of the ghostly realm, he now seems less doubtful of its possible "independent" existence in his decision to allow both characters to participate in it, and even in suggesting, however mutely, something on the order of thought-transference from Alice to Brydon.

The second facet to the tale worth examining is that the *alter ego*, as James here presents it, is unique in literature. Brydon's other self, that is, is an actual alter-*ego* in the sense that Poe's or

Stevenson's, or even Conrad's is not. By this I mean that James reconciles empirically the inherent "contradiction" postulated by the very words "alter" and "ego," and the psychic condition to which they refer, through the positive relationship of polarity at the level of the tale's own unfolding felt life. This basic *kind* of accomplishment is in terms of this study hardly anything new—it is simply James's whole story in his successful work. But we have not yet seen what it looks like, so to speak, when we have a ghostly tale which explicitly posits an *alter ego*. What it means under these conditions is that Brydon *is* his own "other self" throughout the tale in a proceeding and ongoing way not to be found in other "double" literature. And what this in turn means is that throughout the night-stalking and hunting of the tale we can continually measure Brydon's own evolving psychic condition and progress by what he is claiming the ghost has decided; and we can simultaneously measure the actual movements of the ghost by what Brydon himself then decides to do on the basis of the view he attributes to the ghost. Brydon and his *alter ego* are empirically *con*joined in polarity (thereby giving us in effect a "model" for James's own artistic process)—for that conjunction is of course what an *alter ego* really is and means in the first place.

On that unforgettable last night, for example, when Brydon carries on through until dawn, he first stands at the bottom of the staircase looking up, aware that things have "changed":

"He's *there*, at the top, and waiting—not, as in general, falling back for disappearance. He's holding his ground, and it's the first time—which is a proof, isn't it? that something has happened for him. . . . Harder pressed?—yes, he takes it in, with its thus making clear to him that I've come, as they say, 'to stay.' . . . He has been dodging, retreating, hiding, but now, worked up to anger, he'll fight!" [460-61].

These views imputed to the ghost tell us that Brydon himself—"bringing it on, bringing it to perfection, by practice" [459] —has now come to a crisis or psychic turning point in his exploration. The "something" that "has happened for him"—i.e., the *alter*—is in counterpart ratio with Brydon—the *ego*—for they are defining each other in polarity. To take it from the "other side," the ghost has not so much been "falling back" before as not until now been sufficiently induced into active life and presence; each night that Brydon has been coming, gaining confidence and cultivating his habit and routine, has been constituting the "harder press" which inevitably brings forth the occult life he seeks.

It is only a matter of time before someone among James's commentators, trying to explain certain strange "discrepancies" in the text, will hit upon the "discovery" that James has carefully provided just enough clues to show us that Brydon is "himself the ghost" during that climactic night. The opposite argument, that there is no ghost and that Alice Staverton has staged the whole business, has already been offered.[28] There is, in fact, sufficient textual evidence for arguing the case that Brydon and the ghost exchange places shortly after the recognition of the turning point situation just noted. Brydon breaks into a sweat, experiences a tremendous compulsion to flee, and resists the compulsion through sheer will power. He closes his eyes, "held them tight," and upon opening them, is, we are told, "still at the top" of the stairs—i.e., where the *alter ego* was when Brydon underwent the crisis and shut his eyes [462-63]! This tells us not only how Brydon miraculously gets from the vestibule hall to the top of the house, but how the ghost gets to the front hall where he "belongs" for the confrontation that eventually occurs: for the ghost is, in fact, right in the corner where Brydon always goes first to put his walking stick and where he has this night paused in new recognition at the moment in question.

There are several other items in the tale which support this proposal and, certainly, just as many problems with it; and it is not my intention here to become involved in trying to construct an ingenious argument either that Brydon and the ghost exchange places or, another plausible variant, that we actually switch "point of view" from Brydon-*ego* to Brydon-*alter* when we "pick him up" again at the top of the stairs. It is only a matter of time, to repeat, before someone proposes this or some argument allied to it. My point in mentioning such possibilities at all is that they are the inevitable conditions attending a work in which genuine polarity is both psychologically rendered while at the same time an *alter ego* proposed. The polar relationship, which is the only way to genuinely resolve the problem posed by the age-old philosophical principle of contradiction and identity (which is also the problem posed by an *alter ego*, obviously, since it is literally what the words mean), is also the only relationship in which the contraries themselves can and do transform *into each other*, back and forth, in predominance or polar concentration; just as the same contraries transform each other more fundamentally through their given polarity *to* each other. What this means in regard to a story like "The Jolly Corner" is that we are not going to resolve it either by insisting that Alice Staverton hired someone to play the ghost or even by the inevitable discovery that Brydon is "his own ghost"—unless in the second case we understand the positive identity and affiliations, including the possibilites for transference back and forth, found in polarity. And all this means is that it is a work of the creative imagination.

Before turning now to William James's career and examining more briefly a parallel development in his work, there are perhaps two major conclusions to be drawn from the discussion thus far of Henry in this chapter. The first is that he came gradually to take seriously enough the possibility of a supernatural realm that the whole drift of his vision in the late work can be fruitfully looked at in the light of it. The second is that the particular quality of his drift in this regard should remind us once again that he stayed essentially a "realist"; that is, he could only come to his quasi-supernatural realm *his* Jamesian way, through the cultivation of *human* consciousness. James literally ambulated to this "collateral" relationship, which means that he does not disregard or diminish the territory he has traversed. That is in fact the principal reason his view really is *quasi*-supernatural— the realm which that phrase bespeaks is attached to the same "realistic" territory. After our look now at William's development along these lines we will be returning one last time to Henry to hear from him more directly regarding this general issue, in a memorable essay on the subject of immortality which, except for the attention of F. O. Matthiessen, still remains largely ignored and practically unread.

William James's parallel development in these matters is generally more easy to trace and less complicated in nature than Henry's, except perhaps in one facet which will be worth noting. The more familiar facet is, of course, his well known developing interest in psychical research itself and his examination of religious experience, each for him so much the obverse of the other.

In his 1896 essay, "What Psychical Research Has Accomplished," he is primarily attacking what he repeatedly calls the "mechanical rationalism" permeating the scientific community, that same narrow positivistic mentality which he criticizes in "The Will to Believe." In the course of his argument defending the scientific integrity of the Society for Psychical Research and the legitimate hypothesis concerning the reality of "higher phenomena" to be drawn from their meticulous work, he also makes an observation which Henry was to repeat a decade later: he points out that "few species of literature are more truly dull than reports of phantasms"[29]—precisely Henry's point in his retrospective "Preface" to *The Turn of the Screw* (which was written the year following this paper of William's) and the very reason the novelist speaks of Miss Jessel and Peter Quint as belonging instead to the tradition of "elves" and "goblins."

William's principal point, however, is that science needs to respond to the "unclassified residuum," which William himself finds most importantly focused as well as most convincingly demonstrated in the proposition of the "subliminal self." He quotes approvingly the following formulation by F. W. H. Myers: " 'Each of us is in reality an abiding psychical entity far more extensive than he knows—an individuality which can never express itself completely through any corporeal manifestation. The self manifests itself through the organism; but there is always some part of the self unmanifested, and always, as it seems, some power of organic expression in abeyance or reserve.' " It is this proposal more than any other one from the psychical research literature which William personally supports: "The result is to make me feel that we all have potentially a 'subliminal' self, which may make at any time irruption into our ordinary lives."[30] This is, of course, the basic presupposition underlying Henry's ghost*ly* reality, once the generative and psychologically dramatic process of obsession is attached to it. It is even the "quasi-" presupposition for Merton Densher's other "self" at his last interview with Milly, if we assume, that is, that the occasion was truly extraordinary.

William's views in this area come to a head and simultaneously expand in implication with the appearance in 1898 of "Human Immortality," another of his many arguments against the presumptions of scientific positivism. "The whole subject of immortal life," he begins characteristically, "has its prime roots in personal feeling"; [31] but the specific task he sets for himself is to refute the assumption that, since thought, as science knows, is a function of the brain, this necessarily means that the brain either causes thought or contains in its physical structure and mechanism the boundaries of thought or consciousness—so that when the one is eclipsed in death or irrevocably impaired through disease or malfunction, let us say, the other then ceases. His principal rebuttal to this argument lies in a lovely and lucid distinction between what he calls "productive" function and "releasing," "permissive," or "transmissive" function. Thus:

"Steam is a function of the tea-kettle," "Light is a function of the electric circuit," "Power is a function of the moving waterfall." In these latter cases the several material objects have the function of inwardly creating or engendering their effects, and their function must be called *productive* function.

On the other hand:

In the case of a colored glass, a prism, or a refracting lens, we have transmissive function. The energy of light, no matter how produced, is by the glass sifted and limited in color, and by the lens or prism determined to a certain path and shape. Similarly, the keys of an organ have only a transmissive function. They open successively the various pipes and let the wind in the air-chest escape in various ways. The voices of the various pipes are constituted by the columns of air trembling as they emerge. But the air is not engendered in the organ. [32]

William concludes that, whenever we consider the operation of the brain vis-à-vis thought, we are not required to think only of productive function, but are entitled also to consider permissive or transmissive function. He buttresses this argument by pointing out that scientists themselves admit that the production of consciousness "is the absolute world-enigma,—something so paradoxical and abnormal as to be a stumbling block to Nature, and almost a self-contradiction." [33] And then he observes that the transmissive theory has "positive superiorities" in its behalf: it coincides with general idealistic philosophy, with exceptional phenomena ranging from religious conversions to all the data of psychical research, to personal desire, to historical continuity itself.

Such is William's argument for legitimately entertaining the hypothesis of a state or condition comparable to the traditional view of immortality. But what is most striking in his presentation is that his elaboration of the transmission theory begins to have the similar feature of "naming" the drift of Henry's later manner in its ghostly extension, much as his pragmatistic thought does Henry's later style more generally and fundamentally. Speaking of the possibility of some form of "Thought" just "behind the veil," he elaborates:

Only at particular times and places would it seem that, as a matter of fact, the veil of nature can grow thin and rupturable enough for such effects to occur. But in those places gleams, however finite and unsatisfying, of the absolute life of the universe, are from time to time vouchsafed. Glows of feeling, glimpses of insight, and streams of knowledge and perception float into our finite world.

Admit now that *our brains* are such thin and half-transparent places in the veil. What will happen? Why, as the white radiance comes through the dome, with all sorts of staining and distortion imprinted on it by the glass . . . even so the genuine matter of reality, the life of souls as it is in its fullness, will break through our several brains into this world in all sorts of restricted forms, and with the imperfections and queernesses that characterize our finite individualities here below.

. . . .

All abstract hypotheses sound unreal; and the abstract notion that our brains are colored lenses in the wall of nature, admitting light from the super-solar source, but at the same time tingeing and restricting it, has a thoroughly fantastic sound. What is it, you may ask, but a foolish metaphor?[34]

The correspondence of this conception to the internalizing tendency and refractive quality both to Henry's ghostly realm proper and to the later manner itself, particularly after *The Ambassadors*, is apparent. To recur once again to the rendered world of "The Jolly Corner," William's "foolish metaphor" is there brought to life in the house's "likeness of some great glass bowl, all precious concave crystal," in the dome-like "high skylight" which, when Brydon makes his final descent, "created for him a medium in which he could advance, but which might have been, for queerness of colour, some watery under-world"; similarly the apparition he eventually meets stands under a "cold silvery nimbus that seemed to play a little as he looked—to shift and expand and contract"; the ghostly presence likewise stands in "the penumbra" and, when beginning to advance, resembles "one of those expanding fantastic images projected by the magic lantern of childhood" [455, 473, 474, 475, 477].

If, moreover, William's whole conception of this matter as well as his "foolish metaphor" seem somehow already familiar to us, and quite apart from any explicit question of Henry's quasi-supernatural, the reason is that we have seen him use the same metaphor much earlier when describing to Henry the late style itself. In his *American Scene* letter (1907), discussed at some length in the second chapter of this study for its striking appraisal of Henry's method as an expanding "germ," William also compares Henry's style to "the 'ghost' at the Polytechnic," wrought "out of impalpable materials, air, and the prismatic interferences of light, ingeniously focused by mirrors upon empty space."[35] Although William's "ghost" in his letter is obviously not the same "one" he argues for on behalf of psychical research and immortality, they certainly do resemble each other in conception and description. But the real point is, of course, that William writes in such fashion about Henry's late style; and Henry's late style and drift in turn answers to William's formulations, whether in his letter or in his published writings. Such crosscurrent descriptions really serve to remind us of a basic fact about the work of both: William's views in the general area of psychical research and immortality are always closely bound up with his pragmatistic thought; and Henry's drift in the area of the quasi-supernatural is just as closely bound up with his typical "Jamesian" idiom.

This interrelatedness to William's thought is quite apparent in his "Conclusion" to *The Varieties of Religious Experience* (1902), where he gives his famous pragmatic argument for the existence of God: "God is real since he produces real effects."[36] This deceptive and simple-sounding "nugget" is all bound up with his views and reflections over the previous decade in the general area we have just seen, the very interests which determined him to pursue and investigate the phenomena of religious experience—both that of revered saints and religious leaders as well as "cranks" and odd fanatics. William's philosophic rationale for his "nugget" is most clearly expressed when he declares: "that which produces effects within another reality must be termed a reality itself, so I feel as if we had no philosophic excuse for calling the unseen or mystical world unreal."[37] When we arrive at such a statement after his "Human Immortality" essay, we can see, I think, that William has in effect attributed what he would call a "productive" function to the "other side" whose effects are then felt *here*; but he would never make such a proposal had he not previously worked out the argument starting from *this* side—involving "permissive" or "transmissive" function. And he does, in fact, declare most explicitly the direction of his mind over the preceding years:

The whole drift of my education goes to persuade me that the world of our present consciousness is only one out of many worlds of consciousness that exist, and that those other worlds must contain experiences which have a meaning for our life also; and that although in the main their experiences and those of this world keep discrete, yet the two become continuous at certain points, and higher energies filter in. By being faithful in my poor measure to this over-belief, I seem to myself to keep more sane and true.[38]

This entire argument concerning God's "effects" in our lives here, or else the argument for occasional manifestations of "higher phenomena" in an otherwise mundane world, is actually the same basic relationship we have already seen William argue for abstract ideas vis-à-vis the "sea of sense." Ideas, we will recall, create in their steering-function their own "life elsewhere." It would seem now with respect to God or the supernatural realm that conscious life here is in effect *its* "elsewhere." But the difference is that in the case of perception and intellection William could, so to speak, see all the way "round" the whole issue, so that it assumed for him a constantly circular process wherein the outermost boundaries lay always within experience: thus, the experiential relationship itself occurring "transitionally" between perception and thought—the margins between them interpenetrating, and the world of consciousness (which is their "in-between territory") constantly remoulding itself.

Eventually, however, the question would have had to arise for William, given, that is, the "drift" he speaks of regarding his views in the domain of psychical research and religious experience, of whether it was possible to conceive of an epistemological relationship which began at the "other end" and functioned circularly—or at least indeterminantly—in much the same way his usual conception expressed itself when starting from this side. We have arrived now at that less familiar facet of William's thought spoken of earlier: his final exploratory proposals in his doctrine of radical empiricism; or what technical philosophers, I expect, would call the real doctrine of radical empiricism, owing to William's habit of using the phrase in such close connection with his more familiar views on pragmatism and pluralism. Despite this difficulty, however, it is quite clear that William himself came to recognize a real departure involved in his final proposals regarding radical empiricism. In 1896, for example, he speaks of his general philosophic "attitude" as "radical empiricism" in his "Preface" to *The Will to Believe* volume. But in 1907, in his "Preface" to *Pragmatism*, he now writes: "To avoid one misunderstanding, at least, let me say that there is no logical connection between pragmatism, as I understand it, and a doctrine which I have recently set forth as 'radical empiricism.' The latter stands on its own feet. One may entirely reject it and still be a pragmatist."[39] By 1907 radical empiricism had indeed evolved for him from a general "attitude" to a "recently" new and distinct doctrine, for he had published by then "Does 'Consciousness' Exist?" This would eventually become the first in his posthumous *Essays in Radical Empiricism*, the collection he had set apart to argue the doctrine "on its own feet."

This doctrine has both puzzled and ignited the philosophical community. Whitehead's belief that it initiated a new era in thought by its denial of the Cartesian dualism between mind and matter is well known; similarly, it is now increasingly hailed retrospectively as the beginning of modern phenomenology. The heart of the doctrine is that James now denies human consciousness as an entity, reaffirms it as a function, and posits a universe of "pure experience" prior and anterior to its function:

My thesis is that if we start with the supposition that there is only one primal stuff or material in the world, a stuff of which everything is composed, and if we call that stuff "pure experience," then knowing can easily be explained as a particular sort of relation toward one another into which portions of pure experience may enter. The relation itself is a part of pure experience; one of its "terms" becomes the subject or bearer of the knowledge, the knower, the other becomes the object known.[40]

Philosophers will, I am sure, continue to examine this doctrine and attempt further to puzzle it out, especially in view of the effect it has had on Continental phenomenology. For my purposes here, there are one or two issues about the doctrine that should be noted. William's proposal concerning the empirical relationship occurring between the "knower" and the "object known" is most compatible with his theory of ambulation, with which we have been concerned so often. As a matter of fact, the doctrine as proposed throughout the volume is on one side remarkably compatible with the major views we have seen. For example, his proposal that "pure experience" now gets *taken* by us in innumerable ways, functioning in an indeterminate number of contexts for us, remains on good terms with his pluralistic and open-ended viewpoint.

What is truly "radical" about it, however, is its starting point, the given or prior world of experience in which human consciousness participates. It seems clear, however, that this point of departure is his genuine attempt to transfer into the central domain of his work the implications arising from his "drift" in the area of psychical research and religious experience. In point of fact it seems remarkably like his "transmissive" or "permissive" function restated in a secular philosophical context. The only major difference is that, instead of the "higher phenomena" filtering in only on occasion and "at certain points," the "pure experience" gets transmitted constantly and in an indeterminate number of ways. It is a proposition that even has a singular resonance to the traditional view of the *logos*, except that William's *"logos"* is characteristically plural and concatenated in nature, getting itself "known-as" innumerable "contexts" or "functions"—to such an extent that it seems, this pure experience of his, as "piecemeal" in its very expansion as his proposal about God in *The Varieties.* Thus we find in William's "drift," as in Henry's, the gradual transference of his "supernatural" excursions and interests into the center of his work, for the individual essays which make up the posthumous volume were appearing separately from 1905 to 1907. We find, too, his now giving universal sanction to the denial of Cartesian dualism, already effectively denied in the area of cognition by the theory of ambulatory relations. Henry's late work in its natural tendency constitutes the selfsame denial of the subject-object split —best evidenced by its internalizing propensity on the one hand, while at the same time refusing to take the easy "subjective" way by acting as if it were not still a mimetic idiom.

To survey the respective careers of the brothers in regard to epistemology is to be struck by their parallel development and by the distinctiveness of the position arrived at. Thus, they each remained, as was said of William earlier in this book, "Aristotelian" in the sense that each always considered sensation to be a true report of the external world apart from the perceiver—William by precept, Henry (excepting perhaps a book like *The Sacred Fount*) by the mimetic pre-conditions of his art, however internalized or psychological. Yet for each "the hippopotamus and the pea" became increasingly one; each became "ambulatory through and through," each dramatically subversive of the Cartesian subject-object separation. To insist so strongly both ways at once is ultimately to confront a logical contradiction: if denying Cartesian dualism makes mind and matter, subject and object, or knower and known one and the same, how then can we speak meaningfully any longer of "the external world apart from the perceiver"? William's solution, as we have just seen, is to postulate his anterior "pure experience" and then to resubmit consciousness as a function, thereby escaping what would otherwise have been the conclusion that the perceiver and the perceived are indistinguishable because no longer divisible: for the whole thrust of William's thought from the start *had* been to argue for indivisibility and "confluence" in the mind's relationship with its world.

Rejecting Cartesian dualism does not, however, necessarily require William's solution to the logical contradiction just raised. One can deny dualism by proposing that the relationship *itself* between subject and object is vital; that is, that subject and object mutually transform each other in the act of perception and are thereby organically unified. The logical contradiction, in other words, can be resolved through polarity; but polarity is not, as we have seen again and again, a logical principle. Henry, being the artist, was virtually not required to face these philosophical questions. Furthermore, as the brother in possession of polarity, it would have been unnecessary for him to devise anything like "pure experience." But as ambulator and "Jourdain," he was so naturally imbued with the dramatic interrelationship between the percipient and the perceived that, had he to confront the question philosophically, William's notion of consciousness as function rather than as separate entity would have been not only available but even inevitable to him. For *that* conception, unlike "pure experience," begins to "name" the dramatic activity of relationship, of collaboration and participation going on between subject and object, even if it does not address the ultimate unifying principle *of* the relationship—polarity. It may be helpful to keep these considerations in mind as we turn now to the last work by Henry to be examined in this book.

In 1910, the year of William's death, Henry James contributed to a symposium on Immortality an essay which he entitled "Is There a Life After Death?" This document, as I have already indicated, remains virtually ignored. Recently, Leon Edel refers to it briefly and fittingly on the final page of his multivolume biography. He declares there that James denies unequivocally any actual physical immortality while affirming rather the Proust-like immortality, that accrues to the artist who creates "the immortal picture or statue, the immortal phrase whether of music or of words."[41] While this is certainly a fitting testimonial for ending such a monumental biography, and while James does clearly see the whole issue as involving his artistic consciousness, Edel's is nevertheless a rather misleading summation of this remarkable piece of writing. And even F. O. Matthiessen's more probing comments on it in his 1944 study of *The Major Phase* tend to leave the impression that for James the subject of immortality is primarily occasion for his reaffirming, again, like Proust, "the essences of aesthetic idealism."[42] Three years later with the publication of *The James Family*, in which Matthiessen put us in his debt (as indeed his own writings generally indebt us to him) by reprinting the essay and bringing it to our attention, he observes of the two brothers that, "though neither of them became a religious man in any compelling sense, they finally converged, with surprising similarity, upon the question of immortality."[43]

"Is There a Life After Death?" will reward repeated reading as much as, say, one of the late and concentrated tales. It is, of course, about the only time he made, as Matthiessen puts it, "an explicit excursion into philosophy"; [44] and, inasmuch as his only other declarations in this general area seem to be his letters after the death of Minny Temple and the well-known one to Grace Norton, this statement of his views has the added distinction of being his only public one, besides its being considerably later than the others and far more penetrating and elaborate. It is a piece of work, finally, with something of the same authoritative quality of mind and heart found, for example, in Emerson's un-forgettable "Experience," an essay with which it compares fa-vorably and resembles in spirit.

The argument itself puts one in mind of a late quartet by Beethoven or else, say, his final Sonata No. 32, by virtue of James's formal division into two parts, two "movements." Like the Sonata, the first part seems to convey primarily the "storm and stress" of our condition here on earth, while it explicitly ex-amines the compelling reasons against the possibility for immor-tality, making the negative argument so forcefully that, were it to end with Part 1, it would be a most powerful statement against the proposition. The second part not only gives the opposing view in favor of the possibility of immortality, but does so—and this is the quality it shares with the fiction—by virtue of re-traversing the argument of Part 1 and turning it inside out. In this way the positive possiblity ends up singularly constituted of both arguments, possessing the additional power of the first on its own very behalf! In short, James's two parts do not really make so much a dialectic or dialogue as they come to relate posi-tively through polarity.[45]

He begins, as in the fiction, indirectly, and seems at first concerned less with immortality per se than with the fact that so few people would recognize "the appeal of our speculation." This takes him quickly to his first proposal, that perhaps the very extent to which the question itself "more or less torments us," puts us "consciously in presence of it[self]," may in fact con-stitute the measure of our life after death, since it is also the mea-sure of our "general concern with life" and "mode of reaction" under it:

How *can* there be a personal and differentiated life "after" . . . for those for whom there has been so little of one before?—unless indeed it be pronounced conceivable that the possibility may vary from man to man, from human case to human case, and that the quantity or the quality of our practice of consciousness may have something to say to it.[46]

This is of course much akin to William's "piecemeal super-naturalism" at the end of *The Varieties*, except that Henry's sense of the matter is, as Matthiessen would say, more "aristocratic." This is also essentially the position James will arrive at by the end of his essay, but the process by which he comes to it is far more important than even the position itself: I can think of few instances where William's point about the "bridge of intermediaries" has more application.

James admits that the "waste" so many people make of their gift of consciousness may in the eternal scheme be only "to our purblind sight"; but the far graver difficulty, whatever our particular notion of immortality, resides in the overwhelming experience we have that confirms the scientific view of the "laboratory-brain":

We flutter away from that account of ourselves, on sublime occasion, only to come back to it with the collapse of our wings, and during much of our life the grim view, as I have called it, the sense of the rigor of our physical basis, is confirmed to us by overwhelming appearances. . . . they reinforce the verdict of the dismal laboratories and the confident analysts as to the interconvertibility of our genius, as it comparatively is at the worst, and our brain—the poor palpable, ponderable, probeable, laboratory-brain that we ourselves see in certain inevitable conditions—become as naught [205-6].

It is the same issue William had confronted in his essay on "Human Immortality." Unlike William, however, Henry really dwells on the sheer extent to which our own experience conspires to validate the positivists. The proof of our being "the very stuff of the abject actual" is illustrated every hour of our lives in all "the ugliness, the grossness, the stupidity, the cruelty, the vast extent to which the score in question is a record of brutality and vulgarity. . . . The mere fact in short that so much life as we know it dishonors, or at any rate falls below, the greater part of the beauty and the opportunity even of this world, works upon us for persuasion that none other can be eager to receive it" [206, 207-8].

And even were we to find the strength for some larger stoical or tragic understanding of what we see around us, what really "makes, to our earthly senses, for the unmistakable absoluteness of death" is "the disconnectedness of those who vanish from our sight—or they perhaps not so much from ours as we from theirs." And James mocks his own earlier stated proposal: "we may die piecemeal, but by no sign ever demonstrably caught does the 'liberated' spirit react from death piecemeal" [210]. And he notes here that the "trance medium" does not really afford the personal value we seek when trying to establish relations with someone we have lost. What James thinks such mediums *do* afford, however, is well worth hearing:

These often make, I grant, for attention and wonder and interest—but for interest above all in the medium and the trance. Whether or no they may in the given case seem to savor of another state of being on the part of those from whom they profess to come, they savor intensely, to my sense, of the medium and the trance, and, with their remarkable felicities and fitnesses, their immense call for explanation, invest that personage, in that state, with an almost irresistible attraction [211-12].

This is a most important statement, for it amounts to the correlative to his own view and presentation of the quasi-supernatural. What makes the medium such a poor demonstration and argument on behalf of bringing us back someone else is precisely that the medium seems to be able to invoke or induce some dimension of his or her own "subliminal self." That James *does* find "irresistible," for that is also the area his fiction has been inhabiting, as we have seen.

But for the more conventional immortality argument, "we break ourselves against that conception of immortality *as* personal which is the only thing that gives it meaning or relevance." This is what is crucial for James: such a lack of anything like a personal sign from lost ones, and the radical disproportion itself between such apparent "extinction" and the possibly full and intense relationship that may have once existed, comes "little by little" to suggest "some vast sardonic, leering 'Don't you see?' on the mask of Nature" [212-13]. In short:

we begin by pitying the remembered dead, even for the very danger of our indifference to them, and we end by pitying ourselves for the final demonstration, as it were, of their indifference to us. "They must be dead, indeed," we say; "they must be dead as 'science' affirms, for this consecration of it on such a scale, and with these tremendous rites of nullification, to take place" [214].

James's power at building up his negative argument resides primarily in his transforming—as only he would do—a potential "case" against immortality into a dramatic and living *process* argument. For this is what his whole discussion has conveyed: "that our faith or our hope may to some degree resist the fact, once accomplished, of watched and deplored death, but that they may well break down before the avidity and consistency with which everything insufferably *continues* to die" [215].

So ends Part 1—and it is indeed remarkable after all this to hear him open his second part: "I have said 'we argue.' " James very quickly now substitutes for "we" a most emphatic "I" as he begins to make from here on as directly personal a public statement as anything to be found in his autobiographical volumes. With respect to answering the objections raised in the preceding section, "I had best do simply for myself. . . . I speak as one who has had time to take many notes, to be struck with many differences, and to see, a little typically perhaps, what may eventually happen" [216-17].

He informs us candidly that he began with "a distinct sense" that the issue "didn't appeal to me—as it appeals, in general, but scantly to the young—and I was content for a long time to let it alone, only asking that it should, in turn, as irrelevant and insoluble, let *me*." Nevertheless, the question began imperceptibly to reintroduce itself upon him as he got older. The particular context was "resented bereavement" (the very point so powerful in Part 1) which resentment he thought at the time was "one of the exhibitions of life." And so it was. But the form it took was that of realizing more and more the overwhelming difference between the fact of death and "suffering (which means to warmly *being*) on earth." And what *that* brought home to him was that "science" was unequivocally right, and "the universe . . . kept proclaiming in a myriad voices that I and my poor form of consciousness were a quantity it could at any moment perfectly do without, even in what I might be pleased to call our very finest principle. If without me then just so without others" [217-18].

James's reenactment of this whole process begins more and more to resemble the relationship of Spencer Brydon to his *alter ego*. Not only does his request of the question to "let one another alone" recall Brydon's statement to the ghost at the closed door (and we remember how irreversible the process in that instance) but he also speaks of the question as "unaggressive" when young. Even more important, he describes it as "waking up" for him as he grows older—and "waking up" in a direct ratio with his "resentment" followed by the absolute conviction that science is right: thus the final conviction of extinction is what brings forth the question again! James says it began, imperceptibly, and even then little by little "facing me with a 'mild but firm' refusal to regard itself as settled." Once he understood what was happening he began to inquire of himself "why it should be thus obstinate" [219].

What had happened, in short, was that all the while I had been practically, though however dimly, trying to take the measure of my
consciousness—on this appropriate and prescribed basis of its being so
finite—I had learned, as I may say, to live in it more, and with the consequence of thereby not a little undermining the conclusion most
unfavorable to it. I had doubtless taken thus to increased living in it by
reaction against so grossly finite a world—for it at least *contained* the
world. . . . I should perhaps rather say that the more one turned it, as
an easy reflector, here and there and everywhere over the immensity of
things, the more it appeared to take [219-20].

The relationship between these remarks and William's final
doctrine is astounding, as Henry relates in his own way how he
came to rediscover his consciousness as a function instead of an
entity. There is, to be sure, no doctrine of "pure experience" here
as such, no starting out from the "other side," but I think even
that can be accounted for and perhaps is even inevitable, as I
hinted earlier and as we shall see momentarily. The functional
activity of consciousness in William's own distinct sense is, in
any case, here unmistakable:

It is not that I have found in growing older any one marked or momentous line in the life of the mind or in the play and the freedom of the
imagination to be stepped over; but that a process takes place which I
can only describe as the accumulation of the very treasure itself of consciousness. I won't say that "the world," as we commonly refer to it,
grows more attaching, but will say that the universe increasingly does,
and that this makes us present at the enormous multiplication of our
possible relationships with it [221].

These lines, like those before, could have all but come from
William's posthumous volume. But there are two matters here
worth our reflection. In William's last doctrine the innumerable
functions or contexts of "pure experience" in our relationship
with it are always occasioned by our personal needs or the whole
range and spectrum of "affectional facts" (still another area of
compatibility with his other doctrines)—a matter which bears on
Henry's statements above as well as those left to come. The second matter, as I have intimated more than once, has to do with
William's beginning at the "other end" with "pure experience"
vis-à-vis Henry's coming to his functional view of conscious-

ness by going right "into" it more and more. It seems to me that one way of appreciating this difference is, once again, from the standpoint of polarity. If William's final doctrine were really to get itself beyond the "laboratory-brain," he would, in all likelihood, have to start out by postulating at the "other end," or consciously adopting, as I have earlier suggested, his "transmissive function" argument for philosophical purposes. Henry, on the other hand, as a creative artist in possession of polarity, is capable of undergoing this process of discovery or realignment by virtue of nourishing the very strength and conviction opposed to it. Henry's enunciation of how he came to his viewpoint is, we might say, "operatively ironic." William must switch over to the opposite pole for his argument; Henry stays where he is and, by cultivating consciousness, "induces" the opposite possibility as being the very condition of where he is.

James tells us as much in his eloquent and final elaboration of what he has now come to feel since the momentous "rediscovery" of his consciousness chronicled above. He says that it "extends and transforms itself"; and it is here he refers explicitly to his vocation as artist, "carrying the field of consciousness further and further." And in this creative activity especially James insists: "I find myself—I can't express it otherwise—in communication with *sources*; sources to which I owe the apprehension of far more and far other combinations than observation and experience, in their ordinary sense, have given me the pattern of." He says additionally that he cannot make ultimate sense out of the "very provocation offered to the artist by the universe" to *be* an artist and serve it, unless this "being" desires "to get itself personally shared." Once again we can note the Brydon-like relationship: the more James as artist feels a "communication with sources" the more this "being" seems "to show itself for personally sharable, and thus foster the sublimest faith." James is most explicit, moreover, that "I have had admirably and endlessly to *cultivate*" the "renewal of existence," which in turn tells him of a "possible something that shall be better than what we have known here." Otherwise, the power invoked is "worthy but of the wit of a sniggering little boy who makes his dog jump at a morsel only to whisk it away; a practical joke of the lowest description, with the execrable taste of which I decline to charge our prime originator" [223, 224, 225, 226].

"Consciousness," he tells us, "has thus arrived at interesting me too much and on too great a scale—that is all my revelation or my secret." But the revelation and secret have brought Henry James "at this well-nigh final pass" to some rather staggering final proposals. The "cultivation" enables him to wonder if our present world may not be an "experiment" in which our apparent dependency "on our physical outfit" functions

not unlike the sustaining frame on little wheels that often encases growing infants, so that, dangling and shaking about in it, they may feel their assurance of walking increase and teach their small toes to know the ground. I like to think that we here, as to soul, dangle from the infinite and shake about in the universe; that this world and this conformation of these senses are our helpful and ingenious frame, amply provided with wheels and replete with the lesson for us of how to plant, spiritually, our feet [229, 229-30].

James confesses that such a conception "comes back, I recognize," to "the purification and preparation on earth for heaven, of the orthodox theology." He has no objection to the resemblance, which is a superficial one anyway, and mainly goes to show "how neatly extremes may sometimes meet." He is, of course, right. He knows neo-Platonism when he hears it, and refuses to "resent" his mind's association with the "perishable matter of which the rest of my personality is composed"; at the same time he *does* know neo-Platonism when he hears it, admitting that his remarks take "kindly to that admirable philosophic view which makes of matter the mere encasement or sheath . . . of a spirit it has no more concern in producing than the baby-frame has in producing the intelligence of the baby—much as that intelligence may be so promoted" [230-31].

James has qualified *all* of this of course by a repetition of—"I 'like' to think." By the same token he has this to say about his own condition of "desire":

It isn't really a question of belief—which is a term I have made no use of in these remarks; it is on the other hand a question of desire, but of desire so confirmed, so thoroughly established and nourished, as to leave belief a comparatively irrelevant affair. . . . I can't do less if I desire, but I shouldn't be able to do more if I believed. Just so I shouldn't be able to do more than cultivate belief; and it is exactly to cultivation that I subject my hopeful sense of the auspicious [231-32].

Such a viewpoint and argument concerning desire and belief is unmistakably pragmatistic, as is his final expression of having cultivated "the splendid illusion" of actually "doing something myself for my prospect, or at all events for my own possibility, of immortality." At which point he has to throw up his hands and admit that, "again, I recognize extremes 'neatly meet' ": how else can he talk of virtually working out his own "salvation" without having to welcome the "theological" resemblance in operative irony. And he concludes: "No, no, no—I reach beyond the laboratory-brain" [232-33].

This document provides, at least in my judgment, the appropriate analogue and copestone to the Jamesian "drift" which has been the subject of this final chapter. We see here those "intimations" and "collateral" relations with the spiritual viewpoint that surface in the late fiction, those distant "correspondences" with the traditional theological propositions. We see as well the entire foundation for the quasi-supernatural. And we see, even more importantly, the interrelation of the two. But as an interrelationship still it is the second which is the more fundamental, for that amounts to James's own creative process itself and is the very *way* he gets to where he is in regard to the first matter. And where he is, in turn, is not embracing the supernatural per se, but extending the boundaries of human consciousness to now include those "intimations." It is the last of his pragmatistic "inbetween" positions; and if it seems in its "Jamesian" nuance more difficult for us to grasp in its *actual* territory than William's characteristic "mediating" and "cordial" proposals along the same line, we must remember the nature of the relationship between the brothers as proposed throughout this book: William does the naming, Henry the embodying and actualizing.

Epilogue

The reader of this study, having followed my account of the "Jourdain" relationship, may perhaps recall a suggestion proffered back at the close of my first chapter. This was to the effect that, although, within Henry's work, William's thought may be said to correspond to the Coleridgean fancy when viewed in its special relation to the creative imagination, this fact need not preclude the possibility of a relationship existing between them personally like polarity itself. This is a subject well beyond the bounds of this study, and I by no means claim to have demonstrated such a condition in these pages. I am nevertheless drawn to resubmitting it as an implication which suggests itself after we examine their work in its relationship and then put that examination alongside their respective views *about* each other's work. I suggest it also by way of clarifying still another remark from the first chapter: that I hoped to present a case which might be *ultimately* compatible with both the sense of their personal relationship which so many thoughtful scholars who have been drawn to them have felt, on the one hand, and, on the other hand, the more recent argument voiced by Leon Edel.

Inasmuch as the key to polarity is always that of the positive and life-endowing allegiance between the poles which makes for unity, it seems to me that, were there in fact a relationship like that of polarity between the brothers themselves, it is most appropriate that Henry would have been the one who discovered and affirmed the unity in their work. For Henry rather than William, as we have seen, is the one of them in possession of polarity.

The question is, of course, what the nature of the polarity between them was. Perhaps the fact that they were brothers only a year apart, together with their extraordinary mutual genius, not only covers the ground but makes one ponder sometimes that they were not far more "hostile" and in "rivalry" than even the Edel biography insists. Surely, if one has had brothers and/or later on had sons (the present writer knows both experiences), and this without anything remotely like the genius attaching to the Jameses, one can only conclude that they were a pair of awfully good men all in all, both to others and to each other, as well as two of the most brilliant minds in American letters.

There is one aspect to them, however, that seems to suggest itself in the light of the examination of their work in this study. The "Jourdain" relationship itself, once we are conscious of its sheer extent and scope (as I hope this book has had some success at indicating) may point to what might at least have been the sort of polarity between them personally. If the "Jourdain" relationship, that is, consists essentially of William's doctrine—and Henry's embodiment thereof—of the living activity or experiential condition of ideas "happening" in consciousness, that very position is one that has within itself a fundamental polarity to which it can be referred: that of the union or fusion of energy and activity with thought and reflection. Now *within* the unity comprising the "Jourdain" relationship itself, it does seem to me that we can speak most legitimately of basic tendencies in each of the brothers that would comprise polar concentrations or predominances: William more the energy and activity predominance, Henry more the predominance of thought and reflection.

These respective polar-predominances suggest a larger consideration about the work of each. In his well-known 1877 letter to Howells defending the absence of a "cheerful ending" to *The American*, James is revealed to us in effect coerced by an a priori: not his point that Newman and Mme. de Cintre "would have been an impossible couple," but that we "are each the product of circumstances and there are tall stone walls which fatally divide us."[1] It is not surprising that the later James, the "Jourdain" of this study, found *The American* to be an irreparably flawed "arch-romance" precisely because "I was more than commonly enamoured of my idea." James in his "Preface" goes out of his way to reinforce this point by humorously describing himself as a young writer "seated in an American 'horse-car' " getting his first idea for the novel, and "presently to leave that vehicle in full possession of my answer"—that is, that Newman "would arrive at his just vindication and then would fail of all triumphantly and all vulgarly enjoying it."[2] James is, of course, paralleling Newman, who, in an early episode of the novel, tells how he suddenly decided, while seated in a like "vehicle," to forego revenge on a business competitor—thus revealing in advance the novel's ending. The later James believed that his violation by an idea, his coercion by an a priori, was exactly the reverse of a true "germ": there is no "germinating" possible if one is already "in possession" of "the answer" in advance. Perhaps James's later "American humor" in his "Preface" is in direct ratio to his remembrance of young James's serious pronouncements that such "uncheerful" endings confirm the "tall stone walls."

And yet, James's remark to Howells about the "tall stone walls which fatally divide us" *does*, I believe, point to his respective polar-concentration in relation to William, as does perhaps his statement, in the same letter, that "I suspect it is the tragedies in life that arrest my attention more than the other things and say more to my imagination."[3] William's doctrine on behalf of complete open-endedness, novelty, and indeterminacy, and his celebration of confluence and the sheer "flow" of things—these bespeak *his* polar-concentration in relation to Henry. Whether or not these mutually energizing force-fields are referrable ultimately to the tragic and comic visions of man it is difficult to say. Inasmuch as Henry James seems representative of the predominance of thought and reflection over that of energy and activity, and William James of energy and activity over thought and reflection, it does seem proper to think of them as perhaps expressive of the tragic and comic poles. In these terms "tragedy" can be said to occur when the centripetal force of self-consciousness finds or discovers its identity within the *logos*, or world-consciousness—the realization, as Emerson once pointed out, that what we call the Fall of Man is the discovery that "we exist." And "comedy" can be said to occur when the centrifugal force of world-consciousness—the given "pure experience," if you will—assimilates successfully and easily into itself its own pockets and channels and vortices of self-awareness, and holds predominance over them. Put in a less cosmic setting, the characteristic *tone* of the two brothers, especially in their letters to each other, bespeaks these respective polar-concentrations.

In suggesting all of this, however, let me reiterate again that in "assigning" them opposing concentrations, I am not referring to William's thought as one separate pole and Henry's art as the

other. I am speaking rather of a possible po
embedded within the unity between them
dain" relationship. William knew very well,
standing, that his philosophy was not prim
action." And Henry knew, *his* critics notwith
art was anything but a denial of "living." But
these very misconstructions of their work in
to, different predominances within their unity.
sion, one suspects, may often have had its pers
the central matter in all of this is that we *are*
unity, a polarity, and not a dichotomy. And in th
remember again what a polar concentration itself
of its own opposite concentrated at *its* opposite.
therefore, a polarity between the two of them along
suggested, it is, I repeat, appropriate that Henry h
one possessing polarity as a literary artist, would a
the one to affirm the "Jourdain" relationship.

Notes

Bibliography

Index

Notes

I. PERSPECTIVE, METHOD, AND AESTHETIC ASSUMPTIONS

1. Leon Edel, *Henry James: The Master: 1901-1916* (Philadelphia and New York: J. B. Lippincott Co., 1972), p. 298.

2. *New York Times Book Review*, 16 April 1972, p. 36. A continuation of the Barzun-Edel exchange can be found in the *Times Literary Supplement* during the fall of the same year. Especially interesting is Edel's defense, 13 Oct. 1972, pp. 1226-27, in which he cites not only Freud and the "dagger-side of wit and humour" on behalf of his position, but attempts to bolster his argument with a passage from Lionel Trilling's *The Liberal Imagination*, which treats the ideological opposition between William and Henry as that of "America-action" and "Europe-art," and which describes William as "the aggressor." This development in the debate immediately prompted a reply from Trilling, 20 Oct. 1972, p. 1257, who declared himself "wholly in agreement with the opinion expressed by Jacques Barzun," insisted that his and Edel's "respective views of the matter are wholly at odds," maintained that, despite their differences in viewpoint, "the affection between William and Henry was strong and remained unbroken," and concluded that William's letter to the Academy "was perhaps not the happiest example of his easy, genial epistolary manner: he is making a cosy, Brahmin-Boston kind of joke which probably doesn't suit the New York, or generally American, situation."

3. Gay Wilson Allen, *William James: A Biography* (New York: Viking Press, 1967); Ralph Barton Perry, *The Thought and Character of William James*, 2 vols. (Boston: Little, Brown, and Co., 1935).

4. F. O. Matthiessen, *The James Family* (New York: Alfred A. Knopf, 1947). The letters of William and Henry on each other's work, together with Matthiessen's and Ralph Barton Perry's conclusion and other appropriate commentary, will be taken up in the next chapter.

5. Quentin Anderson, *The American Henry James* (New Brunswick, N.J.: Rutgers University Press, 1957).

6. Donald Pizer points out that the Realistic Movement in America is "essentially subjective and idealistic in its view of human nature and experience—that is, it is ethically idealistic." C. Hugh Holman has long maintained that American Realism corresponds to the philosophy of pragmatism. Donald Pizer, *Realism and Naturalism in Nineteenth-Century American Literature* (Carbondale and Edwardsville: Southern Illinois University Press, 1966), p. 4. C. Hugh Holman, *A Handbook to Literature*, 3d ed. (New York: Bobbs-Merrill Co., Inc., 1972), pp. 411-12, 433-34.

7. Matthiessen, *The James Family*, pp. 587-94. This is a most unusual book. Primarily an anthology of writings by William, Henry, and Henry Senior, Matthiessen provides extensive commentary throughout which remains, all in all, the most thoughtful and knowledgeable to date on the interrelationship among the work of the three.

8. The appropriateness of James's comparison of himself to "M. Jourdain" after reading William's *Pragmatism* is discussed in the next chapter.

9. Dorothea Krook, *The Ordeal of Consciousness in Henry James* (Cambridge: Cambridge University Press, 1962), pp. 410-11.

10. See, for example, Peter K. Garrett, *Scene and Symbol from George Eliot to*

James Joyce (New Haven: Yale University Press, 1969), p. 140; also Laurence B. Holland, *The Expense of Vision: Essays on the Craft of Henry James* (Princeton: Princeton University Press, 1964), p. x.

11. Owen Barfield, *Saving the Appearances: A Study in Idolatry* (New York: Harcourt, Brace and World, n.d.), p. 90.

12. Henry James, *The Art of the Novel*, ed. R. P. Blackmur (New York: Charles Scribner's Sons, 1934), p. 45.

13. The case for James's organic and Coleridgean aesthetic was formally argued by René Wellek, "Henry James's Literary Theory and Criticism," *American Literature* 30 (1958): 293-321. Wellek concludes that "James alone in his time and place in the English-speaking world holds fast to the insights or organistic aesthetics and thus consitutues a bridge from the early nineteenth century to modern criticism."

14. See Owen Barfield, *What Coleridge Thought* (Middletown, Conn.: Wesleyan University Press, 1971), pp. 131-43; 158-74; and passim.

15. Compare, for example, the discussion of Goethe's theories in ibid., pp. 135-37; 241-43 (n. 12), to the following passage from the "Preface" to *The Portrait of a Lady*: "These are the fascinations of the fabulist's art, these lurking forces of expansion, these necessities of upspringing in the seed, these beautiful determinations, on the part of the idea entertained, to grow as tall as possible, to push into the light and the air and thickly flower there." *The Art of the Novel*, p. 42.

16. Coleridge, *Biographia Literaria*, chap. 14. This is a basic principle for Coleridge and reappears throughout his writings.

17. Barfield, *What Coleridge Thought*, p. 170. Compare the series of relationships above to Coleridge's distinction (but not division) between *natura naturans* and *natura naturata*.

18. Owen Barfield, *Speaker's Meaning* (Middletown, Conn.: Wesleyan University Press, 1967), pp. 38-39.

19. A new tendency in Jacobite scholarship to be nevertheless more "evaluative" of James's contributions, to acknowledge his limitations as artist and writer, is indicated by two recent publications: Charles Thomas Samuels, *The Ambiguity of Henry James* (Urbana: University of Illinois Press, 1971); and Philip M. Weinstein, *Henry James and the Requirements of the Imagination* (Cambridge, Mass.: Harvard University Press, 1971). Both are valuable additions to the understanding of James's fiction and the second in particular contains excellent individual readings of several of James's novels. Samuels's wish to praise James's satiric gifts at the expense of his idealism tends on occasion, however, to lead him astray, as in his discussion of *The Wings of the Dove*, which he calls a "confusion." The presentation of Milly Theale and the assumptions underlying Merton Densher's conversion are not so confusing if one assumes a polar, as opposed to dichotomous, relationship governing the novel's vision of good and evil, sacrifice and exploitation, and so on. Weinstein's discussion of the "tension" in James between imagination and experience, the "paradox" between actual and vicarious "living," leads him to conclude that James's life and art constitute "an intense but narrow experience" and a "slender though permanent art." Again, polarity has been interpreted as dichotomy. Nevertheless, his extensive readings of *The Portrait of a Lady* and *The Ambassadors* exhibit under the guise of "tension," "conflict" et al. relationships that are essentially polar.

20. This aspect of my argument involving the novelist's "empiricized polarity" will reappear and have its hearing in part 3 of this book. Even then, however, it will remain secondary to the William-Henry relationship. My expectation—or at least my hope—is that it can serve as a positive complement to the central issue of this study.

II. THE BROTHERS: ON EACH OTHER'S WORK

1. Leon Edel, *Henry James: The Master: 1901-1916* (Philadelphia and New York: J. B. Lippincott Co., 1972), p. 295.

2. See Reuben A. Brower, *The Fields of Light: An Experiment in Critical Reading* (New York: Oxford University Press, 1951), pp. 51-53. Brower writes: "There is

one type of assumption in particular that the reader must grasp and define if he is to enjoy the special amusement of irony and if he is to describe and discover the design in any longer piece of sustained irony. He must understand and accept (at least temporarily) *the positive allegiances,* the values through which the individual ironies gain their exact meaning and their force, 'the strength of applied irony being' as Henry James has said, 'in the sincerities, the lucidities, the utilities that stand behind it' " [my emphasis]; Brower also remarks: "To experience . . . irony . . . we must entertain both of the clashing possibilities: therein lies the irony of it. So obvious a point needs stressing, I believe, because some definitions of irony imply that the reader finds the intended or true meaning beneath the apparent, a view that tends to destroy irony both as a literary experience and as a vision of life." Brower's most perceptive comments here bespeak a critical understanding which is (despite the use of the word "clashing") greatly imbued with the recognition in art of polarity rather that just dichotomy—with interpenetration ("the positive allegiances") rather than only juxtaposition. The reference above to James is singularly appropriate: see Henry James, *The Art of the Novel,* ed. R. P. Blackmur (New York: Charles Scribner's Sons, 1934), p. 222.

3. Krook so argues in *The Ordeal of Consciousness in Henry James* (Cambridge: Cambridge University Press, 1962); see also Frederick C. Crews, *The Tragedy of Manners: Moral Drama in the Later Novels of Henry James* (New Haven: Yale University Press, 1957).

4. F. O. Matthiessen, *The James Family* (New York: Alfred A. Knopf, 1947), p. 317. Matthiessen has access to and quotes several exchanges between the two brothers which are not published elsewhere.

5. Ibid., pp. 325, 345; also Henry James, *The Letters of Henry James,* ed. Percy Lubbock (New York: Charles Scribner's Sons, 1920), 2:167.

6. Ralph Barton Perry, *The Thought and Character of William James* (Boston: Little, Brown, and Co., 1935), 1:429. Perry's contention is taken up later in this chapter.

7. Matthiessen, *The James Family,* p. 318.

8. Ibid., p. 338.

9. Ibid., p. 339.

10. Ibid., p. 340; also Henry James, *Letters,* 2:43.

11. Matthiessen, *The James Family,* p. 340; also Henry James, *Letters,* 2:44.

12. Matthiessen, *The James Family,* pp. 341-42; also *The Letters of William James,* ed. by his son Henry James (Boston: Atlantic Monthly Press, 1920), 2:277-78.

13. Matthiessen, *The James Family,* p. 343; also William James, *Letters,* 2:280.

14. Matthiessen, *The James Family,* p. 343; also Henry James, *Letters,* 2:83. Parentheses and ellipses in the original.

15. Leon Edel prints the word "annihilating" rather than "illuminating" in his reference to Henry's response to William's *American Scene* letter: *The Master: 1901-1916,* p. 301. I trust that my discussion of the exchanges above is compatible with either reading, though I have printed from what is apparently Edel's own source.

16. Matthiessen, *The James Family,* p. 344.

17. Ibid., pp. 344-45; also Henry James, *Letters,* 2:140-41.

18. William James, *Letters,* 2:290-91.

19. Perry, *The Thought and Character of William James,* 1:429.

20. F. O. Matthiessen, *Henry James: The Major Phase* (New York: Oxford University Press, 1944), p. 143.

21. Matthiessen, *The James Family,* p. 673.

22. Ibid., pp. 679-80, 683.

23. Ibid., pp. 681, 683.

24. Joseph J. Firebaugh, "The Pragmatism of Henry James," *Virginia Quarterly Review* 27 (1951):434; similarly Henry Bamford Parkes in "The James Brothers," *Sewanee Review* 56 (1948):323-28, argues in reaction to Matthiessen's *The James*

Family: "The main effort of Henry James was to convey, by means of an appropriate aesthetic form, a view of life essentially similar to that which William expressed in philosophy"; more recently Peter Buitenhuis in his study of James's American writings, *The Grasping Imagination* (Toronto: University of Toronto Press, 1970), p. 111, observes that in *The Portrait of a Lady* "Henry James anticipated by some nine years the theory of perception that his brother William was to put forward in his *Principles of Psychology* (1890)"—i.e., that all perception contains a considerable subjective element.

25. Marius Bewley is more satisfying in this respect in *The Complex Fate* (London: Chatto and Windus, 1952), pp. 145-49. Bewley's brief excursion into the William-Henry relationship stresses a parallel "freedom to improvise on the moral plane" deriving from a "pragmatically plastic" universe. He thus puts the emphasis where it should be—on creativity or "improvisation." Robert Reilly in his fine essay, "Henry James and the Morality of Fiction," *American Literature* 39 (1967):20-26, points convincingly to a parallel in William's *Varieties of Religious Experience*. Christof Wegelin in *The Image of Europe in Henry James* (Dallas: Southern Methodist University Press, 1958), pp. 101, 184, n. 12, argues that Lambert Strether, hero of *The Ambassadors*, is a "pragmatist." Although Wegelin is not concerned in particular with William James's philosophy, his presentation of Henry James would, I believe, be very much at home with the James of this study.

26. John Henry Raleigh, "Henry James: The Poetics of Empiricism," *PMLA* 66 (1951):112.

27. Eliseo Vivas, "Henry and William: (Two Notes)," *Kenyon Review* 5 (1943): 580-81.

28. Ibid., p. 582.

29. Ibid., p. 586.

30. Ibid., p. 588.

31. Ibid., p. 589; see also William James, *The Principles of Psychology* (New York: Henry Holt and Co., 1890), 1:255.

32. Vivas, "Henry and William," pp. 590-91.

33. Ibid., p. 592. Vivas's reference is apparently to the third and fourth chapters in "Book Second," which are actually chapters nine and ten of *The Golden Bowl*.

34. There is, however, a further or "terminal" reason which such "alpha-omega" developments in Jamesian commentary derive from, involving the presence of genuine polarity both in Henry's fiction and quite likely, as earlier suggested, between the brothers themselves personally. But this further consideration must be reserved (or at least kept in the background) until later in my argument. The important point about real polarity—it cannot be said too often— is the *positive* relationship which differentiates it from dichotomy.

35. William James, *The Meaning of Truth* (New York: Longmans, Green, and Co., 1909), p. 52.

36. For an excellent discussion of this point see Geoffrey Clive, *The Romantic Enlightenment* (New York: Meridian Books, 1960), pp. 74-95.

37. William James, *The Meaning of Truth*, p. 186.

38. See ibid., pp. 75, 118, and passim. It is certainly not without interest that William, in subtitling this book *A Sequel to "Pragmatism,"* set about to defend himself against the criticism that arose from the previous work, by stressing in general the "humanism" of his pragmatistic thought. Henry, it will be recalled, mentions in his letter that *he* finds William "nowhere as difficult as you make everything for your critics." Henry, characteristically modest when it came to "philosophy," probably thought that if he had no difficulty understanding William, his brother's professional colleagues would surely not. There is a lovely irony in the fact that today the best teachers of philosophy usually must correct the initial and erroneous impression of William's thought precisely in the direction toward Henry's natural grasp of it.

III. WILLIAM JAMES AND AMBULATORY RELATIONS

1. William James, *The Meaning of Truth* (New York: Longmans, Green, and Co., 1909), pp. 138, 139.

2. Joseph Warren Beach, *The Method of Henry James* (Philadelphia: Alfred Saifer, 1954), pp. 178, 179.

3. William James, *The Meaning of Truth*, pp. 139-42.

4. Henry James, *The Future of the Novel: Essays on the Art of Fiction*, ed. Leon Edel (New York: Vintage Books, 1956), pp. 15, 21.

5. William James, *The Meaning of Truth*, pp. 142-44.

6. Ian Watt, "The First Paragraph of *The Ambassadors*: An Explication," *Essays in Criticism* 10 (1960):250-74. After his extensive analysis of James's opening paragraph Watt concludes: "The most obvious and demonstrable features of James's prose style, its vocabulary and syntax, are direct reflections of his attitude to life and his conception of the novel; and these features, like the relation of the paragraph to the rest of the novel, and to other novels, make clear that the notorious idiosyncrasies of Jamesian prose are directly related to the imperatives which led him to develop a narrative texture as richly complicated and as highly organised as that of poetry."

7. Leon Edel and Gordon N. Ray, eds., *Henry James and H. G. Wells* (Urbana: University of Illinois Press, 1958), pp. 245, 246, 248, 249.

8. Ibid., pp. 261-62.

9. Ibid., pp. 263, 266.

10. Ibid., pp. 266-67.

11. Henry James, *The Art of the Novel*, ed. R. P. Blackmur (New York: Charles Scribner's Sons, 1934), pp. 45-46.

12. Ibid., p. 46.

IV. THE "JOURDAIN" RELATIONSHIP (I)

1. Henry Adams, *The Letters of Henry Adams (1892-1918)*, ed. Worthington Chauncey Ford (Boston and New York: Houghton Mifflin Co., 1938), 2:622.

2. F. W. Dupee, "Henry James" in *Major Writers of America* (New York: Harcourt, Brace and World, Inc., 1962), 2:265. It is one of the novelist's most widely quoted and anthologized letters.

3. Henry James, *The Letters of Henry James*, ed. Percy Lubbock (New York: Charles Scribner's Sons, 1920), 2:360-61.

4. See in particular Edward Stone, "The Battle" in *The Battle and the Books: Some Aspects of Henry James* (Athens: Ohio University Press, 1964), pp. 3-60.

5. Nathaniel Hawthorne, *The Scarlet Letter*, ed. William Charvat et al. (Columbus: Ohio State University Press, 1962), p. 37.

6. See especially F. W. Dupee, ed., *The Question of Henry James: A Collection of Critical Essays* (New York: Henry Holt and Co., 1945); also Wayne C. Booth, *The Rhetoric of Fiction* (Chicago: University of Chicago Press, 1961), pp. 311-16; 339-67.

7. Henry James, *The Future of the Novel: Essays on the Art of Fiction*, ed. Leon Edel (New York: Vintage Books, 1956), p. 3.

8. Ibid., pp. 22-23.

9. The notion of the pragmatistic mind as "locally" oriented is one I shall be coming back to most often throughout this and the following chapter. I do indeed mean here to suggest its collateral relations with the post-Civil war "local color" or "regional" movements in fiction, although these matters are beyond the scope of this study.

10. William James, *Pragmatism: A New Name for Some Old Ways of Thinking* (New York: Longmans, Green, and Co., 1907), p. 106.

11. Ibid., pp. 45-46.

12. Ibid., p. 96; last emphasis mine.

13. This is in effect William's doctrine of radical empiricism, a philosophical application and extension of his view, expressed in the *Psychology*, of the relational or transitive state of consciousness, the "stream of thought." See William James, *The Principles of Psychology* (New York: Henry Holt and Co., 1890), 1:224-90.

14. William James, "The Will to Believe," in *The Will to Believe and Other Essays in Popular Philosophy* (New York: Dover Publications, 1956), pp. 8, 9-10.

15. Ibid., p. 16.

16. William James, *Pragmatism*, p. 77.

17. This is the novelist's definition of "operative irony." See Henry James, *The Art of the Novel*, ed. R. P. Blackmur (New York: Charles Scribner's Sons, 1934), p. 222. I shall be returning to this important conception in this and in particular the next chapter.

18. Henry James, *The Ambassadors* (New York: Charles Scribner's Sons, 1909), 21:218. Hereafter cited as New York Edition.

19. Henry James, *The Art of the Novel*, pp. 307, 309.

20. Leon Edel, "Introduction," *The Ambassadors* (Cambridge, Mass.: Houghton Mifflin Co., 1960), pp. viii-ix.

21. William James, *Pragmatism*, p. 201. "Truth *happens* to an idea. It *becomes* true, is *made* true by events. Its verity *is* in fact an event, a process."

22. Wayne C. Booth, *The Rhetoric of Fiction* (Chicago: University of Chicago Press, 1961), pp. 339-74.

23. Again, operative irony; I find most helpful Booth's demonstration of James's inveterate transformations in his works from notebook entry to later entry and so on to the finished piece. I do not, however, interpret this evidence as he does.

24. William James, *Essays in Radical Empiricism* (New York: Longmans, Green, and Co., 1912), pp. 41-42; cf. his "Preface" to *The Meaning of Truth* (New York: Longmans, Green, and Co., 1909), pp. xii-xiii; "The generalized conclusion is that therefore the parts of experience hold together from next to next by relations that are themselves parts of experience."

25. William James, *A Pluralistic Universe* (New York: Longmans, Green, and Co., 1909), pp. 325-26.

26. Leon Edel and Gordon N. Ray, eds., *Henry James and H. G. Wells* (Urbana: University of Illinois Press, 1958), p. 267.

27. See Walter Pater, *The Renaissance: Studies in Art and Poetry* (London: Macmillan and Co., 1924), pp. 246-47.

28. This Kantian notion pervades Carlyle's work. See especially "Pure Reason," bk. 1, chap. 10 of *Sartor Resartus*.

29. Henry James, *French Poets and Novelists*, ed. Leon Edel (New York: Grosset and Dunlap, 1964), pp. 80-81.

30. See, for example, James's review of *Middlemarch* in *The Future of the Novel*, esp. pp. 88-89; he speaks also of Eliot's philosophic mind in his essay "The Novels of George Eliot" in *Views and Reviews*, ed. LeRoy Phillips (Boston: Ball Publishing Co., 1908), pp. 1-37.

31. Theodora Bosanquet, *Henry James at Work* (London: Hogarth Press, 1924), p. 27.

32. Henry James, *Letters*, 1:111-12.

33. New York Edition, 21:14.

34. The first statement is by Edward Stone, *The Battle and the Books*, p. 9. The second and third, by Ralph Barton Perry and F. O. Matthiessen, respectively, were quoted more fully in my second chapter: *The Thought and Character of William James* (Boston: Little, Brown, and Co., 1935), 1:429; *Henry James: The Major Phase* (New York: Oxford University Press, 1944), p. 143.

35. See Henry James, *Literary Views and Essays*, ed. Albert Mordell (New York: Grove Press, Inc., 1957), pp. 61-67.

36. William James, *Pragmatism*, p. 128. I shall return to this important conception of William's in more detail in the next chapter.

37. This quality comes to dominate James's later critical essays on such writers as

Flaubert, Balzac, or Zola. These writers are quasi-fictive projections, or at least impressionistic explorations from James's "felt life." Zola in particular appears in James's 1903 essay on him very much like a Jamesian character: see Henry James, *The Future of the Novel*, pp. 165-71.

38. I am not, of course, suggesting that he did not have pride and esteem for William. But I think he also had genuine feeling for his father, whose writings he says he "can't enter into."

39. Edmund Wilson, ed., *The Shock of Recognition* (New York: Modern Library, 1955), p. 856. Eliot's essay on James first appeared in *The Little Review*, August 1918.

40. William James, *The Will to Believe*, p. ix.

41. William James, *Pragmatism*, p. 257. The italics appear in the original.

42. The very quality in Flaubert we might call, admiringly, his ironic distance James seems to have thought slightly lacking in humanity. See Henry James, *The Future of the Novel*, pp. 145-52. James's own notion of irony is always bound up with engagement and sympathy.

43. Henry James, *The Art of the Novel*, pp. 221, 223.

44. Perry, *The Thought and Character of William James*, 2:668.

45. See Stevenson, "A Humble Remonstrance" in *Henry James and Robert Louis Stevenson: A Record of Friendship and Criticism*, ed. Janet Adam Smith (London: Rupert Hart-Davis, 1948), pp. 93-96.

46. See Henry James, *Hawthorne* (Ithaca: Cornell University Press, 1956), pp. 83-84; also his remarks on the most "genial" of Hawthorne's novels *The Blithedale Romance*, pp. 104-9.

47. William James, *The Will to Believe*, pp. 18-19; my emphasis.

48. New York Edition, 22:266. I shall examine this passage from *The Ambassadors* in more detail in the next chapter.

49. William James, *The Will to Believe*, p. 27.

50. R. P. Blackmur, "Henry James," in *Literary History of the United States*, ed. R. E. Spiller et al., rev. ed. (New York: Macmillan Co., 1953), p. 1051. This really stunning distinction between Adams and James would serve rather well to distinguish the intellectualist or rationalist from the pragmatistic mind. Nevertheless, it should be said that Henry's very pragmatistic mentality is what accounts, I think, for his response, different from that of Adams, to the outbreak of World War I. As Blackmur says in *A Primer of Ignorance* (New York: Harcourt, Brace and World, 1967), pp. 263, 260, "James had nothing but his sensibility, which withstood nothing, but sucked up the horror like a vacuum"; Adams, though as much a partisan as James, was saved this intimate relationship with the horror of the war, because he "generalized *first*" and could incorporate it into "patterns," "lines of force," and the like.

51. Leo B. Levy, "Criticism Chronicle: Hawthorne, Melville, and James," *Southern Review*, n.s. 2 (1966):431

52. Henry James, "A Round of Visits," in *The Complete Tales of Henry James*, ed. Leon Edel (Philadelphia and New York: J. B. Lippincott Co., 1964), 12:435.

53. See Henry James, *The Notebooks of Henry James*, ed. F. O. Matthiessen and Kenneth B. Murdock (New York: Oxford University Press, 1947), pp. 372-415. I am somewhat exaggerating, perhaps, but this extraordinary document does seem at times but a grace note from "*The Ambassadors*: Briefer Version."

54. Peirce's remarks to William sometimes throw an interesting crosslight on William's to Henry; for instance: "he who introduces a new conception should be held to have a *duty* imposed upon him to invent a sufficiently disagreeable series of words to express it. I wish you would reflect seriously upon the moral aspect of terminology"; Perry, *The Thought and Character of William James*, 2:432. Peirce was not always pleased with the Jourdain-like stance William often assumed with *his* doctrine, and eventually called his philosophy "pragmaticism" to distinguish it from William's.

55. William James, *Some Problems of Philosophy: A Beginning of an Introduc-*

tion to Philosophy (New York: Longmans, Green, and Co., 1911), pp. 101-2.

56. Ibid., pp. 102-4.

57. Frank Norris, *The Responsibilities of the Novelist* (New York: Doubleday, Page and Co., 1903), pp. 215-16.

58. William Dean Howells, *Criticism and Fiction and Other Essays*, ed. Clara M. and Rudolph Kirk (New York: New York University Press, 1959), p. 61.

59. Henry James, *The Future of the Novel*, p. 13.

60. *The Golden Bowl* (New York: Charles Scribner's Sons, 1909), 1:22. This is vol. 23 of the New York Edition.

61. See F. O. Matthiessen, *American Renaissance: Art and Expression in the Age of Emerson and Whitman* (New York: Oxford University Press, 1941), pp. 302-4. Matthiessen's point is that James does not take us into "seas of speculation" as do Poe and Melville.

V. THE "JOURDAIN" RELATIONSHIP (II)

1. Allen Tate, "Emily Dickinson," in *Essays of Four Decades* (Chicago: Swallow Press, 1968), p. 287.

2. William James, *Some Problems of Philosophy: A Beginning of an Introduction to Philosophy* (New York: Longmans, Green, and Co., 1911), pp. 147-49.

3. Ibid., pp. 150-51.

4. William James, *Pragmatism: A New Name for Some Old Ways of Thinking* (New York: Longmans, Green, and Co., 1907), pp. 233-34.

5. Ibid., p. 128.

6. F. O. Matthiessen, *Henry James: The Major Phase* (New York: Oxford University Press, 1944), p. 63.

7. Peter K. Garrett, *Scene and Symbol from George Eliot to James Joyce* (New Haven: Yale University Press, 1969), p. 158.

8. Two examples of such "negative" pertinence are: F. R. Leavis's remarks about James's Prefaces in *The Great Tradition*, Gotham Library (New York: New York University Press, 1963), pp. 154-55, where he argues they are not real critical documents but rather "come from the mind that conceived the late work"; and Wayne C. Booth, *The Rhetoric of Fiction* (Chicago: University of Chicago Press, 1961), pp. 339-46, where, as I have earlier mentioned, it is shown meticulously that James kept transforming his conception of a particular work from notebook entry to notebook entry to finished work. Perhaps the classic example of such pertinent adverse judgment is Yvor Winter's celebrated opinion of Robert Frost as "spiritual drifter." If one may speak operatively ironic, such views could not be more wrong for being right.

9. William James, *Pragmatism*, p. 251.

10. Ibid., p. 136.

11. Ibid., pp. 138, 144.

12. Henry James, *The Future of the Novel: Essays on the Art of Fiction*, ed. Leon Edel (New York: Vintage Books, 1956), p. 12.

13. William James, *Pragmatism*, p. 148.

14. Ibid., p. 141; my emphasis.

15. Henry James, "The Beast in the Jungle" in *The Novels and Tales of Henry James* (New York: Charles Scribner's Sons, 1909), 17:71. Hereafter cited as New York Edition. This is, of course, John Marcher's belief about his special destiny.

16. William James, *The Letters of William James*, ed. by his son Henry James (Boston: Atlantic Monthly Press, 1920), 1:288. William's tone, in referring to Henry's "alien" mannerisms, is typically affectionate.

17. Henry James, *The Art of the Novel*, ed. R. P. Blackmur (New York: Charles Scribner's Sons, 1934), p. 45.

18. Ibid., p. xxxi.

19. Ibid., p. xxx.

20. Ibid., pp. 45-46.

21. William James, *Pragmatism*, p. 201.

22. William James, "The Will to Believe," in *The Will to Believe and Other Essays*

in Popular Philosophy (New York: Dover Publications, 1956), pp. 17, 19.

23. Henry James, *The Art of the Novel*, p. 222.

24. Maxwell Geismar has authored the notorious full-scale attack on James and his admirers, *Henry James and the Jacobites* (Boston: Houghton Mifflin Co., 1963).

25. William James, *Pragmatism*, pp. 282-85.

26. Ibid., pp. 286-88.

27. *The Ambassadors*, New York Edition, 22:266.

28. Robert Frost, *The Poetry of Robert Frost*, ed. Edward Connery Lathem (New York: Holt, Rinehart & Winston, 1969), p. 301. The reader should compare the reading of Frost's "Neither Out Far Nor In Deep" that follows with Reuben Brower, *The Poetry of Robert Frost: Constellations of Intention* (New York: Oxford University Press, 1963), pp. 147-51.

29. William James, *The Will to Believe*, p. 27.

VI. PSYCHOLOGY—THE REAL AND THE ETHICAL

1. Henry James, *The Art of the Novel*, ed. R. P. Blackmur (New York: Charles Scribner's Sons, 1934), pp. 309, 52. James, as we know, also fills his famous *Portrait* "Preface" with imagery from architecture; but there is an inherent opposition between his argument from architecture and his insistence that the entire *Portrait* extends the germ of his "unattached" figure of Isabel Archer, a "contradiction" noted, to my knowledge, only by Laurence Holland in *The Expense of Vision: Essays on the Craft of Henry James* (Princeton: Princeton University Press, 1964), pp. 4-5. James's conception of "roundness" or circularity is basically equivalent to the expanding process of the germ, and it does stand in genuine *polar* opposition with the architectural "edifice," the "house of fiction." Were I treating that novel in this study, that is how I should wish to develop my argument, for it corresponds identically to the "tension" between the "autonomous self" that Isabel expounds and the "envelope of circumstances" argued by Madame Merle. In other words James's "contradictory" arguments in his "Preface" are the mirror image of the central polarity that governs that book.

2. Henry James, *The Notebooks of Henry James*, ed. F. O. Matthiessen and Kenneth B. Murdock (New York: Oxford University Press, 1947), p. 18.

3. René Wellek, "Henry James's Literary Theory and Criticism," *American Literature* 30 (1958):321.

4. This is perhaps the major reason for the absence in my final chapter of a fuller, more "ambulatory" reading of either *The Wings of the Dove* or *The Golden Bowl*. In a book with already as much "ambulation" as this one, such a procedure with those two novels would, I suspect, be counterproductive. This decision, moreover, frees me to address the whole question of Henry's quasi-supernatural work in relation to William's views on psychical research and immortality—and to look at Henry's views on immortality as well; it also enables me to present briefly what I feel may be an important link between William's proposals in this area and his final doctrine of radical empiricism—a link possibly of equal interest for students of philosophy as that between William and Henry is for students of imaginative literature.

5. David Toor, "Narrative Irony in Henry James' 'The Real Thing,'" *University Review* 34 (Winter 1967):95-99.

6. Wayne C. Booth, *The Rhetoric of Fiction* (Chicago: University of Chicago Press, 1961), p. 367.

7. See, for example, Henry James, *Notebooks*, p. 105; or Harold T. McCarthy, *Henry James: The Creative Process* (New York: Thomas Yoseloff, Inc., 1958), p. 81.

8. Toor, "Narrative Irony," p. 95. Booth was the first to give an "unreliable" reading to James's "The Liar," pp. 347-54.

9. Henry James, *The Future of the Novel: Essays on the Art of Fiction*, ed. Leon Edel (New York: Vintage Books, 1956), p. 5.

10. Henry James, *Notebooks*, pp. 103, 104.

11. Ibid., p. 102.

12. Ibid., pp. 103, 104.

13. Virgil Scott, *Studies in the Short Story: Instructor's Manual* (New York: Holt, Rinehart and Winston, 1968), pp. 76-79.

14. Booth, *The Rhetoric of Fiction*, pp. 340-45.

15. Henry James, *The Future of the Novel*, p. 13.

16. William James, *Some Problems of Philosophy: A Beginning of an Introduction to Philosophy* (New York: Longmans, Green, and Co., 1911), p. 101.

17. Henry James, "The Real Thing," in *The Novels and Tales of Henry James* (New York: Charles Scribner's Sons, 1909), 18:334. Subsequent references will be to this volume of the New York Edition and will appear in brackets just after the quoted material.

18. William James, *Some Problems of Philosophy*, p. 148.

19. R. P. Blackmur, "Introduction," *The Aspern Papers* and *The Spoils of Poynton* (New York: Dell Publishing Co., Inc., 1959), p. 12. A good summary of critical argument over *The Spoils* and in particular the character of Fleda Vetch may be found in Oscar Cargill, *The Novels of Henry James* (New York: Macmillan Co., 1961), pp. 218-43, supplemented by James W. Gargano, "The Spoils of Poynton: Action and Responsibility," *Sewanee Review* 69 (1961):650-60, and Robert C. McLean, "The Subjective Adventure of Fleda Vetch," *American Literature* 36 (1964): 12-30.

20. Leon Edel, *Henry James: The Treacherous Years: 1895-1901* (Philadelphia and New York: J. B. Lippincott Co., 1969), p. 161.

21. This was the argument proposed in the first of Eliseo Vivas's two notes in "Henry and William (Two Notes)," *Kenyon Review* 5 (1943):580-94, the same essay discussed in the second chapter of this study, though there more for its second note concerning the brothers' epistemological relationship. In *The James Family* (New York: Alfred A. Knopf, 1947), p. 683, F. O. Matthiessen concedes that some readers might believe that Henry was "warning" William in *The Spoils of Poynton*; nevertheless, "Fleda [Vetch]," Matthiessen feels, "though WJ [*sic*] may not have so recognized her, was essentially one of his underdogs," whereas William himself could "have indicated the psychological weaknesses in HJ's free spirits, in so far, at least, as they were represented by the extreme case of Fleda, who was fastidious to the point of being neurotic." Vivas's argument—the moral opposition not the epistemological agreement—is most fully restated by William H. Gass, "The High Brutality of Good Intentions," *Accent* 18 (1958):62-71, in which both *The Portrait of a Lady* and *The Spoils of Poynton* are brought to bear on the issue. For Gass "[t]he impatience which James generates in the reader and expresses through Mrs. Gereth is the impatience, precisely, of his brother: for Fleda to act, to break from the net of scruple and seize the chance . . . but Fleda Vetch understands, as few people in Henry James ever do, the high brutality of such good intentions. She cannot accept happiness on the condition of moral compromise." Finally, Walter Isle in *Experiments in Form: Henry James's Novels, 1896-1901* (Cambridge, Mass.: Harvard University Press, 1968), pp. 86, 110-11, cites Vivas's argument as "central to the moral scheme of the novel" and equates Mrs. Gereth with "pragmatism" and "a pragmatic conception of value"; his point, however, is that James shows the limitations both of Fleda Vetch's "altruistic idealism" and Mrs. Gereth's "pragmatism."

22. Henry James, *The Art of the Novel*, p. 129.

23. Matthiessen, *The James Family*, p. 337. William on occasion could respond positively to Henry's later manner, especially in shorter works. Thus he speaks of the "hard enamel finish" of the collection *The Better Sort* (1903).

24. Yvor Winters, *In Defense of Reason* (Denver: Alan Swallow, 1947), p. 338. Winters nevertheless views the effect of Fleda's morality on the reader as "essentially neurotic," p. 320.

25. The most satisfying discussion to date of this difficult book is by Walter Isle, *Experiments in Form*, pp. 77-119; Laurence Holland, *The Expense of Vision*, pp. 57-113, is also most perceptive and provocative.

26. Henry James, *The Art of the Novel*, pp. 129, 131.

27. Henry James, *The Spoils of Poynton,* in *The Novels and Tales of Henry James* (New York: Charles Scribner's Sons, 1908), 10:46-47. Subsequent references will be to this volume of the New York Edition and will appear in brackets just after the quoted material.

28. Henry James, *The Spoils of Poynton* (London: Penguin Books, 1963).

29. Henry James, *The Art of the Novel,* pp. 129, 131.

30. A good example of this same quality is Fleda's enormously warm response to and "creation" of the character of the deceased maiden-aunt of the dower house at Ricks. See especially her conversation with Mrs. Gereth in chap. 21, where she lauds Mrs. Gereth's artistic arrangement of the maiden-aunt's modest furnishings and then invokes intimately the very moral character of the deceased lady—all of which Mrs. Gereth finds both amusing and yet fascinating, as though "finding herself seated at the feet of her pupil" [249]. It is also true, however, that the maiden-aunt probably inspires Fleda by having lived a life of renunciation and dignity. The sheer extent of this quality in James's heroine can be seen too in her reaction at one point to Owen's dress, when, after responding favorably to his attire, she thinks: "this in turn gave him—for she never could think of him, or indeed of some other things, without the aid of his vocabulary—a tremendous pull" [150].

31. Walter Isle has also noted this "wrong conclusion" from Fleda's declaration, *Experiments in Form,* p. 112.

32. Edel, *The Treacherous Years: 1895-1901,* pp. 163, 164.

33. See, for example, Blackmur, "Introduction," p. 14, and Isle, *Experiments in Form,* pp. 114-17; on the other hand, McLean's reading of the ending, "The Subjective Adventure of Fleda Vetch," pp. 28-29, as the "burning away" of Fleda's "illusion" may seem at first similar to mine, but it is actually as far—even farther—from my reading than the "symbolic" ones I criticize. His entire argument for her "subjective adventure" is, like Toor's reading of "The Real Thing," a matter of reversing things into "unreliability." His casual reference to Fleda's "ethical relativism," p. 19, has no relationship whatever to my discussion of her ethic, and is instead his turning-the-screw on previous "superior" or "absolute" commentary on her morality.

34. See William James, *The Meaning of Truth* (New York: Longmans, Green, and Co., 1909), pp. 142-44; this formulation was discussed in my third chapter.

35. Henry James, *The Art of the Novel,* pp. 33-34.

36. Isle, *Experiments in Form,* pp. 92-93, 108, 117.

37. Holland, *The Expense of Vision,* p. 109.

VII. PRAGMATISM—"REMOULDING" EXPERIENCE AND VIOLATING IDEAS

1. William James, *The Principles of Psychology* (New York: Henry Holt and Co., 1890), 1:234.

2. Henry James, *The Art of the Novel,* ed. R. P. Blackmur (New York: Charles Scribner's Sons, 1934), pp. 307, 308.

3. Ibid., p. 309.

4. Ibid., pp. 309-10.

5. Ibid., p. 310.

6. Ibid., p. 315.

7. Ibid., p. 326.

8. See, for example, Joseph Warren Beach, *The Method of Henry James* (Philadelphia: Albert Saifer, 1954), p. 269; Laurence Holland, *The Expense of Vision: Essays on the Craft of Henry James* (Princeton: Princeton University Press, 1964), p. 238; and Christof Wegelin, *The Image of Europe in Henry James* (Dallas: Southern Methodist University Press, 1958), pp. 88, 102.

9. Henry James, *The Ambassadors,* (New York: Charles Scribner's Sons, 1909), 21:271. Subsequent references will be to this and to the following vol. 22 of the New York Edition and will appear in brackets just after the quoted material; vol. 21 and 22 appearing as I and II respectively.

10. A most explicit critical view of Strether as one who has "quite simply become

a pragmatist" is to be found in Christof Wegelin, *The Image of Europe*, pp. 92, 96, 101.

11. Henry James, *The Art of the Novel*, pp. 317, 318.

12. Ibid., p. 316.

13. Ibid., p. 308.

14. James does allow us a brief glimpse of Strether's own share in Woollett thinking when he first tells of his mission to Maria Gostrey and categorically denounces Chad's mistress (whom he has yet to meet) as "base, venal—out of the streets," and Chad himself as a "wretched boy," who has "darkened [Mrs. Newsome's] admirable life." Strether, James tells us, "spoke with austerity" [I, 55].

15. This has been discussed particularly well in Philip M. Weinstein, *Henry James and the Requirements of the Imagination* (Cambridge, Mass.: Harvard University Press, 1971), pp. 144-52, and Laurence Holland, *The Expense of Vision*, pp. 240-48.

16. At the same time Strether chooses to ignore Maria Gostrey's hint that " '[Chad's] not so good as you think!' " Similarly, though far more subtly, Waymarsh only "glowered at Chad" when he walked into the theater box, making Strether reflect: "The social sightlessness of his old friend's survey marked for him afresh . . . the inevitable limits of direct aid from this source" [I, 171, 137]. Waymarsh's sightlessness no less than Gostrey's worldly knowledge mean that each in a different way is not open to dupery like Strether.

17. Weinstein, *The Requirements of the Imagination*, p. 154.

18. Mme. de Vionnet's sacrificial role has been stressed by F. O. Matthiessen, *Henry James: The Major Phase* (New York: Oxford University Press, 1944), pp. 39-41. The value of giving is most eloquently enunciated by the lady herself in her last interview with Strether when she declares " 'that it's not, that it's never, a happiness, any happiness at all, to *take*. The only safe thing is to give. It's what plays you least false' " [II, 282-83]. This is, of course, the fundamental difference between her and Chad, and one of the principal qualities that attract Strether to her. Her statement is also a parallel to Strether's own final leave-taking of Maria Gostrey and Paris.

19. He reiterates this view again to Maria Gostrey later, when he declares that " 'little Bilham had shown me what's expected of a gentleman.' " He adds: " 'it was but a technical lie—he classed the attachment as virtuous. That was a view for which there was much to be said—and the virtue came out for me hugely.' " And he reflects: " 'I haven't, you see, done with it yet' " [II, 299].

20. This is reiterated again in his final interview with Maria Gostrey. She muses on Chad's future: " 'He's formed to please.' " And Strether replies: " 'And it's our friend who has formed him.' Strether felt in it the strange irony." [II, 325].

21. Henry James, *The Art of the Novel*, p. 57.

22. See Matthiessen, *The Major Phase*, pp. 38-39, and Philip Rahv, "Attitudes Toward Henry James" in *Literature and the Sixth Sense* (Boston: Houghton Mifflin Co., 1969), p. 101. This essay first appeared in 1943.

23. This is the central thesis of Weinstein's *Henry James and the Requirements of the Imagination*. See also Holland, *The Expense of Vision*, pp. 269-82.

24. Wegelin, *The Image of Europe*, p. 88.

25. See Owen Barfield, *What Coleridge Thought* (Middletown, Conn.: Wesleyan University Press, 1971), pp. 41-58 and passim.

26. William James, *The Meaning of Truth* (New York: Longmans, Green, and Co., 1909), p. 186.

27. Henry James, "The Beast in the Jungle," in *The Novels and Tales of Henry James* (New York: Charles Scribner's Sons, 1909), 17:61. Subsequent references will be to this volume of the New York Edition and will appear in brackets just after the quoted material.

28. This objection to the tale has been raised by Allen Tate in *The House of Fiction: An Anthology of the Short Story with Commentary*, ed. Caroline Gordon and Allen Tate (New York: Charles Scribner's Sons, 1954), p. 230.

29. Henry James, *The Art of the Novel*, p. 248. Here are James's final remarks on

the tale in his "Preface," pp. 247-48: "My picture leaves [Marcher] overwhelmed—at last he has understood; though in thus disengaging my treated theme for the reader's benefit I seem to acknowledge that this more detached witness may not successfully have done so. I certainly grant that any felt merit in the thing must all depend on the clearness and charm with which the subject just noted expresses itself." This passage is systematically omitted from, say, casebook treatments of the famous tale, and I grant it is not all that immediately easy to understand. Marcher, however, is the "more detached witness"—i.e., detached *from* James after he "disengages his treated theme" for the reader—who is then unable to successfully "disengage" from, or let go of, his problem. "Witness" is of course one of James's characteristic expressions for his viewpoint character. If James meant here the "more detached witness" to mean himself, the last sentence would make no sense whatever, as well as the obvious syntactical differentiating of "I" from "witness." It is certainly ironic to think that James feels the success of the tale hinges on our appreciating this dimension to its ending. I am afraid we want our irony in his work, but not always his own *operative* kind.

30. Ibid., p. 247.

VIII. RADICAL EMPIRICISM—"BEYOND THE LABORATORY-BRAIN"

1. Henry James, *The Notebooks of Henry James*, ed. F. O. Matthiessen and Kenneth B. Murdock (New York: Oxford University Press, 1947), p. 415.

2. All of these propositions about the three late novels are found in the "Introduction" by R. P. Blackmur to *The Golden Bowl* (New York: Grove Press, 1952), pp. v-xxi; the description of them specifically as "poetic dramas of the inner life of the soul" is on page v. For some allied perspectives see "The Religion of Consciousness" in F. O. Matthiessen, *Henry James: The Major Phase* (New York: Oxford University Press, 1944), pp. 131-51; Christof Wegelin, *The Image of Europe in Henry James* (Dallas: Southern Methodist University Press, 1958), pp. 88, 184-85; Dorothea Krook, *The Ordeal of Consciousness in Henry James* (Cambridge: Cambridge University Press, 1962), pp. ix, 1-25, 393-413. The most rigid argument along these lines is of course Quentin Anderson, *The American Henry James* (New Brunswick, N.J.: Rutgers University Press, 1957)—which no one has accepted.

3. The three principal voices of this newer perspective are Sallie Sears, *The Negative Imagination: Form and Perspective in the Novels of Henry James* (Ithaca: Cornell University Press, 1968): Charles T. Samuels, *The Ambiguity of Henry James* (Urbana: University of Illinois Press, 1971), pp. 61-88, 194-209, 210-26; and Philip M. Weinstein, *Henry James and the Requirements of the Imagination* (Cambridge, Mass.: Harvard University Press, 1971), pp. 1-7, 121-201.

4. Sears, *The Negative Imagination*, pp. 107-8.

5. Oscar Cargill, *The Novels of Henry James* (New York: Macmillan Co., 1961), pp. 340-41. James will speak of himself once again as "poet" and explicitly deny any meaningful distinction "as that between verse and prose" in his "Preface" to *The Golden Bowl*. See *The Art of the Novel*, ed. R. P. Blackmur (New York: Charles Scribner's Sons, 1934), pp. 340-41. He does not speak this way in his "Preface" to *The Ambassadors*. Leon Edel in *Henry James: The Master: 1901-1916* (Philadelphia and New York: J. B. Lippincott Co., 1972), p. 114, attributes the different mode of *The Wings* to the late discovery of the symbolist movement through Ibsen.

6. Matthiessen, *The Major Phase*, pp. 42-43; Cargill, *The Novels of Henry James*, p. 429; Krook, *The Ordeal of Consciousness*, p. 198.

7. Sears, *The Negative Imagination*, pp. 91-98; Edel, *The Master: 1901-1916*, pp. 116-20; Samuels, *The Ambiguity of Henry James*, pp. 61-75; Reynolds Price, "Introduction," *The Wings of the Dove* (Columbus: Charles E. Merrill, 1970), pp. v-xix.

8. Henry James, *The Wings of the Dove* (New York: Charles Scribner's Sons, 1909), 20:343, 342-43.

9. Sears, *The Negative Imagination*, p. 74.

10. Cargill, *The Novels of Henry James*, p. 366.

11. Henry James, *The Future of the Novel: Essays on the Art of Fiction*, ed. Leon Edel (New York: Vintage Books, 1956), p. 16.

12. Henry James, *The Art of the Novel*, p. 25.

13. Henry James, *Henry James: The American Essays*, ed. Leon Edel (New York: Vintage Books, 1956), pp. 27-28.

14. Matthiessen, *The Major Phase*, p. 59.

15. Samuels, *The Ambiguity of Henry James*, p. 71.

16. A notable exception to this division of critical attitudes is Peter K. Garrett, *Scene and Symbol from George Eliot to James Joyce* (New Haven: Yale University Press, 1969), pp. 123-36. Garrett is able to examine and evaluate *The Wings* (and also the other two major novels) approvingly in terms of James's intent; and he can approach all three, along the older critical lines, as a single unit. At the same time, he consistently rejects any view of them as "transcendent" or "poetic" works and insists on our keeping to James's contextual presentation of consciousness itself, pp. 101-23, 136-59.

17. Henry James, "The Golden Bowl," in *The Novels and Tales of Henry James* (New York: Charles Scribner's Sons, 1909), 24:237.

18. Henry James, *The Complete Tales of Henry James*, ed. Leon Edel (Philadelphia and New York: J. B. Lippincott Co., 1964), 12:443.

19. Ibid., 12:373, 390.

20. Quoted in Edel, *The Master: 1901-1916*, p. 501.

21. Henry James, *The Art of the Novel*, pp. 169, 171, 172, 174-75.

22. See, for example, Garrett, *Scene and Symbol*, pp. 98-101; Samuels, *The Ambiguity of Henry James*, pp. 11-22. See also Krook, *The Ordeal of Consciousness*, pp. 370-89.

23. Henry James, *The Art of the Novel*, pp. 169, 175.

24. Ibid., pp. 171-72.

25. Leon Edel in *The Master: 1901-1916*, pp. 315-16, speaks of "The Jolly Corner" in much the same important way with respect to James's own personal and psychological condition—his finally "laying the ghost" of his American past, his "old rivalry with William," and so on. Inasmuch as his entire quasi-supernatural drift is fundamental to his major phase and has very personal roots indeed, I much agree. But the relationship with William in all of this, although "rivalry" is perhaps not ultimately inaccurate in one sense, just does not begin to cover the ground between them.

26. Henry James, "The Jolly Corner," in *The Novels and Tales of Henry James* (New York: Charles Scribner's Sons, 1909), 17:440-41. Subsequent references will be to this volume of the New York Edition and will appear in brackets just after the quoted material.

27. Quoted in Edel, *The Master: 1901-1916*, p. 316.

28. John A. Clair, *The Ironic Dimension in the Fiction of Henry James* (Pittsburgh: Duquesne University Press, 1965), pp. 17-36.

29. William James, "What Psychical Research Has Accomplished," in *The Will to Believe and Other Essays in Popular Philosophy* (New York: Dover Publications, 1956), p. 317.

30. Ibid., pp. 316, 321.

31. William James, "Human Immortality," in ibid., p. 3. "Human Immortality" was a separate publication from the essays in the original *Will to Believe* volume. It appears in the Dover Edition I have been citing immediately following the reprinted *Will to Believe* collection; and, being also a reprint, the page number above refers to the original edition.

32. Ibid., pp. 13, 14.

33. Ibid., p. 21.

34. Ibid., pp. 16-17, 19-20.

35. William James, *The Letters of William James*, ed. by his son Henry James (Boston: Atlantic Monthly Press, 1920), 2:277.

36. William James, *The Varieties of Religious Experience: A Study in Human*

Nature (New York: Longmans, Green, and Co., 1903), p. 517.

37. Ibid., p. 516.

38. Ibid., p. 519.

39. *The Will to Believe*, p. vii; William James, *Pragmatism: A New Name for Some Old Ways of Thinking* (New York: Longmans, Green, and Co., 1907), pp. viii-ix.

40. William James, *Essays in Radical Empiricism* (New York: Longmans, Green, and Co., 1912), p. 4.

41. Edel, *The Master: 1901-1916*, p. 564.

42. Matthiessen, *The Major Phase*, p. 148.

43. F. O. Matthiessen, *The James Family* (New York: Alfred A. Knopf, 1947), p. 588.

44. Ibid., p. 592.

45. Although James's "Life After Death" paper—about which I am conscious here of making such extraordinarily high claims—is still without appreciable recognition or praise among his critics, James himself revealed his feelings about its worth in a letter to his publisher. Apologizing to Elizabeth Jordan, editor of *Harper's Bazar*, for his delay in sending the essay, James explained that he was "to find the little business distinctly difficult, so that I had—it being a sort of thing that is so little in my 'chords', to work it out with even more deliberation than I had allowed time for. . . . It is too long—I don't mean for what it is, but for what I said it would be; and yet, having taken the most exquisite pains with it, I now proceed to supplicate you, first, dispassionately (if not better passionately!) to read it, and then to print it as it stands. . . . I won't take time with attempting to explain, with persuasive eloquence, how I came to beguile myself into stretching it out—the simple truth being that I didn't seem to make it at all worth while except by saying what I wanted and what I seemed to *have* to. If I can take anything out in proof I heroically will—I should like of course very much to *see* the proof. But meanwhile it seems to me to hang very tightly together, as my stuff always does; and in short I throw myself on your patience." Henry James, "Henry James and the *Bazar* Letters," ed. Leon Edel and Lyall H. Powers in *Howells and James: A Double Billing* (New York: New York Public Library, 1958), pp. 54-55.

46. Henry James, "Is There a Life After Death?" in *In After Days* (New York and London: Harper & Brothers, 1910), pp. 200, 201. Due to my extensive quotation from the text of this work subsequent references to its page number in *In After Days* will appear in brackets just after the quoted material.

EPILOGUE

1. Henry James, *The Selected Letters of Henry James*, ed. Leon Edel (New York: Farrar, Straus and Cudahy, 1955), pp. 68, 69.

2. Henry James, *The Art of the Novel*, ed. R. P. Blackmur (New York: Charles Scribner's Sons, 1934), pp. 21, 22.

3. Henry James, *Letters*, p. 69.

Bibliography

I. Books

Adams, Henry. *The Letters of Henry Adams*. Edited by Worthington Chauncey Ford. 2 vols. Boston and New York: Houghton Mifflin Co., 1938.

Allen, Gay Wilson. *William James: A Biography*. New York: Viking Press, 1967.

Anderson, Quentin. *The American Henry James*. New Brunswick, N.J.: Rutgers University Press, 1957.

Barfield, Owen. *Poetic Diction: A Study in Meaning*. New York and Toronto: McGraw-Hill, 1964.

————. *Saving the Appearances: A Study in Idolatry*. New York: Harcourt, Brace and World, n.d.

————. *Speaker's Meaning*. Middletown, Conn.: Wesleyan University Press, 1967.

————. *What Coleridge Thought*. Middletown, Conn.: Wesleyan University Press, 1971.

Beach, Joseph Warren. *The Method of Henry James*. Philadelphia: Alfred Saifer, 1954.

Bewley, Marius. *The Complex Fate: Hawthorne, Henry James and Some Other American Writers*. London: Chatto and Windus, 1952.

Blackmur, R. P. *A Primer of Ignorance*. Edited by Joseph Frank. New York: Harcourt, Brace and World, 1967.

Booth, Wayne C. *The Rhetoric of Fiction*. Chicago: University of Chicago Press, 1961.

Bosanquet, Theodora. *Henry James at Work*. London: Hogarth Press, 1924.

Brower, Reuben A. *The Fields of Light: An Experiment in Critical Reading*. New York: Oxford University Press, 1951.

————. *The Poetry of Robert Frost: Constellations of Intention*. New York: Oxford University Press, 1963.

Buitenhuis, Peter. *The Grasping Imagination: The American Writings of Henry James*. Toronto: University of Toronto Press, 1970.

Cargill, Oscar. *The Novels of Henry James*. New York: Macmillan Co., 1961.

Carlyle, Thomas. *Sartor Resartus: The Life and Opinions of Herr Teufelsdröckh*. Edited by Charles Frederick Harrold. New York: Doubleday, Doran and Co., 1937.

Clair, John A. *The Ironic Dimension in the Fiction of Henry James.* Pittsburgh: Duquesne University Press, 1965.

Clive, Geoffrey. *The Romantic Enlightenment.* New York: Meridian Books, 1960.

Coleridge, Samuel Taylor. *Biographia Literaria.* Edited by J. Shawcross. 2 vols. London: Oxford University Press, 1907.

——. *The Friend.* Edited by Barbara E. Rooke. 2 vols. London: Routledge and Kegan Paul; Princeton: Princeton University Press, 1969. Part 4, *The Collected Works of Samuel Taylor Coleridge.* Edited by Kathleen Coburn.

Crews, Frederick C. *The Tragedy of Manners: Moral Drama in the Later Novels of Henry James.* New Haven: Yale University Press, 1957.

Dupee, F. W., ed. *The Question of Henry James: A Collection of Critical Essays.* New York: Henry Holt and Co., 1945.

Edel, Leon. *Henry James: The Master: 1901-1916.* Philadelphia and New York: J. B. Lippincott Co., 1972.

——. *Henry James: The Treacherous Years: 1895-1901.* Philadelphia and New York: J. B. Lippincott Co., 1969.

——, and Ray, Gordon N., eds. *Henry James and H. G. Wells: A Record of Their Friendship, Their Debate on the Art of Fiction, and Their Quarrel.* Urbana: University of Illinois Press, 1958.

Frost, Robert. *The Poetry of Robert Frost.* Edited by Edward Connery Lathem. New York: Holt, Rinehart and Winston, 1969.

Garrett, Peter K. *Scene and Symbol from George Eliot to James Joyce: Studies in Changing Fictional Mode.* New Haven and London: Yale University Press, 1969.

Geismar, Maxwell. *Henry James and the Jacobites.* Boston: Houghton Mifflin Co., 1963.

Grattan, C. Hartley. *The Three Jameses: A Family of Minds: Henry James, Sr., William James, Henry James.* London, New York, and Toronto: Longmans, Green, and Co., 1932.

Hawthorne, Nathaniel. *The Scarlet Letter.* Vol. I of the Centenary Edition. Edited by William Charvat et al. Columbus: Ohio State University Press, 1962.

Holland, Laurence Bedwell. *The Expense of Vision: Essays on the Craft of Henry James.* Princeton: Princeton University Press, 1964.

Holman, C. Hugh. *A Handbook to Literature.* 3d ed. New York: Bobbs-Merrill Co., 1972.

Howells, Wliam Dean. *Criticism and Fiction and Other Essays.* Edited by Clara Marburg Kirk and Rudolph Kirk. New York: New York University Press, 1959.

Isle, Walter. *Experiments in Form: Henry James's Novels, 1896-1901.* Cambridge, Mass.: Harvard University Press, 1968.

James, Henry. *The Art of the Novel: Critical Prefaces.* Edited by R. P. Blackmur. New York: Charles Scribner's Sons, 1934.

——. *Autobiography: A Small Boy and Others; Notes of a Son and*

Brother; The Middle Years. Edited by Frederick W. Dupee. New York: Criterion Books, 1956.

———. *The Complete Tales of Henry James*. Edited by Leon Edel. 12 vols. Philadelphia and New York: J. B. Lippincott Company, 1962-64.

———. *French Poets and Novelists*. Edited by Leon Edel. New York: Grossett and Dunlap, 1964.

———. *The Future of the Novel: Essays on the Art of Fiction*. Edited by Leon Edel. New York: Vintage Books, 1956.

———. *Hawthorne*. Ithaca, N.Y.: Cornell University Press, 1956.

———. *Henry James: The American Essays*. Edited by Leon Edel. New York: Vintage Books, 1956.

———. *The Letters of Henry James*. Edited by Percy Lubbock. 2 vols. New York: Charles Scribner's Sons, 1920.

———. *Literary Reviews and Essays*. Edited by Albert Mordell. New York: Grove Press, 1957.

———. *The Notebooks of Henry James*. Edited by F. O. Matthiessen and Kenneth B. Murdock. New York: Oxford University Press, 1947.

———. *The Novels and Tales of Henry James*. 24 vols. New York: Charles Scribner's Sons, 1907-9.

———. *The Selected Letters of Henry James*. Edited by Leon Edel. New York: Farrar, Straus and Cudahy, 1955.

———. *The Spoils of Poynton*. London: Penguin Books, 1963.

———. *Views and Reviews*. Edited by LeRoy Phillips. Boston: Ball Publishing Co., 1908.

James, William. *Essays in Radical Empiricism*. New York: Longmans, Green, and Co., 1912.

———. *The Letters of William James*. Edited by his son Henry James. 2 vols. Boston: Atlantic Monthly Press, 1920.

———. *The Meaning of Truth: A Sequel to 'Pragmatism.'* New York: Longmans, Green, and Co., 1909.

———. *A Pluralistic Universe*. New York: Longmans, Green, and Co., 1909.

———. *Pragmatism: A New Name for Some Old Ways of Thinking*. New York: Longmans, Green, and Co., 1907.

———. *The Principles of Psychology*. 2 vols. New York: Henry Holt and Co., 1890.

———. *Some Problems of Philosophy: A Beginning of an Introduction to Philosophy*. New York: Longmans, Green, and Co., 1911.

———. *The Varieties of Religious Experience: A Study in Human Nature*. New York: Longmans, Green, and Co., 1903.

———. *The Will to Believe and Other Essays in Popular Philosophy*. New York: Dover Publications, 1956.

Krook, Dorothea. *The Ordeal of Consciousness in Henry James*. Cambridge: Cambridge University Press, 1962.

Leavis, F. R. *The Great Tradition: George Eliot, Henry James, Joseph*

Conrad. New York: New York University Press, 1963.

McCarthy, Harold T. *Henry James: The Creative Process.* New York: Thomas Yoseloff, Inc., 1958.

Matthiessen, F. O. *American Renaissance: Art and Expression in the Age of Emerson and Whitman.* New York: Oxford University Press, 1941.

———. *Henry James: The Major Phase.* New York: Oxford University Press, 1944.

———. *The James Family: Including Selections from the Writings of Henry James, Senior, William, Henry, & Alice James.* New York: Alfred A. Knopf, 1947.

Norris, Frank. *The Responsibilities of the Novelist.* New York: Doubleday, Page and Co., 1903.

Pater, Walter. *The Renaissance: Studies in Art and Poetry.* London: Macmillan and Co., 1924.

Perry, Ralph Barton. *The Thought and Character of William James.* 2 vols. Boston: Little, Brown, and Co., 1935.

Pizer, Donald. *Realism and Naturalism in Nineteenth-Century American Literature.* Carbondale and Edwardsville: Southern Illinois University Press, 1966.

Samuels, Charles Thomas. *The Ambiguity of Henry James.* Urbana: University of Illinois Press, 1971.

Scott, Virgil. *Studies in the Short Story: Instructor's Manual.* 3d ed. New York: Holt, Rinehart and Winston, 1968.

Sears, Sallie. *The Negative Imagination: Form and Perspective in the Novels of Henry James.* Ithaca, N.Y.: Cornell University Press, 1968.

Stone, Edward. *The Battle and the Books: Some Aspects of Henry James.* Athens: Ohio University Press, 1964.

Tate, Allen, and Gordon, Caroline, eds. *The House of Fiction: An Anthology of the Short Story.* New York: Charles Scribner's Sons, 1954.

Wegelin, Christof. *The Image of Europe in Henry James.* Dallas: Southern Methodist University Press, 1958.

Weinstein, Philip M. *Henry James and the Requirements of the Imagination.* Cambridge, Mass.: Harvard University Press, 1971.

Wilson, Edmund, ed. *The Shock of Recognition: The Development of Literature in the United States Recorded by the Men Who Made It.* New York: The Modern Library, 1955.

Winters, Yvor. *In Defense of Reason.* 3d ed. Denver: Alan Swallow, 1947.

II. *Essays and Articles*

Barzun, Jacques. "Letters to the Editor." *New York Times Book Review*, 16 April 1972, p. 36.

Blackmur, Richard P. "Henry James." In *Literary History of the United States*, edited by Robert E. Spiller et al, pp. 1039-64. New York: Macmillan Co., 1953.

——. "Introduction" to *The Aspern Papers* and *The Spoils of Poynton,* by Henry James. New York: Dell Publishing Co., 1959.

——. "Introduction" to *The Golden Bowl,* by Henry James. New York: Grove Press, 1952.

Dupee, F. W. "Henry James." In *Major Writers of America,* edited by Perry Miller, 2:137-48, 264-65. New York: Harcourt, Brace and World, 1962.

Edel, Leon. "Introduction" to *The Ambassadors,* by Henry James. Cambridge, Mass.: Houghton Mifflin Co., 1960.

——. "The Jameses." *Times Literary Supplement,* No. 3684, 13 October 1972, pp. 1226-27.

Firebaugh, Joseph J. "The Pragmatism of Henry James." *Virginia Quarterly Review* 27 (1951):419-35.

Gargano, James W. "*The Spoils of Poynton:* Action and Responsibility." *Sewanee Review* 69 (1961):650-60.

Gass, William H. "The High Brutality of Good Intentions." *Accent* 18 (1958):62-71.

James, Henry. "Henry James and the *Bazar* Letters." In *Howells and James: A Double Billing,* edited by Leon Edel and Lyall H. Powers, pp. 25-55. New York: New York Public Library, 1958.

——. "Is There a Life After Death?" In *In After Days: Thoughts on the Future Life,* pp. 199-233. New York and London: Harper and Brothers, 1910.

Levy, Leo B. "Criticism Chronicle: Hawthorne, Melville and James." *Southern Review,* n.s. 2 (1966):427-42.

McLean, Robert C. "The Subjective Adventure of Fleda Vetch." *American Literature* 36 (1964):12-30.

Parkes, Henry Bamford. "The James Brothers." *Sewanee Review* 56 (1948):323-28.

Price, Reynolds. "Introduction" to *The Wings of the Dove,* by Henry James. Columbus, Ohio: Charles E. Merrill, 1970.

Rahv, Philip. "Attitudes Toward Henry James." In *Literature and the Sixth Sense,* pp. 95-103. Boston: Houghton Mifflin Co., 1969.

Raleigh, John Henry. "Henry James: The Poetics of Empiricism." *PMLA* 66 (1951):107-23.

Reilly, Robert J. "Henry James and the Morality of Fiction." *American Literature* 39 (1967):1-30.

Stevenson, Robert Louis. "A Humble Remonstrance." In *Henry James and Robert Louis Stevenson: A Record of Friendship and Criticism,* edited by Janet Adam Smith, pp. 86-100. London: Rupert Hart-Davis, 1948.

Tate, Allen. "Emily Dickinson." In *Essays of Four Decades,* pp. 281-98. Chicago: Swallow Press, 1968.

Toor, David. "Narrative Irony in Henry James' 'The Real Thing.'" *University Review* 34 (Winter 1967):95-99.

Trilling, Lionel. "The Jameses." *Times Literary Supplement,* No. 3685, 20 October 1972, p. 1257.

Vivas, Eliseo. "Henry and William: (Two Notes)." *Kenyon Review* 5 (1943):580-94.

Watt, Ian. "The First Paragraph of *The Ambassadors*: An Explication." *Essays in Criticism* 10 (1960):250-74.

Wellek, René. "Henry James's Literary Theory and Criticism." *American Literature* 30 (1958):293-321.

Index